"I have worked with Rick on many projects over the years. There is no one better at using video to get people to take action. In his book *Video Persuasion*, he shares and explains the video marketing techniques that have worked for him, so successfully. You need to be using video in your marketing and if you do, you need this book."

> – Rowland Hanson, CEO & Founder of The HMC
> Company; former Vice President of Corporate
> Communications for Microsoft where he is credited
> with the naming & launch of Windows

"Rick Cesari's *Video Persuasion* celebrates how the potency of video empowers the marketer to capture customers' hearts and minds, and convert these customers to buy the brand."

> – James Thomson, Partner, Buy Box Experts; co-founder
> of PROSPER Show; former business head of Amazon
> Services

"A pioneer of using Direct Response Video as an effective brand-builder, Rick Cesari demonstrates how to influence consumers by creating and leveraging compelling stories on video. In this book, Cesari also takes it a step further, applying 35 years of know-how toward promoting social good through video marketing."

> – Ann Nikolai, Director, Osher Lifelong Learning
> Institute at CSU, Chico

"Rick has guided me through a series of insightful branding and marketing concepts in his previous two books. *Video Persuasion:*

Everything You Need to Know was the missing piece in a brilliant series of the most innovative and breakthrough ideas in direct marketing. I apply video testimonials throughout my entire organization in Central and South America, helping me build client loyalty, build awareness with future clients, and increase overall profitability."

– **David Ricardo Suárez, Head of Marketing, Finance, IT and HR in LATAM, Grupo Salinas**

"Obscurity is the biggest challenge every brand faces today. Millions of ideal prospects would buy your product or service if they only knew about you. *Video Persuasion* is THE playbook on how to effectively and efficiently leverage video to break through the noise and connect with your ideal customers. It clearly explains how to connect, convert, and nurture prospects into high value, profitable, long term customers. After reading it the first time, we fundamentally changed and vastly improved our video strategy with-out adding a dime to our existing budget."

– **Tom Schwab, Chief Evangelist Officer, Interview Valet**

"Rick Cesari is the absolute master at *Video Persuasion*. Reading his book was as enlightening and educational as his entire career has been. Highly recommend this one!"

– **Eric Yaverbaum, Best Selling Author of eight books including Leadership Secrets of the World's Most Successful CEO's and PR For Dummies**

"Rick Cesari's *Video Persuasion* delivers a 'how to' on writing, producing and marketing videos that grab attention and deliver compelling sales messages. Take one part direct marketing genius, who has sold millions products and services, plus one part video production guru plus expert interviews and you have a must read detailed primer on how to produce videos that sell."

— Peter Levitan, Former Head of New Business for Saatchi & Saatchi Advertising, Agency owner, Author and New Business Consultant

"Video is deceptive. Sure, video is everywhere but that doesn't mean it's useful for its creator. In fact, most video is just noise. However, when done correctly, and persuasively, as outlined in this incredible resource, the results can be explosive as evidenced by Rick's $4 billion dollar track record. If you're learning how to put together video from your neighbor's kid, you're wasting time. Do the smart thing, get this book and start tapping into and leveraging over 30 years of wisdom making videos profitable."

— Dustin Mathews, Chief Education Officer, WealthFit.com

"Rick brilliantly combines the art, science, and psychology of marketing into practical tips for anyone who wants to take their brand to the next level. As a pioneer in the industry, he reveals his secrets for success and also teaches us through his own mistakes how to create videos that sell. I've personally used many of his proven techniques with my own brand with impressive results."

— Dr. Michele Burklund, NMD, MBA

"I'm a retired Oral Surgeon and I witnessed these concepts work first-hand. Rick made a video for me that helped sell a large ranch in Florida. Whether you're a college student or a CEO, Cesari's book is a must read for anyone interested in video marketing and sales."

— Gerry Williams, DDS

"Rick is already a well-known branding expert so I knew *Video Persuasion* would be powerful, but Rick supposed my already high expectations. This book is a perfect combination of actionable tactics combined with the winning strategy of incorporating video into the DNA of a brand. From the billion-dollar brands to the emerging brand Rick has delivered example after example of winning ideas along with exact steps that a reader can take to implement the concepts. This is a fresh approach marries the skill building that is required to understand the concepts with precise action steps including contacts, resources and even templates the readers can implement instantly. I love this book and you will too!"

> — Steve Simonson, Serial Entrepreneur, Podcaster and
> Founder of, www.stevensimonson.com,
> www.awesomers.com, www.empowery.com,
> www.parsimony.com, www.catalyst88.com,
> www.symoglobal.com, www.sellerchatbot.com

"Rick has the rare combination of deep experience and a "beginner's mind" ready to re-apply that knowledge to our ever-evolving world. It might be because Rick's professional work, every direct response effort, has always been measured in units or sales in a precise way that strips away the false notions. Rick started from the wisdom of the industry giants, and refined that through decades of A/B message testing. This marketing experience and wisdom is only becoming more relevant and valuable in our increasingly Internet and Amazon centric world. Rick generously shares the secrets he has learned in this book."

> — Bernie Thompson, Founder and CEO of Plugable, Inc.

"Nobody has been doing video marketing longer or better than Rick Cesari. In his new book *Video Persuasion* he shares the techniques and experiences that have helped make him and his clients successful. With video content exploding across social media platforms, you need to read this book to learn how to use video to your advantage. I highly recommend it."

> – Larry Benet, "Chief Connector", Co-Founder/CEO | SANG, The Power of a Connected & Socially Conscious Community

"Video is essential for any marketing campaign but it's extremely difficult to get right. In *Video Persuasion*, Rick turns decades of experience into an actionable guide on how to craft marketing videos for maximum success. This book will help any entrepreneur turn prospects into customers, regardless of the sales channel."

> – Roy Krebs, CEO & Co-founder, NaturalStacks.com

"Beautiful but non-productive video material is an unnecessary business expense and a missed opportunity! *Video Persuasion* is the path to the alternative – success! Rick Cesari, one of the true masters of the craft, has written a beautifully organized, comprehensive, interesting and truly informative book including, most importantly, practical, can-do specifics for effective video marketing. I today paused our company's video production schedule until our key marketing and video management have read, digested and discussed *Video Persuasion* as the foundation of our video materials agenda moving forward."

> – Bob Lamson, CEO, Precision Appliance Technology, Inc.

"Rick is one of the top experts in the world using direct response video to sell. I was looking to feature the top marketers in the world for the InspiredInsider podcast and when I asked many of the top entrepreneurs who I should consider Rick's name kept coming up over and over. He has helped sell more than 2 billion dollars worth of product and launched over 30 brands including Sonicare, Oxiclean, George Foreman Grill, Juiceman, GoPro camera and many more. If you are just launching a new product or already have an existing product and want to generate more sales using direct response video, then you should read this book and listen to what Rick says!"

> — **Dr. Jeremy Weisz, Cofounder of Rise25, Founder of InspiredInsider show**

"Rick Cesari has sold BILLIONS with video persuasion, based on rock-solid marketing principles that never change. If you're making videos for your business without first reading this book, you're building castles on sand—a huge mistake. Before you finish chapter 3, you'll be motivated to do new, better things with video marketing. It's that valuable."

> — **Kevin Donlin, Copywriter + Marketing Optimizer**

"Rick's *Video Persuasion* is an excellent read for those looking to use the video marketing avenue or to supplement their current strategy. He does an excellent job laying out the key elements of video marketing in a way that is understandable to the non-technical/marketing person. I have followed his career for awhile and know his track record in marketing is second to none. I plan to use this as a blueprint to promote my business which until now has not had this

valuable video component! Highly recommend this read for anyone considering video media marketing for their product or business."
 – **Rob Brown, President/Owner, BNT Ormond LLC, Property Management**

"There are many people who claim to be video experts but very few with the track record of Rick Cesari. His successful TV and video campaigns are a who's who of marketing success stories…and thank goodness he decided to share many of them in *Video Persuasion*. He combines real world success with proven direct marketing principles and the result is a step-by-step blueprint to using video strategies to sell more product, help grow your business and build your brand."
 – **Brian Kurtz, Titans Marketing and author of** *Overdeliver*

"Thanks, to Rick Cesari, we've come a long way from simply uploading assembly videos on Amazon product details pages. His proven methods for producing product video that sells developed and perfected during the height of the Direct Response TV glory days, translate perfectly to the digital era. Rick's methods have helped my own business, as well as my clients' businesses, hit every required touch point needed to convert sales. Videos that Rick produces convert infinitely better than any other video we've used. Simply put this book is a must-read for the digital era."
 – **Jason Boyce, Founder/CEO, Ave 7 Media**

"This book is essentially a mini-MBA on Video Marketing in the Digital Age. Packed with insights, strategies, and 'in-the-trenches' experience from experts who have been-there, done-that, *Video Persuasion* not only offers practical step-by-step advice on testimonials, production, copywriting, offers, and much more – it blends solid how-to with powerful stories that will motivate and inspire. It's comprehensive, compelling, and entertaining from start to finish."

— **Jack Turk, Copywriter, jack@writekillercopyfast.com**

"Rick Cesari's expertise in the realm of video marketing is second to none. With years of direct response marketing and billion dollar successes, no one else comes close to his track record. Video is everywhere on social media but you need to learn how to stand out from the crowd and utilize it effectively. There is no one better to learn from than Rick. I highly recommend his book, *Video Persuasion* to anyone looking for more exposure and customers for their business."

— **Adam Payne, Founder of VideoMarketingInsider.com**

"The science of *Video Persuasion* has been revealed sharing the secrets of video marketing no matter how big or small – from Instagram to infomercial."

— **Dr. John Douillard, Former NBA nutritionist and founder of LifeSpa.com with 9 million+ YouTube views.**

VIDEO PERSUASION

Rick Cesari

VIDEO PERSUASION

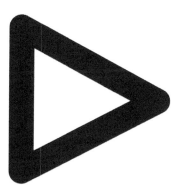

EVERYTHING YOU NEED TO KNOW

HOW TO CREATE EFFECTIVE
HIGH LEVEL PRODUCT
AND TESTIMONIAL VIDEOS
THAT WILL GROW
YOUR BRAND,
INCREASE SALES AND
BUILD YOUR BUSINESS!

Books may be purchased for educational, business, or sales promotional use. For information please write: Arcie Publishing, LLC, 7829 Center Blvd. #191, Snoqualmie, WA. 98065

First Edition

ISBN-13: 978-0-578-50046-1

To my sister, Susan, who was there at the beginning of my business journey and was always available when I needed help. I am very proud of your accomplishments.

To my wife, Martha, for putting up with me during this process and helping me every step of the way.

CONTENTS

ACKNOWLEDGMENTS

First and foremost, I would like to thank Susan Gilbert for giving me the idea and the encouragement to write this book. My editor, Joni Fisher, who took a whole lot of my words and made them make sense. Jane Schloth, for helping me record the interviews and for contributing some of the content. I'd also like to thank all the experts, Paul Miller, Mark Swaby, Jason Boyce, Bernie Thompson, Kevin Donlin, Jack Turk, Matt York, Kurt Bullock, and Jeff Turley, who took the time from their busy schedules to speak to me about the video concepts that are currently working for them in the marketplace.

CHAPTER ONE
Introduction to Video Persuasion

"Persuasion is often more effectual than force."
—Aesop

I'm going to introduce you to a new term I call Video Persuasion. Video Persuasion combines all the elements of good video production, the ability to create interesting, engaging, and watchable videos, with scientifically-proven direct response marketing strategies. Using the video persuasion techniques in this book will help make all your video's "work better" regardless of the goal you are trying to achieve.

I made my first marketing video in 1984. The only videos being made back then were for TV advertising or product information tapes sent out through "snail mail". The video I made was for a 30-minute television show, an early "infomercial" used to promote a real estate seminar. Up until that time other people promoting real estate seminars had only been using newspaper ads. By using this new marketing platform and a powerful video, I helped to quickly build one of the largest real estate seminar businesses in the country. I was "hooked" on the power of video. Since that time, I have used video production, video marketing combined with direct response strategies to sell more products direct to the consumer than just about anyone alive.

I also made a lot of expensive mistakes along the way, because video *was so costly to produce at that time.* I like to look at those mistakes as learning experiences that helped me get better at what I do. It was the combination of mistakes and finally the many spectacular successes that I have had over the last thirty years that helped me create the concepts of Video Persuasion in this book.

VIDEO ALCHEMY

I like the definition of Alchemy—*A science or philosophy that transforms something ordinary into something meaningful, often through mysterious means.* Video Persuasion is both an art and a science, designed for getting the viewer to take the specific action you want. I have used video persuasion techniques to create television and online ads that drove millions of dollars in sales and built many brands you might use in your home today, products like: the Juiceman juicer, the Philips Sonicare toothbrush, the George Foreman Grill, OxiClean, Clarisonic, Rug Doctor, the Momentus Golf Swing Trainer, the GoPro camera, and many more products leading to over $4 billion of Direct-to-Consumer sales. With video persuasion, you will transform all your videos into something more meaningful. I'm going to take out the mystery of how to do that.

STUDY MARKETING HISTORY

I did not invent the direct response marketing concepts that are used as part of video persuasion, I might have improved on them or helped refine some of them, so they work better, or tailored them specifically to a video format, but please be aware there is a long history of successful direct marketing concepts, starting with print catalogs and direct mail sales letters that form the foundation of many of the principles I am going to share with you. If you study marketing history you will see there is a direct line connecting the concepts that worked for Direct Mail to Direct Response TV to Home Shopping to Online marketing, successful e-commerce sales, Facebook and Instagram ads, and now videos on Amazon. Don't reinvent the wheel. The techniques that successfully sell products on QVC will be the same techniques that help you sell your products on Amazon using their new live streaming service. I will be pointing out these techniques, and more importantly, explaining why they work, taking out the mystery so you can add your own level of creativity when scripting your videos and building your product offers.

KNOWLEDGE IS KEY

It's important to get all the information that you can—knowledge is the key to success. I want to mention two books that had a profound influence on me as I learned the concepts of video persuasion, the first is *How to Win Friends and Influence People* by Dale Carnegie, which I talk about in more detail in chapter five. The second book is *INFLUENCE: The Psychology of Persuasion* by Robert Cialdini, Ph.D., which I draw from for some of the techniques I share in chapter six.

It is no coincidence that both these books use the word *Influence* in their titles. After all, isn't that what you are trying to do when someone watches a video that you produce? You are trying to educate and influence the viewer to your way of thinking and guiding them to the action you want them to take.

WHY WRITE THIS BOOK?

As you will soon learn, video is powerful. Its reach and use grow every day. This book was written for those who want to start making video a part of their marketing plans, even if you have absolutely no previous video production experience. The information in this book will help you use video to increase your sales, to grow your business, to create more customers and/or clients, to generate more leads, and to build your company, product, or personal brand.

HERE IS SOME OF WHAT YOU WILL LEARN:

The foundational old school marketing concept that far too often gets lost in the chaos of ever-changing advances in technology and how not knowing this can cost you sales.

The four keys to making your next video compelling, engaging, and effective in making the sale. When you put them all together in the right way, your video becomes practically irresistible!

The startling similarity between couch-surfing and online media consumption and how to overcome the core sales challenge posed by each.

How to build engagement with your message in a way that's natural, affirming, and powerful.

The perfect context for product testimonials inside your videos—where to place them for maximum effectiveness.

The core elements to include with every call to action (CTA). It's like building a bridge, you really can't afford to miss a single one.

The 4-step formula I'm going to explain in detail is for anybody creating videos for Facebook, Instagram, YouTube, Amazon, and any other online media.

If you sell anything online, **there's nothing that can compare with the power of video.** Video makes you stand out from your competitors in the marketplace. But if you want your videos to drive sales and deliver bottom-line results, you must do them right.

At a recent conference, I was having breakfast with two large Amazon sellers who do millions and millions of dollars a year in sales. They noted that Amazon has finally embraced the idea of using videos to promote products. But it was clear from the event that most have no clue how to make a video that gets people to respond, like order their product. However, one client of mine found that leveraging the video design principles I'll reveal in this book increased customer engagement by over 800%! My client was raving about these results all throughout the show. He still talks about that. The essence of what I helped him do you'll discover over the following pages.

We will take a detailed look at the three steps of video production and the things you can do to save money while still producing great looking videos

You will learn the best way to gather and videotape powerful testimonials that will sell your products for you…and why they are such a powerful marketing tool.

Learn how to create tutorial and demonstration videos that set you apart from the competition.

You'll hear from the top experts in video production and video marketing that I work with day in and day out, directors, producers, editors, lighting and sound experts, and art directors who can make your product shine. They share their knowledge, experience, and secret insider tips for your benefit.

I will show you how to incorporate direct response into your marketing videos to create a much higher return on investment (ROI). Whether you end up producing videos yourself or hire someone to do it, you will have all the knowledge, shortcuts, and money-saving ideas right at your finger-tips.

PERSONAL STORY: HOW VIDEO CHANGED MY LIFE!

I come from a family of entrepreneurs. My grandfather came over as an immigrant from Italy in the early 1900s. America then and now, being the land of opportunity, allowed him to open a small grocery store in Valhalla, NY. Just like any other small business owner, through hard work and long hours he created a successful life. He was able to open several other small businesses and invest in real estate, which is still a great formula for success!

My father ran a successful restaurant and eventually took over the grocery store. I was number six of eight brothers and sisters. My earliest working memories were of stocking the shelves, being a cashier, taking inventory, and helping with grocery deliveries. Yes, we were doing this forty years before Amazon and Instacart. I learned about customer service and the proper way to deal with people. My early life was about as perfect as it gets, filled with a nice house, great schools, and plenty of friends. That all changed quickly when my dad passed away from a heart attack. He was only 46 years old. My mother was left to raise and support eight kids by herself.

It got worse. Two years later my youngest brother drowned. What had once been such a great home environment to live in changed almost overnight. It was a struggle for my Mom to deal with two family deaths and try to keep the household with seven kids above water. When times are tough, sometimes you need to relocate to a less expensive place to live, so my mother decided to move to Daytona Beach, Florida. I spent a year and a half there before leaving again for college.

I attended a small school in Western Pennsylvania called Westminster College. I was more interested in partying and playing football than studying. I played linebacker on my college team that won the NAIA national championship in 1977 and 1978. I graduated with a Bachelor of Science degree in Biology, not the best preparation for a lifelong career in marketing!

I did not learn anything about video production, selling or persuasion, but through sports, I learned about teamwork and winning. The reason for studying biology was part of a plan to go to dental school. One of my best friends in High School, Dr. Rick Brown, DDS, and I were sitting in his bedroom our senior year in high school and talking about the future. We both decided to become dentists. He followed through, but I decided I had had enough of school, so I moved back home to Daytona Beach and became a bartender and a lifeguard. My Mom was not too happy with this career choice, but I started to learn a skill that would help me the rest of my life—how to sell and overcome objections.

As a pool lifeguard, the only way I would make money was to sell the local brand of suntan lotion called Hawaiian Tropic to tourists. If I didn't sell, I didn't get paid, and I didn't eat. That was a strong motivator! After having fun for a year, I realized these jobs were probably not good for my long-term success. Looking for something I could do with my life, I started reading books about how people made money and became millionaires. The overwhelming majority of them had made their money by investing in real estate. I decided I would learn everything I could about investing in real estate by reading books, attending seminars, and getting head first into investing, even though I had very little money at the time. One personality trait that has followed me throughout life was I hated being told what to do. Not a good trait if I ever was going to work for someone else. Investing in real estate allowed me the freedom of working for myself while doing something that was rewarding.

MY FIRST VIDEO

I'm a big believer of learning from other peoples' experiences, and that is exactly how I got started in my video marketing career. I attended a real estate seminar in Orlando being conducted by a young man named Tom Vu. Tom's family came to the US as boat people after the Vietnam war. Starting with nothing, Tom built substantial wealth through investing in real estate. He was now teaching others, through seminars, his method of investing. I figured if he could do it so could I. After the seminar I did what he told me and bought a distressed house and resold it in two weeks, making about $12,000!

I was so grateful and amazed that I called a local business magazine called *Florida Trend* and told them about this guy who had arrived penniless and was teaching others how to make money. They wrote a story, and it helped his seminar business take off. He asked me to work for him and offered me a lot of money. I said, "Why not?" That was the start of my direct-to-consumer marketing career as a seminar promoter. There was already another large successful real estate seminar business out there that was pioneering the use of direct response TV to drive people to their seminars. We figured if it worked for them it would work for us. But how do we get started?

At that time, if you wanted a TV show, you had to go to where they made TV shows, so we headed to Hollywood. After some due diligence, we found a writer and producer, which was easy to do, because everyone in Hollywood is either a writer or producer and got started on our project. I was never a very technical person and am still not when it comes to cameras, and sound, and lighting. Other people have always done this part of the process. I found I had a knack for creating the right content and show structure to produce a show that successfully promoted our seminar business. I would sit in the editing bay hour after hour, day after day—this was before digital editing—working with the editor to choose which sound bites would produce the desired results we were looking for. That is the skill set that I have been able to nurture, fine tune, and expand over the years. It is the basis for what I share in this book.

The first 30-minute show we made was a tremendous success, but it was mostly done by others. After that, we knew a little more, and we created a second show that was even more successful. This one was a 60-minute program called "The Secrets to Success with Mason Adams." I was in charge from beginning to end. My responsibilities included writing the script, producing, finding guest experts and testimonials to interview, finding a host and negotiating his contract, hiring video crews, directing the taping and all post-production. I found I had a passion for this. It was a crash course in video production and video marketing that was better than could be learned in any school!

MOVING ON

While I really enjoyed what I was doing, I was still working for someone else. There were two problems. First, all my hard work and effort were going toward making someone else rich and second, the guy I was working for started to behave unethically, so I decided it was time to move on and start my own business. My employer was not happy with that decision and tried to stop me from leaving. I guess he did not want to lose the Golden Goose that was making him a lot of money, so he sued me and tied me up in court and legal fees that I could not afford. Not understanding the legal system and how it's not always about truth, justice, and the American way, I borrowed money in the form of a second mortgage against my mother's home to fight him. Slowly my small resources were drained, and I was forced to declare bankruptcy to stop the lawsuits, I lost my home and everything I owned at the time, and I still needed to pay my mother back, or she would lose her home.

IT GETS WORSE

I needed to do something to generate revenue. My only skillset was in creating videos, so scrambling for what to do next, I decided to go to the local bookstore. It was always a good place to generate new ideas. There I found a book called *How to Make a Million in the Stock Market.* I figured that I could make the same type of show we had been using to promote real estate but do it with the stock market as the wealth-generating vehicle instead. I was not an expert in this field, but I could provide the marketing vehicle so the expert could reach more people. The only problem was that I was flat broke and in debt. I called Dale, a friend from college who was living in Seattle,

Dale was in the fishing business and doing quite well. He agreed to finance the project to the tune of $10,000. I was able to pull in favors and made a show that normally would have cost $50,000 for only $8,000. We decided to use the remaining $2,000 for media time to test the show to see how well it worked. I would move to Seattle from Florida to run the business.

I arrived in Seattle with two suitcases, a lot of debt, and nothing else. It was the middle of the summer and prime fishing season, so Dale was up in Alaska, and I was to fly up to join him and help work as crew on one of his boats. I didn't even unpack but left my suitcases in his apartment and caught the next flight to Kodiak, Alaska. Talk about a culture shift, from Tampa, Florida to Kodiak in less than 24 hours. Now if you have ever watched the Discovery TV series called the "Deadliest Catch" you might have some idea what happened next. We were fishing for Halibut way out in the Aleutian Islands and got caught in the storm of the decade. The boat I was on sank in the storm, we had to put on our survival suits and were rescued by the coast guard. I remember sitting in the coast guard station in Kodiak, happy to be alive, but depressed at losing everything else. I think this was one of the lowest points of my life. What else could go wrong?

VIDEO SUCCESS!

The stock market show was scheduled to test while we were out fishing. I was curious about the results, so I asked to use the phone at the coast guard station to call the telemarketing company to see if we had any orders. After a long delay, they told me we had sold 27 units. I did the math, 27 units x $300 each = $8,100! Our original investment of $2,000 in media time multiplied to over $8,000. The show was a big success and eventually was able to pull me out of all my financial difficulties. It would not be the last time that a video project was going to bail me out from a tough situation. That was thirty years ago, since that time I have used video to promote some of the world's best-known consumer brands, products like Sonicare, Clarisonic, the George Foreman Grill, OxiClean, Rug Doctor, and the GoPro camera. With every product or project, I was always learning a little more about certain video elements and how they might affect human behaviors, why people respond to certain video sound bites, but not others. This information is not theory, but market-tested over many years to many different demographics and many different product categories. There are certain video persuasion secrets that will help any marketing campaign, and I am going to share those with you in this book.

HOW TO USE THIS BOOK

In my consulting and speaking engagements I educate people about how to build their product or company brand using video persuasion techniques. You'll soon learn why video is so powerful and why its reach is rapidly growing. I will show you specifically how to do your own video production, but if choose not to or you're not able to do so, I also explain how to hire the right person or production company that is able to deliver what you need, inexpensively, for your business to grow using video. I'll show you which video content people are watching, and you'll learn about the three most popular types of online videos and the ones to use in your marketing for the best results. We will look at writing video scripts, crafting powerful offers and the underlying principles and why these offers work so well. Then we will look at how best to use video on social media channels and on Amazon.

Combined with the video production and marketing information I will be sharing, I end each chapter with interviews of industry experts and how they are using video to help grow their businesses. Not only is the information they provide valuable, but you will also see, first-hand, how I interview people, an important skill to have when producing marketing videos.

Here are experts you will hear from:

- Paul Miller, the Founder and CEO of Cozy Phones, on how he uses video ads on Facebook to grow his business.
- Bernie Thompson, the Founder and CEO of Plugable, a top 200 Amazon seller and how he uses YouTube videos to help grow his business.
- Mark Swaby, the Founder and CEO of Net Media Group and Ladders.com, on how he uses video to increase sales and conversions on his e-commerce sites.
- Matt York, the Founder of *Videomaker* magazine, on his thirty years on the cutting edge of video production and how he is now using that video knowledge for social good on a global scale.
- Susan Gilbert, the Founder and CEO of Online PR Success, on using video on social media channels and how to properly set up your YouTube channel.
- Jack Turk, a high-level copywriter, who shares his insights into writing video scripts that get people to respond.
- Kevin Donlin, the Founder of Client Cloning Systems. The former webmaster at FedEx is now one of the nation's best copywriters. He shares valuable information on making

offers and persuasion techniques he uses with his clients that have generated millions in sales.

- Jason Boyce, the Founder of Avenue 7 Media, an agency that helps people sell their products on Amazon. Jason shares the latest on using video on Amazon to increase sales and buy box conversions.

- Kurt Bullock, the Founder and CEO of Produce Department, an agency that specializes in Facebook and Instagram advertising. He shares what types of videos are working for him on those platforms.

- Jeff Turley, the Founder and CEO of GoNetYourself, on how his company is revolutionizing the video production process and making high-level videos both repeatable and affordable for everyone.

The first-hand information of what's working in the marketplace right now—shared in these interviews—is worth every penny and more than you spent on this book!

VIDEO PERSUASION

The world of video today is more exciting and growing more rapidly than ever before. Over the last thirty years, I've had an amazing level of success integrating video production with video marketing and direct response principles to create video persuasion secrets that work. Now I'm sharing that knowledge and experience with you. The more you can start using this knowledge, the further ahead of the competition you will be. So, let's get started!

CHAPTER TWO
Why Video?

"Tell me a fact and I'll learn.
Tell me a truth and I'll believe.
Tell me a story and it will live in my heart forever."
—Native American Proverb

WE ARE LIVING IN A VIDEO-FIRST SOCIETY

Technology now allows everyone to create a video, simply, easily, and quickly.

We have shifted to a video first society. Our society does not include a lot of reading, but it does include a lot of watching. Just look around you. You will almost always find someone deeply engrossed in watching a video on their computer or cell phone. Video is taking over the world, and the statistics are staggering.

- Every second almost 17,000 hours of new video will be produced.
- Forbes reports that there's been more videos produced in the last 30 days than the television networks have produced in the last 30 years.
- By 2019, Research shows that nearly 80 percent of all internet traffic will be made up of videos. With the surplus of videos already all-over social media, websites, and the internet in general, this statistic is already proving to be true.
- From April 2015 and November of the same year, the average amount of video views per day on Facebook went from four billion to eight billion.

Simply put, you are falling behind if you aren't putting video to use for your own benefit.

VIDEO IS POWERFUL

Did you know these facts?

- Viewers retain 95% of a message when they watch it in a video, compared to 10% when reading it in a text (Wirebuzz)
- Social video generates 1200% more shares than just text and images combined (SmallBizTrends)

The reason video is so powerful is that when you are watching a video, you are engaging two of your senses rather than just one. Another reason is we have all been programmed to watch video because of our TV viewing habits. Almost all of us grew up watching TV. We tend to believe what we see on TV, so we are very used to video as a vehicle to deliver the information we might be curious about and want to know more about.

- The human brain has the ability to process visual content 60,000 times faster than it can text. With a simple fact like that, if you're still using text and not video, then you could be losing out on customers in this fast-paced digital world.
- People like doing business with brands that they know and trust. Videos are effective in getting your potential customers to connect with a human face or voice, as well as a personality. This allows emotions to be communicated through video in a much more powerful fashion than with text alone.

These statistics show that marketers who don't incorporate video into their programmatic platform are missing the opportunity to convert a sophisticated crowd.

VIDEO MARKETING IS EVEN MORE POWERFUL

- Using video in an email leads to a 200-300% increase in click-through rates. (Hubspot)
- Including a video on a landing page can increase conversion rates by 80%. (Unbounce)
- 64% of consumers purchase after watching branded social videos. (Tubular Insights)

Social media is all about engaging with your audience. The more you can get your followers to share your posts, the more reach you have. Research shows that video is one of the best ways to do this. In fact, your followers are ten times more likely to engage with your post and share it if it consists of a video. How are you engaging with your audience? A great example of this was the marketing campaign I did for the GoPro camera. We used video ads to drive people to the GoPro website when people got there and watched all the cool videos, they shared them with their friends creating a viral effect that helped grow the business.

Everyone wants that front page position on Google. Well, one way to get it is by using video content. Statistics show that you can boost your odds of getting your website on that front page by 50 times by adding videos to your site. Are you increasing your odds by incorporating video into your website?

These statistics show that marketers who don't incorporate video into their marketing are missing the opportunity to engage convert new customers or clients

ARE YOU USING VIDEO?

So, the question now is: Are you using video to the best of your advantage? Are you using video to get ahead of your competitors? Are you using video to catapult yourself to the first page of Google's search engine results page?

If you are involved in e-commerce, selling products on Amazon, or advertising on Facebook or YouTube, you had better understand how important it is to be incorporating video into all your marketing. The two key questions you should be asking yourself are:

1. With so much video content being produced, how can I make my videos stand out?
2. How can I make my marketing videos perform better?

I want to clarify. I'm not talking about videos for entertainment. There are thousands of people and companies creating this kind of content. What I'm referring to is something more important, something that I've been doing for over thirty years and at a higher level than most. And that is to create videos that are designed for the viewer to take a specific action like visiting a landing page, ordering a product, or pushing the BUY button on Amazon.

In the upcoming chapters, I will be going into specific steps in all things related to creating video content that engages the viewer and creating video content that sells your product or service. We will take a detailed look at the three steps of video production and the things you can do to save money while still producing great looking videos.

You will learn the best way to gather and tape powerful testimonials that will sell your products for you, how to create tutorial and demonstration videos that will set you apart from the competition. You will learn from the top experts in the video production that I work with day in and day out – directors, producers, editors, lighting and sound experts and art directors – who can make your product shine, will share their knowledge and experience to help you produce compelling videos. I will show you learn how to incorporate direct response into your marketing videos to create a better return on investment (ROI). Whether you end up producing videos yourself or hire someone to do it, you will have all the knowledge, shortcuts, and money-saving ideas right at your finger-tips.

INTERVIEW WITH PAUL MILLER, FOUNDER OF COZY PHONES

Paul is the founder of Cozy Phones, www.cozyphones.com. I met Paul after I gave the Keynote speech at the Prosper Show for Amazon Sellers. He was just starting his business selling kid's hcadphones. I have been an advisor to him for the last several years. Here is a short interview we did about how he has used video to help grow his business.

PAUL

As you know, I started in e-commerce in 2015 on the heels of ... basically looking for a Plan B, because my multi-unit restaurant franchise was basically failing. I was looking for something else to do.

I basically took a course on how to sell products on Amazon. Studied up and found my first product which I was interested in sourcing from China. It was a sleeping headphone, adult sleeping headphones, something that I had personally used in the past. It's a soft, stretchy headband with speakers inside. I've used one from another vendor quite a while ago, but it had broken. It was a product that I was familiar with, and there just wasn't much of a selection on Amazon.

I found a supplier in China, and I followed all the rules of what we had been taught, to make a better listing, take better pictures, better descriptions, bullet points, and so forth. I had some pretty nice success with that very first product.

Few months later, I was doing a photo shoot with some models and a photographer of different styles and different colors of those sleeping headphones. My photographer put them on her ten-year-old daughter with her iPad in her hand and took a couple of shots that way. That was just kind of my "aha" moment, right there. I said, "What if I could make a fun, colorful, interesting headband headphones for kids?"

I came home to my house, my family. I asked my own daughter if she could come up with some character designs for me. I had my daughter draw up a couple of different versions. One was a frog and the other a cat. I sent those drawings off to my supplier. I said, "Can you try to make this for me?" I think it was November of '15, I launched my first children's product. Nothing like that was on the market. Whole new category.

We got traction right away. It turns out that we solved a lot of problems for kids and parents about headphones. The younger kids, preschoolers and so forth, were using tablets and doing either educational programs or watching movies. They don't like big, bulky headphones or earbuds. This is a great solution for them. We also added volume limiting in our speakers, so it's a safe product for the kids. The headphones stay on. They can fall asleep in the car with the headphones on. They're great for traveling. We just met all these needs that we really didn't know existed in the beginning.

From there, we took off and created more styles, more originals. As you know, along the way I got some advice from a friend who said, "You should look into licensing."

We executed our first license, I think, in 2016, a children's book character called the Whatif Monster. That led to some initial success in licensing. I decided to go pursue that further, and in 2017 we ended up with our first big license with Nickelodeon. It just kind of went crazy from there. That opened up some more opportunities, and we developed more licenses within Nickelodeon. We have three other licenses besides the Nickelodeon "Paw Patrol." We have "Teenage Mutant Ninja Turtles," JoJo Siwa, and "Shimmer and Shine."

Now we're developing a bunch more licenses. We think that that's just a great strategy to grow and protect your brand, and you're riding the coattails of those major entertainment properties that the kids already know and love. That has really propelled our business forward in a major way and allowed us to continue to just add more styles, and more product, and more licenses.

From '16 to '17...we were able to double our business. Actually, that's already out there. In '17, I did about $4.5 million. The year before that, in '16, we did about $2 million, so we doubled our business. Then, this year, we're on track for another high growth year.

RICK

When did you first start using video, tell me a little bit about that, and when you decided to incorporate video into what you were doing?

PAUL

I knew that we had an opportunity to advertise on Facebook, and the Facebook video was a big thing. One time, early on, in 2016, I think, is when I made my first Facebook video. I wrote a very simple script. It was all just a bunch of still images and music put together with a brief narration track. That was the first video that we did.

I think at that time I was probably just using Adobe Premier. I think it was Adobe Premier. I just used ... I didn't even shoot any new video stock, really. I just used still video, motion stills, a little bit of music in the background track, and a narration track. Then we also captioned it. That's important, especially on Facebook, where people aren't necessarily playing the volume. At least, as you're scrolling through it, you can see what the words are, and the first one was pretty successful. I was very happy with that. I actually hired a guy to help me with the Facebook ads, defining the audience, and managing the Facebook budget. Optimizing the Facebook ads. He did a great job with that first one.

RICK

What were you asking people to do with the Facebook video ads? Driving them to Amazon, or driving them to your website?

PAUL

We were driving them directly to our product page on Shopify, CozyPhones.com.

We would drive them directly to there, which ... Some people say, "Drive them to an information page," or something like that. There's obviously all kinds of ways you can do it. But we were just basically trying to get a purchase out of that.

RICK

Did you get the ad to pay for itself? Was it a positive ROI (return on investment)?

PAUL

Absolutely, yeah. On that first one, it was positive ROI. That was a long time ago. I can't remember exactly, but I think we were getting somewhere in terms of a three to one return on our advertising spend.

RICK

Did you do any more video ads?

PAUL

We did one last spring in March of '17. One Saturday morning, I had the idea of ... I think, actually, it was my Facebook guy had told me about a video that they did something like "Top Five" or "Top Ten Reasons" for another product. That planted the seed, and I said, "Let me just do another video," "Top Five Reason Why Kids Love CozyPhones."

I actually used a lot of real-life ... Again, it was a series of stills made into video, I used product shots that we had taken for our catalog listings of kids using the CozyPhones, and a combination of real customers' kids using CozyPhones, for people that I already had permission to use those photos with. As a matter of fact, I believe that the real kids' use cases were from my photographer, who has five young children. She takes pictures of her kids using CozyPhones all the time.

RICK

How did you create that video, what did you use?

PAUL

For that one, I used a really simple program, extremely simple program anybody can use without video experience. It's called Lumen5.

What that software can do ... You can point it to a blog article that you have, and if you have photos and text in the blog article, it'll actually scrub your site and put together a sample video for you.

But, for my purposes, since I knew what I already wanted to say, I just imported the stills ... I had about ten still images, and about five text bullet points, along with a music track. No narration at all. That video just took off. It just started with "Reason number five," "four," "three," "two," "one."

It really showed kids demonstrating the product. The parent could get it immediately. They could envision their kids using that product in that way. In the car. On the airplane. At home. They could see how that would solve problems that they have every day with their kids using headphones.

RICK

About what do you think was your budget for that video? You produced it for $1,000, or $500?

PAUL

Less, I think I even used the free version of the software, plus about two hours of my time.

RICK

Pretty much zero, right?

PAUL

That one was a pretty much zero budget one. Obviously, some of the photos I had already paid for. But those were sunk costs.

RICK

Where do you find music? How important is music to it?

PAUL

I think the music was helpful, but in this case, Lumen5 comes with a music license. They have a library in there that you can choose from.

RICK

That's awesome. Do you have numbers now from Facebook or approximate numbers?

PAUL

That particular video, I think I finished it on a Saturday. I sent it to my Facebook guy.

He ran it for a few hours. He says, "Paul, I think this thing is really hitting nicely. Do you want me to scale it up?" I said, "Sure, go ahead."

In the beginning, we were getting like three or four times return on our investment. For every dollar spent on Facebook, we were getting three- or four-times sales dollars back. Then, as he scaled it up and we find the audience, we got to a peak of about eight times return on our spend. Then that trickled off over time.

RICK

What about the time frame, when you said it trickled off over time, are you talking about a year? Six months?

PAUL

It was more like about three or four months.

Yeah. With the peak being in sixty days, probably. We were just crushing it for that first month. My sales on Shopify, Cozy-Phones.com, went from about $1,000 a day to about $10,000 a day. I 10x-ed my ... We could just say "10x-ed", probably better than the dollar figure, on my website. ... I 10x-ed my Cozy-Phones.com sales.

The very interesting part of this was we had what we called the halo effect on Amazon or the ripple effect. People would go, they'd see the product on CozyPhones.com, and then they would leave, and they'd go buy it on Amazon. During that peak time, I actually doubled my sales on Amazon also without ever directing any traffic there.

RICK

That's awesome. It's so funny how advertising works. We had the same exact halo effect when you run an infomercial on TV. It pushes all the other channels that people shop in.

PAUL

Yeah. The same thing, Walmart.com, we also had a big lift there. You can see it across the board. During that time, that video got over ... During that first 90, 120 days, we got over five million views.

A lot of that was sharing, people sharing or tagging people in Facebook. What you would see, typically, is you'd see in the comments, somebody would tag their friend with small children because they thought they might like the product. That would generate another view, right there. Some folks would share it, as well.

At one point, in advertising on Facebook, we were spending as much as $8,000 a day. On average I would say we were spending several thousand dollars a day on Facebook ad spend. I finally had to pull it back because of inventory.

RICK

That's a good problem to have. Amazing story Paul, thanks for sharing.

PAUL

Now, here's a tidbit for you. I did two highly produced videos recently and spent a lot of money on a budget. Neither one of those is performing as well as my homemade video.

RICK

I see that happen sometimes. What it shows you is, it's more about the messaging than production values. In other words, you can have low production ... you were using stills, and you did it yourself. But the message hit home as opposed to, maybe, those other ones. The production quality was way up, but maybe the message was not the one that people were looking for. The other thing ... I don't know how much the production company did the script, or you did it, or whatever, but the one coming from you, that you wrote, obviously worked really, really well.

PAUL

Yeah. I agree with those things. Sometimes the simplest of video could be more impactful than a $20,000 video production. It is about the message. It's about relating to those folks.

RICK

Is there anything you want to add?

PAUL

I think it's evolving. What I have found is you have to keep trying different video, and different messages. Just, sometimes, it can be really hard to figure out what will work. Don't get discouraged. You may have to make ten videos before one hits. But, when that one hits, and you get 5 million views, and it 10x-es your sales, then it's worth the effort.

RICK

Paul, thank you again, this has been great!

CHAPTER TWO SUMMARY

- You do not need to spend a lot of money to make a video that works.
- Content and messaging are more important than pretty pictures (high production values).
- A positive ROI will allow you to scale your advertising and grow revenue.
- All successful video advertising campaigns will have a "Halo" effect on other distribution channels.

CHAPTER THREE
The Most Effective Video Content

"Persuasion is clearly a sort of demonstration since we are most fully persuaded when we consider a thing to have been demonstrated."
—Aristotle

SHAREABILITY

One of the most appealing aspects of online video is its inherent shareability. Video gets you access to huge platforms like YouTube, which serves over 1 billion unique visitors per day. If you make something interesting, people will share it. A great example of this was for the company I worked with that created the GoPro camera. They created thousands of user-generated videos that were posted on their site that people loved to share.

We helped fine tune the process by branding each video with the GoPro logo at both the beginning and the end, something I highly recommend. We then helped create traffic to their site by running a contest giving away one of everything they make every day. We created awareness for the contest by using 30-second brand response TV spots driving people to the site, again using user-generated footage. This was an all video marketing campaign that helped grow the business to over one billion dollars in sales!

One of the main reasons the campaign worked was that the videos were so interesting that people wanted to share them. How do you make your video content more interesting, more appealing, more engaging, and more effective? Simple. *Find out what people like to watch and then give them that type of content.*

To do that let's start with some online viewing statistics.

According to Curata (Source: Curata), the top three most effective types of video content are:

- Customer testimonials (51%);
- Tutorial videos (50%);
- Demonstration videos (49%)

Let's look at these different types of video content, what they are and how to make them.

TUTORIAL, INSTRUCTIONAL OR HOW-TO VIDEOS

I want to start with tutorial videos because they are by far the easiest to make from a content standpoint. Tutorial videos are used more for teaching and for customer service.

Here is how Wikipedia describes a tutorial: "A **tutorial** is a method of transferring knowledge and may be used as a part of a learning process. More interactive and specific than a book or a lecture, a tutorial seeks to teach by example and supply the information to complete a certain task."

Video is the perfect format for tutorials. 'A picture is worth a thousand words' or 'show me don't tell me' are two good statements that show why video is so effective for tutorials.

Here's another statistic to consider, **90% of users** say that product videos are helpful in the buying decision process (Source: Hubspot). Make sure you create videos for each of the products you sell. Illustrate how to use it, the benefits, features, and specs. *The more you educate your viewing audience on the product's use, the better success they'll have once they purchase your product.* I am a strong believer in *selling through education.* This will lead to fewer returns and happier customers who are more likely to re-order from you in the future.

71% of consumers say that video is the best way to bring product features to life. A great example of this is a company I work called Plugable, https://plugable.com/. Every time they introduce a new product, they make a new product video. Is it effective? They are an Amazon top 200 seller, so they must be doing something right. Go to their website and see how they use tutorial videos.

Making a tutorial is easy, start with the premise that you are explaining to a friend how to use your product. Use simple words. I always like to think that I'm speaking to a sixth grader, a twelve-year-old. Keep it simple. Record this dialogue into your phone. You've just created the script. Create a storyboard of the steps, then just use the camera on your phone to record these steps and you are done!

There are many wonderful guides on how to create tutorials that you can find online. Here are just a few.

- https://www.incomediary.com/ultimate-guide-making-online-video-tutorials
- https://www.techsmith.com/tutorial-camtasia-how-to-make-a-video-tutorial.html
- https://www.creativebloq.com/video-production/make-tutorial-video-2131915

DEMONSTRATION VIDEOS—BEST FOR SELLING

Definition of *demonstration:* a showing of the merits of a product or service to a prospective consumer.

Demonstration videos are how you sell your product. There is no better way to sell your product or service than show its capabilities in use. Another feature of demonstration videos is that they have a call to action or CTA embedded in the video. This is extremely important. *You must show a person where they can get your product or service after you get them excited to buy with the demonstration.*

Let's look at some more statistics;

- Including a demonstration video on a landing page can *increase conversion rates by 80%* (Source: Unbounce)
- After watching a demonstration video, **64% of users** are more likely to buy a product online (Source: Hubspot)

Demos work! Sometimes you can build an entire business off of a good demo video. Let me give you two examples, the first video was one that I created for OxiClean. It shows Billy Mays, one of the best pitchmen ever, with a large aquarium of clean water. He puts some stained white sheets into the water then proceeds to add many different staining ingredients until the water looks filthy brown. He then adds two scoops of OxiClean and stirs the water, magically, right before your eyes the water turns clear, and when he removes the sheets, they are clean. This one video demo helped propel Oxi-Clean to over $100 Million in sales!

If you want to see the demo here is the YouTube link. You can also find all the videos mentioned in this book on my YouTube channel, rickcesari.tv.

http://bit.ly/3Video1

I first created this in video 1996, it was Billy Mays very first infomercial. There have been many imitations done since then, but this was the original demonstration.

Another highly successful series of demonstration videos are for the Blendtec blender. The most memorable was when the demonstrator put a cell phone into the blender and turned it into dust, with over 12 million views sales skyrocketed!

Here is the Blendtec Video Link:

http://bit.ly/3Video2

Food and recipe videos are another area of demos that are a very successful way to sell the product that is being demonstrated. Two products that I had great success with using demonstration videos are the Juiceman juice extractor and the George Foreman Grill.

Here is a video I created, with over 1.2 million views, of Jay Kordich, aka The Juiceman, making Orange Juice:

http://bit.ly/3Video3

Because of doing video demos like these and running TV ads we were able to create a huge juicing phenomenon that swept the country and created over $100 million in juice extractor sales!

Here is the famous demonstration of George Foreman Grill's slanted surface draining the fat away from the food being cooked.

This video helped create the brand and tagline, "knock out the fat," a product that went on to sell over 100 Million units! http://bit.ly/3Video4

Again, this was the very first demonstration that George ever did on TV. There have been lots of copycats since then. Two things that I want you to learn from this video is that I combined three very effective techniques which I discuss in detail in the book.

1. The actual Demo showing the fat draining away, using extreme close up shots for more emphasis.
2. Having the spokesperson, George Foreman, describe what is happening during the demo. More on this is in Chapter 7.
3. Backing up the demo with testimonials of people using the product experiencing the same thing being described. More on this is in Chapter 3.

If you combine all three aspects above, you will be able to create very engaging and effective videos.

CREATING A GREAT DEMO VIDEO

Here is a simple guide on how to make a great demo video in 5 easy steps:

1. Introduce your product or brand
2. Tell us who this product is for.
3. Demo-show how the product is used. Show close-ups.
4. Cover the Main Features of the product backed up with benefits to the end user.
5. Call to Action-ask the person watching to purchase or visit your website.

I created a video that shows you these exact steps: http://bit.ly/videodemosteps

One last example of the effectiveness of demonstration videos is for a product called The Sous-Vide Supreme, sousvidesupreme.com. This is a product that was trying to introduce a brand-new way to cook using a "water bath."

The secret to launching and growing this business was to make many different recipe videos showing how you could create delicious meals using the Sous-vide Supreme. The company created over 200 different video recipes of different chefs, cooks, and people using the machine. It is a great lesson in content marketing. My good friend and co-author of *Building Billion Dollar Brands*, Barb Westfield has been instrumental in the success of this company.

AUTHENTIC CONSUMER TESTIMONIALS

This is your most powerful marketing tool. Over the last twenty years, I have been using different types of video marketing (persuasion) to help grow businesses and create brands like Sonicare, Clarisonic, OxiClean, and GoPro. The videos, regardless of how they were deployed, were trying to have a specific impact on viewer behavior. That behavior might be to purchase a product, visit a website, attend a live or online webinar, drive the viewer to brick-and-mortar retail stores, to the top of a sales funnel, go to Amazon or other online stores, or simply for lead generation. I've found that the single most powerful tool to do this successfully, that I've used over and over again, is finding and creating authentic video testimonials. These are real consumers who have purchased your product or service tried it and are happy to talk about it in front of the camera.

Testimonials are not a new concept. They have worked effectively for generations in every type of advertising vehicle ever used from direct mail, to print ads, on radio or TV, and websites for e-commerce. Amazon uses the testimonial concept with their product reviews, which are effective, but not as good as using a real video testimonial.

Surprisingly, I've found that most business owners never talk to their customers proactively, but only do so when the customer reaches out to them. Let's look at why this seemingly obvious marketing tool is so often overlooked or not done correctly.

First, I am going to share with you, why testimonials work so well and second, how to find and create authentic video testimonials that will help sell your product or service more effectively.

TESTIMONIALS OVERCOME OBJECTIONS

People will see a product or service you are offering, their first reaction will be something like this, "It works for him/her, but that won't work for me because…" and then a series of excuses will follow: "I'm too young," "I'm too old," "it takes too much time," "It's too hard," "It's too easy," "It's too expensive," and so on. Breaking down these mental barriers and overcoming these objections are a normal part of the sales process that needs to be addressed. Testimonials are a quick, easy, and effective way to do that.

If you are the product owner or manufacturer, people are going to be skeptical about what you say or claim about your product or service. You have a vested interest in selling the product, so why should they believe you or your advertising? But, if they hear how well a product or service works from people they can closely relate to, it will help overcome their objections. That is what third-party testimonials can do for you.

Let me give you a few examples. When we were trying to sell the Juiceman Juice Extractor, one objection to purchasing that we heard over and over again was that people thought it would be too hard and time-consuming to clean up after juicing. In many cases, that was just an easy excuse for not committing to buy. To overcome this, we videotaped many customers who had already purchased the product talking about their experiences using the machine, how simple, fast, and easy to use and easy to clean it was. The payoff was delicious—healthy juices that gave them more energy and made them feel great. We shot B-roll (extra video footage of the action people describe in their testimonial) of each of the people using the juicer, cleaning the machine and finally enjoying the juice they had just made. We use the "B-roll" to enhance the viewing, giving each testimonial a real look and feel and so they were not just a talking head.

Another good example was the testimonials we taped for the Sonicare toothbrush. People complained that the sonic brush was too expensive, a common objection for many products. When Sonicare was first introduced, it cost $150, which was expensive compared to paying a couple dollars for a toothbrush.

We interviewed and videotaped many happy Sonicare customers. They all talked about the price point as being expensive at first, but that the product was the best investment they had ever made as it actually saved them money by having better dental check-ups.

Others talked about how squeaky clean their teeth felt and others how Sonicare actually made their teeth brighter by removing stains. Oprah probably said it best when she held up a Sonicare on her show and said, "It makes your gums hum!" Yes, that kind of celebrity testimonial led to millions in sales!

There are several things happening in the examples above. One key is that I was talking to actual purchasers of the products, not actors. The authenticity of the testimonial will be apparent when it is a real customer, and you hear first-hand about their experiences using the product. I have always found that genuine answers in response to good targeted questions always turn out better than having actors read lines.

The second key is the actual interview questions being asked and how they are presented. When I interview someone, I never tell them what to say. Instead, I ask them questions that will lead them in the direction I want to go or the information I want to cover to reach the goal of the video I am creating. Also, I start with very general questions to get people comfortable speaking in front of the camera. Start with very broad questions and then get more specific about the points you are trying to cover as a person gets more comfortable. I usually ask 15-20 questions (see list below) of each person. The good testimonials, ones that are saying great things, you talk to longer. Ones that are a struggle to get information out of you cut the interview shorter.

I can't tell you how many times I was having a great conversation with someone and as soon as the camera started rolling people clammed up and looked like a deer in the headlights. It's not comfortable for most people to speak in front of a camera. Many try to think about the right thing to say instead of how they truly feel about a product. I always say, "Forget about the camera and talk to me like you're telling your neighbor about this wonderful new product you found and what you like about it." You want a good testimonial to feel like an intimate conversation between two people, but it's caught on video to be replayed over and over to potential new customers. This is word of mouth advertising, amplified! For some people, the camera can be so intimidating that they just won't open up.

A technique we use in a situation like that is that I tell the cameraman to start rolling using a hand signal while I'm just having a normal conversation with them. I usually don't make small talk before an interview, because you never know when that great sound bite will come out, and you want to have the camera rolling when it does. Once the interview has started, I normally ask about the individual that I'm interviewing first as it's easy for people to talk about themselves and a great way to break the ice.

TIPS AND TECHNIQUES ON INTERVIEWING

Get your subject talking first; don't ask whether they like or dislike your product. Just ask how they feel about it.

Be ready for a classic deer-in-the-headlights response, which is most people's initial reaction to being filmed. They're liable to shut down to simply answering "yes" or "no" if you give them the opportunity, so don't. Instead, ask questions that require them to speak at more length. One technique we use is to have the camera rolling when the person first sits down. As you are greeting them and having a normal conversation, the interviewed customer will be at ease unaware the camera is rolling.

Always ask people to include your question in their answers. Don't put words in their mouth as the answers tend to come out stilted and fake. Here's an example:

> Question: Would you recommend Sonicare to your friends?
>
> Answer: "I would recommend the Sonicare to my friends because…"

When you get people who want to talk, don't interrupt with more questions. Let them talk. Nod, be responsive, take notes to show you're listening, but let them talk. You can go back and ask more specific questions based on what they've said. For instance, let's say you were interviewing people about the George Foreman Grill. The conversation could go like this:

> Response: "I like the fact that it's very convenient. I can just come home from work, grab something out of the re-frigerator, throw it on there, and two minutes later it's ready."
>
> Question: "So, what you like about it is the fact that it's convenient. It saves you time," and see how they respond.

Focus on the benefits and use what the consumer has said as a prompt for your next person's interviews. "Tell me about how convenient this product is to use at home. How does it help you when you come home from work? How does it help you prepare meals for your family?" Hone in on one particular benefit of the product. Another consumer might say, "I can't believe how great the food tastes when it comes off the grill." That gives us the prompt for the next interview: "Why do you like the taste? What's different about the flavor the food has, cooking it this way versus the way you normally cook food?"

Be alert to any negative answer trends coming out of the inter-views. If we're interviewing thirty consumers and all thirty say, "I don't like the fact it takes too long to heat up," or something like that, then that's information that should go back to the manufacturer. "You've got to do something about this. People are waiting ten minutes for your grill to heat up and it's going to be an issue." That feedback can provide vital help in fine-tuning the product and making it better. You're not going to have a successful brand if there are issues out there that people are concerned about.

You should always try and just have a conversation with the person you are interviewing, not an interrogation. A person's answer should lead to your next question or comment just like a conversation. Never try to put words in their mouth or tell them what to say.

Here is a list of sample questions I might use to interview someone about the Sonicare toothbrush. These questions can be adapted to any product:

- Tell me your name and what you do.
- How did you hear about Sonicare?
- What made you want to try Sonicare?
- How did you feel after first trying it?
- What did you like best? Why?
- Is there anything you did not like? Why?
- Did your teeth feel cleaner? Whiter?
- Have you been to the dentist since using Sonicare?
- Did you get a better checkup? How did that make you feel?
- What do you think of Sonic technology?
- Did you know that the brush vibrates at 32,000/second?
- What do you think about the cost?
- Is it a good value for what you paid? Why?
- Would you recommend Sonicare to your friends? Why?

- If you were talking to your neighbor about this product that you just purchased and were happy with, what would you tell them?
- Anything else I didn't ask that you would like to share?

This conversation would probably last 30-45 minutes. Out of it you might get one or two great sound bites to use in the video you are creating. All the additional footage can be used as content for the website, YouTube channel, or social media. You should always have enough content to build an individual story about each person.

TESTIMONIALS ESTABLISH CREDIBILITY

Why should a consumer believe the claims you are making for your product or service? Good authentic testimonials come from certain targeted people who can influence others who have bought or tried your product and have great things to say about it. This will help establish the credibility needed to break down the barriers to purchase. The key here is to establish trust in your product and in your company. You can do this by tapping into trust that has already been established by influencers already using your product.

For example, with the George Foreman Grill, we claimed that it could cook your food quickly and that the food tasted great. Why should people have believed us? They didn't have to! One of our customers was the head chef at Tavern on The Green in New York. He loved using the grill and raved about how great the food turned out—especially fish. He even started using it in the restaurant at work. Of course, we asked him if we could videotape him using the grill and place that footage in our advertising. It was good promotion for them and great credibility for us. People might be skeptical about us making our own claims, but now we had a respected professional chef who was *substantiating our claims for us*. Something like this has a huge impact on a person's thoughts and decision-making process, "If it's good enough for him to use this product must really work!" We were even more fortunate when the *New York Times* decided to run a story featuring the Chef and the George Foreman Grill. We got permission from the *New York Times* (it was expensive!) to use the article, and we placed it strategically as B-roll over the Chef's testimonial, further enhancing the credibility of the video we created. I go into more detail about how we did this in my previous book, *Building Billion Dollar Brands*.

Another example again was with the Sonicare toothbrush. One of the marketing claims we were making for the product was that regular use of the Sonicare toothbrush could help reverse gum disease. Our best testimonials to support this claim were from the many dental professionals who were using the product and seeing great results in both themselves and their patients. Targeting some of these dentists for video interviews led to many great professional, authentic endorsements for the product.

One of my favorite places to get many testimonials in a short time for your product or company is at your booth at an industry tradeshow. Always bring a camera crew to this type of event, and you will be able to gather more video content than at any other single place. Tradeshows work so well because you have both existing customers and new customers coming up to your booth and they almost always will be willing to say great things about your product or company. Also, the atmosphere of a tradeshow when someone is being interviewed in front of your booth with activity going on in the background creates a sense of authenticity that is hard to duplicate in any other environment.

Sonicare had a booth at one of the largest dental trade shows at the time. It was being held in the Moscone Center in San Francisco. At that show, we were able to get high-level testimonials from people like the head of the dental schools at Harvard and USC as well as many of the top periodontists in the country.

TESTIMONIALS WORK WELL BECAUSE OF SOCIAL PROOF

This is actually based on a psychological concept that has been studied extensively. It says that in certain situations, in the absence of any other guidance, people will look to what other people are doing as a way to guide their own behavior. P.T. Barnum, The Greatest Showman on Earth and one of the best marketers ever, has a famous quote which sums up social proof: "Nothing draws a crowd quite like a crowd." That's a really simple insight into human behavior. Amazon does this with product reviews. If you are looking at similar products on Amazon and one has many good reviews, and the other doesn't which are you going to buy? I have promoted live health and nutrition seminars where people would come to a meeting room and listen to a presenter for 90 minutes. At the end of the lecture they were supposed to get up and go to the back of the room to purchase the product, but often people just sat in their chairs and asked questions. We started having members of our staff sit in the audience. When the lecture was over, they simply stood up and went back to their regular seats at the registration table. People would see this and feel that it was okay to stand and follow them back. Conversions and sales increased by as much as 30 percent with this one simple strategy. You should be using this concept in all your marketing, including your website, which should be filled with testimonial videos of happy customers who have purchased your products. If you start creating and deploying authentic video testimonials, your sales and conversions will go up, guaranteed!

FINDING GREAT TESTIMONIALS

When an ordinary consumer tries your product and loves it enough to send you a testimonial, it establishes valuable third-party credibility you can use. This is taking word-of-mouth advertising to the next level. Ad agencies often hire actors to perform scripts that sound like testimonials, but they lack authenticity and can misfire with consumers, or leave them indifferent. You get authenticity when you videotape actual customers to find out what they really think. If it's a glowing review, find a way to feature that video in your product marketing promotions.

Great product or company testimonial videos should be used throughout the company website and in your PR and social media channels. How do you find these great testimonials? You need to become proactive and not reactive. I cannot tell you how many businesses I run across that are not reaching out to their existing customer base and specifically asking them if they would be interested in doing a testimonial for the company or product they are selling. I've been creating great consumer video testimonials for over 25 years, and I promise you that if you ask, people will be eager to help you out.

CURRENTLY IN BUSINESS

Your customers or clients are the best sources of honest feedback about your product or service. The first place to look is your own database. When we are gathering testimonials for a marketing campaign, I will usually schedule two taping days, one on the east coast and one on the west coast. This is done to create a diversity of testimonials being taped and to find relatable people for any potential new customers who might be viewing them.

We look through the existing customer database for the ZIP codes for an area where the customers are more densely populated. The reason we are looking for many people in the same area has to do with production costs when you are setting up your testimonial taping days. We usually book a local home or studio, a central location where everyone can get to at the appointed time. This way your camera crew can set up their gear and not have to waste valuable time going from location to location. Doing it this way I find that we can comfortably interview ten to twelve people in a single day instead of two or three if you have to move around to different location each time. It makes it a much more cost-effective and efficient way to gather video testimonials.

We then send a series of emails to the people telling them we would like them to participate in our testimonial taping. Many people who like your product or company will be happy to do so if you just ask! We have an email sequence that we use for existing databases that we have refined and developed over the years. It always works well for us. I will share it with you later in the chapter.

NEW PRODUCT LAUNCH OR START-UP

If you are just starting and you do not have a customer database, then you will have to give some of your product away to people and have them use it for thirty to sixty days and then go back and videotape them based on their experiences. As a bonus for doing this, I always let them keep the product for their efforts. If you can show people the improvement customers have experienced from using your product in before-and-after videos, it makes a compelling argument for buying what you are selling.

From the very first moment you start selling yourself or your product, you should be collecting testimonials. For example, you could send out a "Tell Us How We Did" postcard to new customers with a grading scale and a final question along the lines of, "Finally, what would you say to someone else considering using <YOUR NAME / PRODUCT NAME>?"

Every chance you get, gather feedback. Eventually, you'll have an entire library of testimonials. This is incredibly valuable. You'll find that you will have one that fits any type of advertising you do to any type of demographic.

Getting testimonials that will sell your product for you is always a numbers game. To get three or four really great testimonials for your product or service you need to interview at least ten to twelve people. We find that to get ten to twelve people at our shoot days we need to send out a minimum of 500 emails to the database. If you are having trouble finding enough people in the local area, our next step is to expand the email solicitation to a wider geographical area. Once people show interest, we do a pre-interview by phone, and if we feel the people will be good on camera, we fly them in to help fill out the testimonial shooting day's schedule.

INTERVIEW WITH MARK SWABY, CO-FOUNDER/CEO NET MEDIA GROUP, BASED IN SALT LAKE CITY, UTAH

RICK

Hi Mark, please give me a brief overview. What's the name of your company and what do you do?

MARK

Well, the name of our company is Net Media Group, https://www.netmediagroup.com/ and it's an incubation company for e-commerce opportunities and projects. We had been a digital ad agency for a couple decades, and over the years we've compiled quite a portfolio of customers and experience in a lot of industries. We got tired of working for other people. We just thought let's just start drinking our own Kool-Aid. It's funny as soon as you start thinking that way opportunities start coming your way. So we had the opportunity to take over the supply side as well as inventory and selling of things that we were very familiar with. So Net Media

Group became a holding company for bigger distribution opportunities.

We receive distribution rights globally, and then we apply our e-commerce knowledge and trade skills towards that in developing these brands. So once a brand becomes sizeable, or a dot-com becomes sizeable under Net Media Group, we then roll it out into its own corporation, and it takes a life of its own at that point.

RICK

That sounds like fun! Let's back up for a little bit and let's talk about when Net Media was an online or digital agency. What are some of the services that you offered?

MARK

So, every digital agency would rattle off a similar skill set of search engine assistance, whether it's the FCO organic or any sort of paid media. Today paid media—you used to be able to say paid search—but now it's PLAs. It's paid marketing with the social channels, you could go on and on and on, but our main offering was we really taught clients how to spend appropriately in those channels so that you weren't betting against yourself, you had a plan in how you wanted a search engine to appear.

It wasn't always about maximizing every channel; it was about maximizing the right channel for the right amount of money with the right message. Affiliates come into play here, now influencers come into play here. We always refer to the search engine results as an ecosystem, and you have to manage the ecosystem. It's all about controlling the ecosystem from a paid marketing standpoint. And then as a footnote to that, you're also controlling the eco-system by controlling your price, so that was also a big component of what we brought to the table was bringing pricing integrity across all the channels as well as balancing your marketing spent within the channels.

RICK

This book is about using video to get people to take specific actions, whether that video is deployed on TV, on an e-commerce site, on Amazon, as a Facebook ad, et cetera. One of the things that I talk about is starting with a foundation of direct response principles. Do you use those principles in what you do?

MARK

Well the short answer is absolutely. It's one of the most relatable disciplines that I can think of to digital marketing. *In fact, to me, Direct Response Marketing is what saved the internet.* You might remember back in the 90s when the dot-com bomb happened, the bubble burst. No one really knew how to monetize. Everyone just ran around saying "Put banners on your site and charge people for banners." But, *the reality is people didn't know how to position a product with a call to action and an offer, solicit the response, and produce an ROI.* And the Direct Response Principles ultimately saved the internet, in my opinion, along with a lot of great innovation of course. But *it was the companies that knew how to speak in the language of ROI that ultimately rose from the ashes and succeeded.* So, I'd say Direct Response Marketing and the modern internet today, go hand-in-hand.

RICK

That was very well said. I've been trying to kind of beat that drum for a long time, but that was a very succinct way of putting it. Let's talk a little bit about how video fits into what you do from a marketing perspective, e-commerce perspective?

MARK

Well it's really crucial, especially when you start talking about price points that are several hundred dollars or several thousand dollars. It's one thing to go buy a charging cable for your iPhone on Amazon when you just have a static image. But it's quite another thing to solicit a response for something that is complex. I'll give you an example. We sell a lot of fitness equipment, and there's no shortage online for fitness equipment. They're complex. There's a lot of moving parts. A lot of technology that needs to be explained and demonstrated and video is the best way to do that. One of the biggest projects we're doing right now in our warehouse is that we have dedicated space that we're using to build out a photo and video bay.

We realized just how important it is to document every inch, every angle of your product. And so rather than outsourcing that, which is not a bad idea, but for us, *it just made more sense to go all in on detailed video and photography because we know that ultimately, it's what sells our product.* So again, yesteryear you could get away with a picture, but I think the companies, the dot-coms that really excel, Zappos is a great example, the individual short little videos make me want a pair of shoes. Who would have thought a pair of shoes you could take into that level of detail? But it worked, and I just think *that if you're really going to succeed online, especially if you're controlling or operating a brand, you really need to articulate it and let people see it via video.* Bandwidth and download time is not an issue like it was ten years ago. People were always scared of content that was too heavy, and how it takes too long to load on your slow internet speed. Those problems are mostly over with, so embrace the content.

RICK

That's awesome. So, when you were doing the agency, what you're doing today, you basically are saying that video is pretty much a part of any online marketing campaign. Can you get more specific about how maybe you might deploy the video?

MARK

Yes. You video something that's five minutes long or ninety seconds long, or whatever it needs to be, and then from that content, you can digest and cut up and slice and dice and make really, I think the common phrase now is "digestible content." So, whether you're on Facebook and you're doing a 15-second tease or YouTube, you can make the video once, but then use all the raw footage or B-roll as they say, to make more digestible content, depending on what platform you're in. It's not as daunting as people think. Sometimes you think, "Oh that's 35, 40 different pieces of content." Well, *just find your message, find your voice, tape it as such and then cut it up as you go. That's ultimately the more cost-effective way to approach it.*

RICK

You have a great way of simplifying everything and I think that's a barrier to many people when it comes to using video is the video production process, which we cover and give people lots of resources in other chapters of the book. But it sounds like you were doing it externally earlier, but now you're making the move to bring that internally, which probably shows you how important video is.

MARK

Exactly. It's paying for itself. It's a no brainer. But people shouldn't feel that's their only option. I think some of the best video content out there is raw and organic cell phone footage. Someone pulling their cell phone out saying, "Let me walk you through this X, Y, Z, setup process here." It's real, it's not scripted. That stuff is so credible, and people sometimes think they need a creative director to produce video for them. You don't. There are incredible examples of powerful brands that just use raw, organic cell phone footage to produce video content.

RICK

That's a great point. I like to use the word authenticity. It's authentic, it's not a fake, it's not an ad. It is what people see on social media every day, so they respond better to that. That's what I'm trying to help people do in this book is to show how easy it is to make video and more important what to focus on from a content standpoint to make those videos work better. Just to reemphasize, why do you think that raw iPhone footage works so well in your opinion?

MARK

I think sometimes we can spend too much on production. It becomes corporate, or we over think things. But when you put a camera in your face and it's just kind of mind to mouth, and you're going with it, I think there's like you say, authenticity there. I'm not saying it's always your best choice, I just encourage people to get involved and try that step one and dip your toe in the water. Ultimately you might need a more polished production, but maybe you don't.

RICK

I agree! You spoke about deploying the video and creating digestible content. If you shoot a video for one of your pieces of exercise equipment, what are some of the different ways that gets deployed then through e-commerce or social media?

MARK

Many of our fitness equipment pieces take a lot time to be set up. So for an example, we filmed one of our product technicians putting together a weightlifting power rack. And as he was doing it, he was explaining it, "be sure to tighten this bolt, be sure to do this," and we thought that was the content we were after, like a real step-by-step video presentation of explaining how this went together. Not very exciting but important to the consumer. Then, something we just decided to do this on a whim, because that video lasted 10 minutes, we just decided to speed it up, not slow motion, like fast motion, and we suppressed obviously the audio, so he didn't sound like a chipmunk. And we just showed the setup while we played some music. It was the same piece of video, but we sped it up to 60 seconds total, and that was ultimately what people chose to watch was the sped-up version of him setting up the rack that took 60 seconds with no audio, and that was just a happy accident that we just stumbled on. *We thought we wanted a 10-minute how to set it up video. Turns out the consumer chose the quick and dirty 60-second version.* We just took the one piece of content we'd shot and just put our creativity hats on and decided to do something different with it.

RICK

That's a great example. I see recipe videos that do that. They basically do an overhead shot of a bowl or cutting board, and they just show everything speeded up to make the recipe and then it's a finished product. It really captures your attention because it's something that's different than ordinary and that's something I tell people to do, be different. That's a fantastic example of something people can do to really stand apart from the competition and what other people are doing.

MARK

Yes, and you never know the mindset of someone. You don't know how much time someone has to make a decision. The latest trend online are very in-depth product reviews. Product reviews that can take 30 minutes to review *and the search engines give those really in-depth articles a whole lot more credence and so from an FCO perspective that's kind of a trend right now.* Really good articles which contrasted a few years ago where people were just putting up quick Amazon type reviews and moving on.

It's the same with video. Some people want to sit down and watch 30-minute explanation on something. But you look at how Facebook and Instagram and these platforms have evolved where it's just an 8-second, 10-second clip of something because that's ultimately what the masses will digest the quickest and the easiest. *And so, if they digest that and still like it, then they can go to the longer content. But whether it's video or even in print, I say do both.* Because you never know what audience or what potential customers you're talking to.

Some have a lot of time, a little time. Where are they in the decision-making process? Are they just starting the process, or have they already been researching this for months and you just need to kind of persuade them with one last little 30-second hit that's digestible? So once again I think I know the answers, but then *we produce this stuff in different lengths, on different platforms, and we learn what the consumer tells us.*

RICK

That's a great point. I always urge people to *listen to what the consumer is trying to tell you.* If somebody comes to you, wanting to market a product and you were setting up their website, how would you do that so that the website would include video? Is it a video from the founder? Is it about the product? A long instruction video? What are some of the uses on the actual site where you like to see video?

MARK

That's a good question. I really think that price point plays a role. Nowadays we buy all our office supplies on Amazon or Costco.com or something, and we don't think twice about what copy paper we need. We already know what copy paper we need. But funny, if I'm researching a printer, I might like a 5-minute video. I really think price point has a lot to do with it in the psyche of the consumer. When you start spending a certain amount of money, you're inclined to research it that much more, and product videos help.

RICK

So, commodities, like office paper, printer paper, toilet paper, paper towels, no brainer stuff obviously you don't need a video. What I was referring to because you were talking about fitness equipment and I know you're involved in selling ladders, things that require more explanation. So you're doing a higher price point, more complicated product, what would you like to show them when it's a high price point product?

MARK

Yes, we've had the privilege of working with Little Giant Ladder for many years, and I learned a lot from them and *one of the things the founder, Hal Wing was a big proponent of was demonstrating the ladder,* which you may recall, this is an articulating ladder. This broke the mold. Can you think of the last innovation in a ladder over your lifetime and Little Giant comes along? And it needed to be demonstrated. And this is before the internet. But Hal Wing traveled the country and demonstrated this ladder for people. And when people saw what it could do, I mean the rest is history. So I always remember that example, *that there are just some things that you can't read about. You need to look at it, you need to see it, you need to have your eyes open wide when the wow factor hits.*

So, if you think you've got a product or a unique selling proposition that can do that, really start embracing the demonstration and the deep elaborate explanation. If your audience wants to read that, fine. But my experience is most people want to see it.

RICK

That's a fantastic answer! You've already identified two of the types of video content that are the most popular online. We talked earlier about a ***tutorial video,*** how to set up a piece of fitness equipment, a weight lifting set. To me that's a tutorial video, you happened to speed it up. The second type of content that's really popular, which you just talked about, are **demonstration videos.** And the third, believe it or not, and you'll get a kick out of this, and probably the most popular are **testimonial videos.** How important are product testimonials videos, and how do you incorporate that into your e-commerce?

MARK

Testimonials are so important. Unfortunately, it's also a very manipulated part of the internet these days. I remember reading articles about how Amazon's conversion rate was so, so, alarmingly low in the early days and that's because people were coming there to read the reviews and then go buy at brick-and-mortar stores. Amazon knew people were just using their site for reviews, and of course, many people stayed around and purchased and now everyone stays around and purchases on Amazon.

RICK

Yes, shopping habits tend to change. People were used to brick and mortar; now they've made the transition to online, but they're still using the reviews for the same reason.

MARK

Exactly. So reviews are crucial; they're not going anywhere. The trick is how do you make them seem believable? So you've got to really walk the line there. Being honest, someone can always game the system, but I think a customer knows it when they go to a website, and they see and read an honest review.

RICK

I agree 100 percent with what you're saying. I spend a lot of time talking about the type of testimonials we used to film for the Direct Response TV and everything I emphasize in the book is *using authentic testimonials, where you're reaching out to an actual customer who has purchased your product, and they love it, and you're just capturing what they say on video and then deploying that type of thing on the website.* People can say, "Well, that might be an actor or something, that happens." But if you do that at a trade show and you have a trade show booth and people are coming up to your booth, and they're just raving about your product or service, those are the types of authentic testimonials I'm referring to.

MARK

I agree. That's a good point. You're harnessing the enthusiasm of a happy customer and you want to relay that to the masses, and that's a very good way of putting it. I like how you said that. It's just when you say reviews it can mean so many different things to someone looking on the internet. But when you say testimonial the way you did, I think it means something entirely different. I think that's a worthy distinction.

RICK

OK, let's dive a little bit deeper. Talk to us about when you're doing a tutorial video, for people that maybe have never done one of those. What should they do?

MARK

Our tutorial videos started from our customer service people on the phone. Our customer service people would be frustrated because people would call in and say, "This treadmill belt is kind of making a squeak here or a squeak there. What do I do?" We'd say, "We will send you a video."

So now if they could send a quick video, they could text it or email it, the customer service person looks at it and rather than say, "Oh yeah, yeah, great, here's how you fix that." Our guys just started walking to the back of the warehouse where we had all the products set up and whip the camera phone out and just shoot a quick response back. It was just so organic. We thought, *in order to save on customer service resources, let's start posting all these responses we're doing via video in some sort of library within our service department, within our needing-help-assistance links on our website.*

You say tutorial, we didn't necessarily start out thinking they were tutorials because often times you think that tutorials is just what you sell features and benefits on or something. But we grew our video library out of servicing our product, and as we showed us servicing our product, those naturally evolved into more of a showcase or a selling video. So it's interesting to note, we didn't get into the whole video world thinking we were going to do it for selling sake; we got into it for customer support sake.

RICK

That's an awesome answer. That's really amazing. Let's transition for just a second. The tutorial videos stemmed from customer service which makes all the sense in the world. But let's take a look at the marketing side. If you want to create a demonstration video, can you talk about that? You mentioned the ladder example which was fantastic. What's going to get somebody excited about the product itself?

MARK

It's all about honing in on that USP, your Unique Selling Proposition. I've seen videos talking about the powder coating on something, and I thought it was so boring and then I looked at the data on it, and people really cared about the powder coating. I don't know. You might think that you have a USP? Customers might think that you have a different USP. A demonstration video is what I think the USP is and I try to explain the features and the benefits. *People don't buy based on features; they buy based on what the benefit of the features are to them, and that's ultimately what a demonstration is.*

RICK

I always say Features tell, Benefits sell.

MARK

There you go. Yes, that's far more eloquent. The Unique Selling Proposition, you have to have one. If you don't have one, you're in the commodity industry, and you don't know it. So if you don't understand your Unique Selling Proposition, all you've got to offer people are service and price, service and price. So if you can sell copy paper in a more convenient way at less money, you're probably going to outsell your competitor. That's no way to grow a business in my opinion; it's just a race to the bottom of the profit margin.

RICK

With Amazon, it accelerates that race to the bottom and if you're a commodity. It's like it's a downward spiral the whole way. So I'm 100 percent aligned with defining your product, our company USP and making people aware of that. I'm focusing on the video aspect of it, but it really holds true for any part of a business.

MARK

I talk to a lot of people that ask me, "How do you identify a good opportunity because there's a lot of products out there?" Ultimately what it comes down to, do I believe there's a Unique Selling Proposition in place for this product because we don't want to be in the commodity business, because I'm telling you what, Amazon is always going to do it better than you. A mass retailer is always going to do it better than you. So I have to make sure that we believe there's a Unique Selling Proposition in the product and that's what I know I can do well is explain that online, whether using video or Affiliate's testimony. Everything we've discussed. If that USP doesn't exist, we just walk away.

RICK

That's awesome. Also reinforces what I've been trying to hammer home to people as well so to hear it from you who's out there on the front lines selling product every day online, that's great information. Everything you're saying is really fantastic information. That's the reason I'm doing these interviews with different experts like you, is that you're on the front lines, you're out there, you're selling products every day, you're seeing what works, what doesn't work. Is there anything I didn't ask you about that you want to talk about that would be useful for someone that might be reading this book?

MARK

Yes, I can maybe end with this. I was surprised and honored when you wanted to interview me, and inevitably all conversations around when people talk to me kind of start off with, "Oh, you're a digital or online guy, or you've got experience in this." Kind of where I am now is, I don't think you can just be a digital or an interactive or a web guy. I think you need to be a big picture guy. Just because most of our sales take place online, I can't afford just to be an interactive digital guy. I have to think about pricing across all channels. I have to think about dealers. It's amazing how the business can never be ignored. You can't just have an oversimplified, technological website and think that's ultimately going to be what works for you. In my opinion, we had to become experts in the entire business field like I talked about. Identifying Unique Selling Propositions, pricing strategies, pricing equilibrium, the eco-systems online That's a savvy business person and no longer is it just an internet digital guy. I think that you have to have the big picture in mind.

RICK

Yes, absolutely. First of all, very well said, not to oversimplify what you said, but it's like an omni-channeled marketing model. You need to understand all the potential distribution channels and how they work together, and for the business to succeed how you can make them work together seamlessly or synergistically, you're always going to get the biggest bang for your buck. I do a lot of work with large Amazon sellers and Amazon does everything for them, and they're all scared to death that their business is going to evaporate overnight, which does happen to some people. They need to learn exactly what you said, which is all aspects of the business and other channels. Anyway, we could write a whole other book about that.

MARK

Well, I've been in meetings with you, back when we had our agency hats on, and you'd be in a client's boardroom, and there'd be three or four other agencies there and everyone's fighting for their piece of the client's budget. The television guys want this, the web guys wanted that, the print guys wanted this. Everyone was pursuing money based on their own agency's interest, and it wasn't until you got a very savvy marketing person that realized and understood the ecosystem, that there was a role for all of this. You had to be intelligent about how you deployed all of this and the agencies that ultimately won, were the people that understood that environment and advocated for that environment, even if it meant less budget for their own agency and their own projects.

RICK

Yes, absolutely. You have to do what's best for the client, and the product and their business and not what's best for your agency. All right this has been fantastic. I'll tell you what, it's kind of like an MBA, a short MBA course in online marketing because just the information you gave, someone can walk away with any one of numerous tips and it will improve what they're doing. So, thank you very much for sharing that, and I really appreciate it, Mark. One last thing, you talked about what your business did at the beginning of this conversation. If you had to say what your ideal client or business customer is, that you might be looking for in the marketplace if you could give a brief description of that and then maybe how someone could contact you if they wanted to follow up.

MARK

Sure, thank you for the opportunity. We're looking for brands, brands that we can build and have exclusive relations on. We're not interested in doing all of the heavy lifting and then have someone than deal behind our backs to someone that could do it differently. We're looking for brands that we can ultimately sink our teeth into and grow. But crucial to that, that brand has to have Unique Selling Proposition, then this sounds really self-serving, but it's got to have margin. So we like brands that we have exclusivity on, tangible Unique Selling Propositions and margin. And if we have those things in place, then I can deploy overhead and my strategy and my team into place, and you feel confident we can build a brand.

RICK

Oh, that's fantastic. Again, every time you say something it leads to another thought because it's something that I haven't really mentioned very much, but it's really the key to a lot of these giant successes that you and I have worked on in the past. You just brought up margin. Can you just take a minute and tell people why margin is so important because I know both of us have experienced what may be perceived as a good product but you know it cost you ten dollars to make and you can only sell it for fifteen dollars, that's never going to grow into a business.

MARK

No, and I'm a direct-to-consumer retailer. I do have wholesalers and partners I work with, but for the most part, we're direct-to-consumer.

If you are a wholesaler, then this discussion is even that much more important because your retailer partner is taking the majority of the margin, so you've got to make sure your wholesale margins are healthy. What people don't understand, even in a direct-to-consumer world, how quickly your profit gets eaten up by Amazon fees, merchant account fees, Google expenditures, paid expenditures within social channels. And that quickly, three percent here, three percent there, fifteen percent there, can put you in a position where you can't afford to take risks and make mistakes.

And what I mean by that is, take some risks on building out, putting money behind your photography budget. These are all things during this whole interview we've been discussing. But I know that I've got margin in a product that's going to allow me to take some of these risks. If that margin isn't there, it handcuffs me to take risks and to invest the way we've been talking about. Margin's important, and you've just got to realize it. There are so many ways to eat up your margin selling direct-to-consumer, the expenses are there. So I like to have some cushion so I can feel like I can make some mistakes.

That brings me to my most significant point is when I talk about ecosystems and pricing integrity, I like to control all the pricing. I want to know I'm setting the price on Amazon, I'm setting the price on my website. If I have dealers, they sign contracts that they will sell at certain prices. I have to protect my margin for everybody because the moment someone steps out of line or drops their price by a quarter or a dollar or a hundred dollars, it upsets the whole ecosystem and that goes all the way to margin, and eventually, that's going to come back to bite me. So, margin is key, set the ecosystem, pricing integrity, and as long as that situation is in place, you'd be surprised how much cushion you have and how much leeway you have to make a few mistakes.

RICK

That was awesome. Thank you for that answer. I promise I won't go off on any more tangents. Tell us how to get in contact with you. You described the type of product you're looking for, the company you're looking for, and did a really great job. If someone wanted to contact you, how do they do that?

MARK

NetMediaGroup.com. Email is mswaby@netmediagroup.com. And at Net Media Group you can see all the different projects and brands that we're working on.

RICK

Thanks Mark for your time, I really appreciate all the great information that you shared.

CHAPTER THREE SUMMARY

- Give people the content they are looking for.
- The three most popular types of online video content are Tutorials, Demonstration videos, and Testimonial videos.
- Tutorials are how-to or instruction videos good for teaching and customer service.
- Demonstration videos are marketing videos and good for selling.
- Always make sure your demo videos have a call to action, CTA.
- Always try and use authentic testimonials in all your marketing videos.
- The absolute most effective videos to sell your product or service will combine demos with testimonials.

CHAPTER FOUR
How to Create a Technically Great Video

"In making a speech, one must study three points: first, the means of producing persuasion; second, the language; third the proper arrangement of the various parts of the speech."
—Aristotle

Remember the formula; Video Production + Video Marketing + Strategic Direct Response Principles = Video Persuasion. This book is primarily about creating video content that will move or persuade your viewer to the action you desire. It is not about, how to do video production, BUT that being said, having helped create, shoot and edit thousands of hours of video footage over many years I've learned a thing or two about video production. I'd like to pass along some of this information that I had to learn the hard and expensive way. It might help save you both time and money in your own video production process.

GETTING STARTED, THE 3 BASIC STEPS

Creating a video has three distinct steps or phases.

1. Pre-production, this is the planning phase.
2. Production, this is the execution phase.
3. Post-production, this is the editing phase and the place where the entire project comes together.

Of all these steps, by far the most important is in Pre-production. When this is done correctly, the final two steps will flow easily, and you will finish with the outcome you are looking for on time and on budget. If not done correctly I guarantee you will get frustrated during the process, spending more time and money than needed and not always end up with a video you are happy with. These three steps remain constant no matter how small, or large your budget or video project may be.

COST

I like to compare video production to building a home. They come in all shapes, sizes, and costs. You start with a dream or idea of what your finished home will be or look like, then you or the architect creates the blueprint as a guide to the building process, then you or the general contractor hires sub-contractors to execute each step of the process. The video producer is like the general contractor, responsible for hiring the people that will execute the blueprint or script.

One question everyone always asks is how much does it cost to produce a video? It's totally dependent on the script you are trying to produce and the quality of the video. Houses come in a variety of styles from a starter home (cheap) to mansions (expensive), you end up getting what you pay for. With videos, there will be corresponding budgets that vary widely for creating both lower-end and higher-end videos. I'm a big believer in spending as little as possible to get the job done correctly. You can do this if you have a clear goal of what you are trying to accomplish and an organized plan to reach that goal.

PHASE ONE, PRE-PRODUCTION

Be prepared! A successful video shoot starts here.

A direct result of how good a video you produce is ALWAYS contingent on how well you are organized going into your shoot day. This organization process starts in the pre-production phase.

In my business consulting practice, I always give new business owners the same advice, **start with the end in mind.** What is it you are trying to accomplish? This is also a good rule of thumb for any video you are producing.

- What is the video you are making trying to accomplish?
- What is your goal for the video?
- How will this video be distributed?
- What is the result that you are looking for?
- What action do you want the viewer to take?

Once you are clear on the goals of your video you can move on to the scripting phase.

CREATING A SCRIPT, YOUR BLUEPRINT FOR SUCCESS

The script is your guide or blueprint for everything you want to accomplish on the shoot day. It lets you plan out how many shots or set-ups you will need and in which locations. You can then figure out how long each shot will take helping you organize your shoot day into segments. This is called creating a Shot List. The more camera moves and lighting set-ups you have, the less you will be able to accomplish in a day of taping.

A script can be as simple as just an outline that you follow or full-fledged word for word, scene for scene document. It is always a good idea to plan out ahead of time everything that you need to capture. Once you get to the editing phase, if you missed something on the shoot day, it might be prohibitively expensive to go back to capture the missing shot or footage, or just impossible because the people involved are no longer available. You either cannot finish your video correctly or end up spending a lot more than planned. When in doubt it is always better to have too much footage to work with than too little.

Here is an example of an actual script for a fitness product I am currently helping to market called Slip Gym. In this spot, the product is being demonstrated by the inventor, long-time fitness guru, Kurt Wolfe.

Project: *SlipGym* (Short Form spot)
Client: SlipGym Productions, LLC
Version: :120 (2 min.) spot – V.1

	VIDEO	AUDIO
1	FADE UP TO: KURT WOLFE DOING PULL-UPS IN HOME GYM	*Believe it or not, I'm 73 years old, and I've been in the fitness industry...*
2	CUT TO: QUICK MONTAGE OF B&W (Black & White) IMAGES OF FITNESS PRODUCTS	*for over 50 years and I've seen it all.*
3	CUT BACK TO: M.C.U. (Medium Close Up) KURT WOLFE DIRECT TO CAMERA	*But now, there's a revolutionary innovation that I guarantee will change your body and your life...forever.*
4	FX TRANSITION TO: SENIOR COUPLE WALKING AND USING THE SLIPGYM. CUT TO: SIDE BY SIDE SHOTS: LEFT FRAME 40'S MALE ON TREADMILL & RIGHT FRAME 50'S FEMALE WALKING IN PARK	*KURT WOLFE VO:* *And here it is... the **SlipGym** total body workout jacket!" It's the world's first body gym that you can use anywhere, anytime!*
5	CUT TO: KURT WOLFE SLIPPING ON SLIPGYM, THEN MONTAGE OF SHOTS OF KURT SHOWING VARIED EXERCISES	*You just slip it on, and now you've got the easiest, most convenient and effective way to get your body into tip-top shape ever invented!*
6	CUT TO: GRAPHIC ANIMATION OF ALL 4 SIZES CUT TO: SIDE BY SIDE: LEFT FRAME SMALL WOMAN USING SLIPGYM,	*With multiple sizes available, it doesn't matter if you're petite... or extra elite!! The SlipGym will fit you like a glove and get you the body you'll always love!*

		RIGHT FRAME LARGE MAN USING SLIPGYM	
7	CUT TO: SHOTS OF VARIOUS IN-SHAPE PEOPLE USING THE SLIPGYM IN A VARIETY OF SETTINGS		*And it works the same for everyone… no matter what age or shape you're in.*
8	CUT TO: C.U. (Close Up) RESISTANCE BANDS AS HANDS GRAB BANDS AND STARTS MOVING BACK AND FORTH CUT TO: SCROLL OF GFX SHOWING NAMES OF EXERCISES ON LEFT WITH IMAGES MATCHING THE EXERCISES WITH PEOPLE USING THE SLIPGYM		*The built-in Pro Resistance Bands deliver dozens of upper body exercises for your chest, back, arms, biceps, triceps, and even your core… and MORE!*
9	CUT TO: SHOT OF WOMEN PLAYING TENNIS SHOT OF GUYS PLAYING FOOTBALL IN PARK CUT TO: GOLFER IN ACTION BOWLER GETTING A STRIKE SOFTBALL PLAYER HITTING MARTIAL ARTIST WITH COACH		*And if you're a sports enthusiast or weekend warrior, SlipGym will not only get you into game shape, but it will actually improve your game, whether you golf, bowl, play softball or are seriously into martial arts.*
10	CUT TO: SENIOR FEMALE INDOORS		*And for a total body workout, just slip on the SlipGym and go*

	AS SHE PUTS ON SLIPGYM DISSOLVE TO: SAME FEMALE NOW WALKING AND WORKING OUT WITH A FRIEND BOTH USING SLIPGYM OUTDOORS	*for a walk! Now you're not just walking, you're total body rocking!*
11	CUT TO: TESTIMONIALS (EXAMPLES LISTED)	*TESTIMONIAL EXAMPLES:* *SENIOR COUPLE: (Female) SlipGym works great for both of us. (Male) And it transformed my wife from couch potato to hot tomato!* *MID 40'S MALE: With the SlipGym, now I've got more energy and stamina than when I was in my 20s.* *SENIOR FEMALE: With the SlipGym, I turned my daily walk into a full body workout. And it's hands-free, so I can even walk my dog at the same time!*
12	CUT TO: M.C.U. KURT WOLFE DIRECT TO CAMERA CUT TO: GENERIC SHOT OF BUSY GYM IN B&W WITH BIG RED "X" OVER IT	*KURT WOLFE VO:* *There's no cords, cables, batteries, recharging or replacement parts needed. And you'll never have to drive to a gym, wait for a machine or pay excessive monthly club fees ever again.*

13	CUT TO: SHOT OF SLIPGYM EXERCISE, THEN TWO, THEN 4, THEN 8, THEN 16... ALL SHOWING DIFFERENT EXERCISE MOVEMENTS	*In fact, the SlipGym offers all the same exercises as any major gym... and more!*
14	CUT TO: OFFER/ORDER CARD PHONE # + URL ONLY $99 *LIMITED TIME OFFER AT THIS PRICE INSET WINDOW: REPRISE SHOTS OF VARIED PEOPLE USING THE SLIPGYM **ALTERNATE: only 4 payments of $24.95**	*Call or click now to get this limited time introductory offer to order your very own SlipGym, for just one single payment of only $99 dollars! You heard right, just $99 dollars. That's less than the cost of an annual gym membership!* *ALT; Only 4 payments of $24.95*
15	SAME OFFER CARD CUT TO INSET WINDOW: KURT WOLFE USING SLIPGYM WHILE ADDRESSING DIRECT TO CAMERA PHONE # + URL ONLY $99 *LIMITED TIME OFFER AT THIS PRICE	*KURT WOLFE: (To Cam)* *The SlipGym is absolutely the best fitness product I've ever seen. As my good friend Jack LaLanne would say, "Your body is your slave... it works for you!". But with the SlipGym, now you're moving and grooving, staying active and I guarantee you'll see amazing results in just a few weeks... or send it back for a full refund.* *That's how sure I am the SlipGym is the real deal! Order yours, right now!*

16	FINAL OFFER/ORDER CARD PHONE # + URL ONLY $99 *LIMITED TIME OFFER AT THIS PRICE **ALTERNATE: "Only 4 payments of $24.95**	*ANNOUNCER:* *Call 1-800-xxx-xxxx and get the incredible SlipGym and the total body results you deserve. That's 1-800-xxx-xxxx… call now!* **ALTERNATE: "Only 4 payments of $24.95**

You can write the script yourself. I have a sample script template you can use. This is more **Free Bonus** content you can get at my website, https://www.RickCesari.com/VPBonus, or you can hire a good direct response copywriter to do it for you.

Here is a short list of some good direct response writers that I have used for some of my projects:

- Kirk Gross, krg@kreativeresourcesgroup.com
- Jack Turk, jack@jackturk.com
- Kevin Donlin, k@clientcloningsystems.com
- Tess Clark, Tess@tessclark.com

VIDEO PERSUASION TIP: If you are writing your own script, don't try to entertain or be humorous. You will fail miserably. Instead, try to educate and inform your viewer about your subject or topic. Your most important viewers will find your videos entertaining because they are interesting to them and they are learning something new. There are more great scriptwriting ideas in the interviews at the end of chapters five and six.

Once you have your script or outline finished here are some things to consider.

- SHOT LIST: Create a shot list from the script. This is called "breaking down the script." Do the biggest most complicated shots first then work your way down to the smaller shots.

- STORYBOARDS: Create storyboards, hire someone who can sketch each scene of the video. This makes it easier to visualize each shot and what it will take to set it up. You also might be able to eliminate some scenes to save time and money.

- LOCATION: Finding a location. Your script will call for a location or several locations. With a few exceptions, I primarily tape in two places, in a home or on a stage either with a set or white/green background. If you are using a house a good place to look is VRBO (Vacation Rental By Owner) or Air BNB.

- TALENT: Finding and hiring talent, use real people that match your target demographics, not pretty models that people cannot relate to. Unless it's an aspirational product like Skincare or an exercise product.

- TESTIMONIALS: see Chapter 3.

- WARDROBE and MAKE-UP: This might seem like an easy budget area to cut costs by not having a make-up person on set, but I find working with a make-up person not only makes people look good on camera, they can also make people feel good and comfortable before going on camera. This is very important before taping, especially with people who are not used to being in front of a camera. You will get better results.

- PHOTOGRAPHER: Consider having a still photographer on set to capture stills for any other marketing you might be doing. These will come in handy to use on your website and any social media you are doing.

Be realistic about what you can accomplish. Don't try and cram 15 hours of work into a 10-hour day. The crew will get frustrated, you'll end up going into overtime and paying time and half for the same service. Plus, I find you always get diminishing returns the longer you are on a set or shoot location after ten hours.

Now, if all this sounds a little overwhelming to take on yourself, especially if you-are just starting there is an easy solution.

SECRET TO SUCCESS, HIRE A GOOD PRODUCER

What is a video producer and what do they do? Very simply a video producer works to coordinate all aspects of video production. This is a person who is very organized, can get things done quickly and efficiently, and pays attention to the details. This person is great at putting out fircs and dealing with the unexpected. A good producer is vital to getting the video shoot organized and completed on time and on budget. The producer can help with every aspect of the list we just went through.

Here is a partial list of what a good producer does:

- Manages the production budget.
- Plans the video project and accepts it will not go according to plan.
- Accepts responsibility when no one else does.

- Plans for any and all resources needed to get the job done.
- Maintains a healthy state of paranoia. ("What did I forget? What is missing?")
- Is obsessed with staying on schedule.
- Always checks a download link personally before sending to the client.
- Is ultimately responsible for the success or failure of a video project.
- Double checks work again before sending to the client.
- Under-promises.
- Over-delivers.
- Develops a very thick skin.
- Identifies the most creative and most organized on the team (both needed).
- Checks frustration and ego at the door when communicating with the client.
- Never names any file "Final," which is the equivalent of wishing 'good luck' before a performance.
- Understands the client's terminology and has read the client website thoroughly.
- Understands each function of the production and every production job.
- Acts as a video project team cheerleader when necessary.
- Acts as a video project team hammer when necessary.
- Knows that often the most creative people are difficult to deal with.
- Is willing and able to roll up sleeves and get his or her hands dirty in a production.
- Reviews every change to the content, no matter how minor, before sending to the client.

- Praises in public and punishes in private.
- Has trouble sleeping the night before a shooting day.
- Hires everybody on the video production team.
- Oversees talent scouting.
- Keeps track of client tasks and acts timely to remind them when late.
- Fires anybody on the video production team when necessary.
- Oversees location scouting.
- Looks for creative ways to cut cost out of the budget.
- Ensures everyone eats.
- Ensures everyone gets paid.
- Is married to a cell phone or other communication device.
- Keeps track of what went wrong, performing a post mortem to avoid repeating mistakes.
- Keeps client confidential information secure.
- Wears comfortable shoes.
- Prepares for the first meeting with a client by thoroughly reading the client's web marketing.
- Picks up coffee and bagels if no one else can.
- Always asks about power, restrooms, and building access in preparing for on-location shooting.
- Answers emails while walking to and from the car.
- Knows who is traveling to/from location shoots and when as well as how to contact them on the road.
- Stresses when something DOESN'T go wrong… anticipating the storm.
- Removes logistical obstacles, so they don't become a drain on the remote team.
- Asks to see in-progress work often, offers constructive criticism without micromanaging.

- Inspires efficient creativity.
- Discourages lethargic routine.
- Hires people much more creative than himself or herself.
- Hires people much more technically competent than herself or himself.
- Always asks "Do my people on location have food/water?"
- Doesn't deliver content he or she knows the client doesn't want. Takes responsibility for client success in this regard.

Credit for this list–Tubular.

I've been fortunate to work with one of the very best video producers for over twenty years, Jane Schloth. She once told me that she knows when she's done a good job preparing for production when nobody is looking for her or calling out her name on set. If you ever have any questions about the production process you can contact her at jane@directbranding.com.

THE PEOPLE AND TITLES INVOLVED IN VIDEO PRODUCTION

- Executive Producer: Responsible for funding the project and responsible for financing and paying all the bills.
- Director: Involved in every aspect of the video production and responsible for the look and feel of the video. The producer and director work closely together.
- Producer: see list above.
- Writer: Creates the script based on your vision and goals.
- Director of Photographer: Known as the DP. Works with the director and the lighting crew to set up the shots and makes sure they look great.

- Lighting, Gaffers, and Grips: Responsible for lighting and lighting equipment.
- Audio: In charge of sound.
- Production assistants or PAs: Assist the producer in all aspects of the production.

This list of production people can get much larger and much more detailed based on the size of the production. To give you an idea of one major extreme, next time you go to a movie sit all the way thru the end of the film when the credits roll and see how many people can be involved in a large project.

Always try to have the right size crew for the job; otherwise you will waste time and money. You might be producing a simple, low-budget video with your iPhone and might fill all the roles yourself, writer, director, producer. When I go to a trade show to get testimonials, I just bring a cameraman to do the taping, lighting, and audio himself, so there are just two people involved, me and the technical person. I'm looking for the right video persuasion content, while the camera operator is making sure we get the footage.

Here is Your Third FREE BONUS

This is an example of a Producer's Call Sheet, listing all crew members for a recent testimonial video-taping we did in Orange County, California for one of my clients, Puriya, www.puriya.com. You can see the testimonial videos I produced for them on my YouTube channel, rickcesari.tv.

You can use this form to guide in when you hire a production company or individual crew members. It is available as a FREE download on my website, https://www.RickCesari.com/VPBonus.

PHASE TWO, PRODUCTION

This is where all your advance planning comes into play, and everything should go very smoothly if you have followed all the steps outlined in Phase one. Your director is the key person in this stage. It's his job to execute the script, make sure all the scenes are covered and everything looks good.

The biggest difference I see in a video that is shot by beginners versus working with a crew really falls into two areas, lighting and sound. Increase the production level in these two areas, and your videos will have a more professional like and feel.

PRODUCTION TIPS

Always overshoot the amount of video footage you think you need without creating overtime or losing efficiency. It will always be better in post-production to have more footage to work with than less. Working with more experienced cameramen and directors, I learned very early to shoot an establishing or wide shot first, then move in for tight shots to highlight the action. Always shoot a person or scene from different perspectives (wide, medium, closeup) to give the video editor a wide selection of shots to use. For example, in producing 30-minute informercials we would normally be working with 30-40 hours of footage.

Shoot lots of B-roll. This is the supplemental or alternate footage intercut with the main shot in a video to help tell the story visually. B-roll can be used as cut-aways, showing a different image while a testimonial is talking. B-roll is really useful to cover an audio edit to string together two or more good sound bites without the viewer seeing the edit. Good B-roll will enhance what is being said on camera.

So whenever you're planning a video production, take time during the pre-production process to map out what B-roll may be suitable. Any extra footage can be used for more than one project. You should divide your taping between recording interviews and capturing B-roll. Done correctly, it makes what the testimonial is describing through their audio much more realistic and interesting to the viewer. The person viewing this video sequence will picture themselves using the product in the same way to solve their problem, and they will probably take the next step which is to go and Google the product to see how they can purchase it for themselves. But we will make it easy for them by including the URL in the video along with some type of offer, giving them the incentive to buy now!

As a general rule, B-Roll can include animation, graphical elements, photographs, and any extra footage.

What are 2D or 3D Animation and Graphic Effects (GFX) and why do I need them?

This is not to be confused with "explainer" videos, which have become very popular. You can find resources to create these kinds of videos by just Googling "explainer Video."

I use video animation in many product sales videos that I create. Its best use is for when I am trying to take a complicated process and make it simple for the viewer to understand. This will always help in the sales and conversion process. This animation can be produced in 2D or 3D, which is more lifelike and realistic, depending on your budget. Some examples are:

- Hunter Fan produced an air purifier that could remove up to 98% of bacteria and debris from the air you breathe. This would be almost impossible to capture on video, but with a 3D animation, this was easy to show. We start by using a real video shot and zooming in to the machine's filter, we cut to the animation showing the bad particles being removed, while the announcer or voice over (VO) talks us through the process. The easiest way to create good animation is to write exactly what you want to see happen, the VO script, and use this as a guide for the animator to build the sequence of pictures.

- Sonicare used animation to show the "sonic technology" of this new product. The bristles of the brush vibrate at 32,000/second, much too fast to see with the naked eye. By using 3D animation, we can slow down the process and see the sonic wave action taking place as the brush cleans teeth and helps destroy plaque bacteria. When we did this 3D animation in the mid-nineties, computer technology was not as advanced as it is today and once the animation was set up, the editing house pushed a button, and we had to wait two weeks for it to render! With time constraints like that, you better make sure you have the sequence of pictures worked out perfectly because making any little change was very costly and time-consuming.

Product animation works so well because, like the old saying goes, "a picture is worth a thousand words."

PHASE THREE, POST PRODUCTION:

I have spent thousands of hours in "Post," and I feel that I can have more impact on the outcome of the way a video performs from the decisions made in post-production than in any other area of production. Again, not being a technical person and not knowing how to actually use the editing equipment myself, I always work with a good video editor. My definition of a good video editor is someone who understands not only the technology of editing but also understands basic direct response principles. As mentioned above I always "overshoot" footage in the production phase, so I have more choices to work with once I start editing. To give you an example, when we are taping individual testimonials, I might interview each person for 20 to 30 minutes. Out of that footage, we are looking to make a 1 to 2-minute video, and sometimes we were just looking for one good 15 to 20-second sound bite.

TIP: It's always a great asset to have your editor on set during rehearsal and production to assist the Director with technical considerations. Often, the editor can prevent any oversights that cannot be fixed in post-production.

MAKE TRANSCRIPTS

One thing that always facilitates the editing process is to have transcripts made of everyone who is recorded during the taping, including "timecodes." This lets you quickly find the best material to work with. I then read through the transcripts and highlight everything that looks like a good soundbite. I bring these notes into the edit bay or send them to the editor, and the editor picks the selections I have outlined. This way we can quickly review the best of the best sound bites and decide which ones will go into the final video. If you want to, you can also do a "paper edit" using the transcripts. This allows you to piece together material on your own and get organized before working with your editor. This will save you time and money.

The transcription service I use is Rev.com. Another good, inexpensive, and fast transcription service is Temi.com.

Here is a list of common mistakes to avoid that will help the process flow smoothly. **5 Mistakes** That happen during Production from an editor's point of view.

1. Have your editor on set or location during the shoot. This acts as having a second set of eyes for the Director. An editor can help overview the shots and instinctively know how the edit can come together without needing to be in front of the edit bay. This could save thousands in unnecessary pickup shoots to fix the issue that could have been prevented if the editor was engaged earlier in the Production process.

2. Not enough crew on set. Sometimes money is an issue for Production and cutting crew cost might not be the best solution. Try saving money on locations instead of the crew. Keep in mind the crew is there to help you get the look and feel you are after and if you don't have enough of them to execute the look then the overall production can be hindered.

3. Preserving 4x3 safe on commercial spots. Lots of times we see all this real estate left and right of the frame and think that we need to close the shot up and take out the negative space. By doing this, you are limiting the editor to fit

necessary graphics on the screen which end up making the scene look like an afterthought in post-production.

4. Finalize the script before shooting begins. Not "locking" the script before a shoot can lead to missing coverage and an unhappy crew that isn't organized for the next shot. Locking the script and creating a clear shot list will make your production go much smoother and you will retain a happy crew that will most likely want to work with you again in the future.

5. Fix it in POST. If you are around production very much a common statement you will hear is, "I'll fix it in post." If someone says, "we can fix it in post," it means they did not capture footage that they said they would, or the footage that was needed to complete the video correctly. This usually means you or the director or the producer screwed up somewhere in phase one or two. It's almost always easier and less expensive to fix it on set while shooting than to spend days trying to fix it in post. Keep this in mind the next shoot you are on and check with all parties to see if you are able to troubleshoot on location or if it really is easier to just fix it in post.

Some great video editors:

- Colby Wayne, Colby.wayne84@gmail.com
- Dan Riley, dan@rylow.com
- Jonah Vigil, runningstillsprod@gmail.com

STOCK FOOTAGE

We talked about getting B-roll earlier to help your video come alive and be more authentic. If you find yourself in post and are looking for some B-roll that you might not have shot, that's when I turn to using stock images or footage. You almost always can find the right picture/video clip you are looking for, and it saves the time and cost of going out to shoot it yourself.

Some stock footage companies I use are:

- Pond 5
- Adobe Stock
- iStock

MUSIC

One last thing, adding music to your videos will enhance the emotion and watch-ability of the video and help keep the viewer engaged. This is always added at the very end of the post process, once the final content is "locked."

Online music services I use:

- Premium beat
- Killer tracks

And for original music I use:

- Pat Rickey, Downpat music, http://downpatmusic.com/
- Bryan Miller, Sensory Overload, www.sensory-overload.com

NEW WAYS TO CREATE VIDEO

Until recently video production could be a very expensive process. In this chapter, I have outlined the way that I produce "high end" videos that are used for TV or online brand building. I feel it is important to understand the video production process as it will help you in whatever way you choose to make your videos. One of the nice things that has happened in the last several years is the creation of many online services that let you create a video, using templates, very quickly and inexpensively. Several of these services and companies are mentioned in the interviews in this book. Here are the ones mentioned and a few more.

- **Waymark**, https://waymark.com/
- **Lumen 5**, https://lumen5.com/
- **Animoto**, https://animoto.com/business/
- **Movavi**, https://www.movavi.com/
- **Wochit**, https://www.wochit.com/
- **Offeo**, https://offeo.com/

Production Apps—Just Google video production Apps and you will get many more services that you can check out to see which you like best.

And this next interview will introduce you to yet another inexpensive way you can create great videos.

INTERVIEW WITH JEFF TURLEY, FOUNDER OF GONETYOURSELF

RICK

Tell me the name of your business and what it does?

JEFF

It is GoNetYourself. GoNetYourself is all one word. GoNetYourself provides video production in a streamlined way that allows for companies to use our studios in a shared studio model so that they don't have to build their own studios; they don't have to edit their own videos. They can come in and use our studios, and then basically streamline the process of video production from start to end. I think what I would say is we have streamlined the systems of video production.

RICK

What does that do for the end user, then?

JEFF

Our kind of core model is affordable, repeatable, and executable. It allows people and companies to make high-end videos in a very affordable way, but also make it very repeatable, because ultimately, in today's world, video is more than one video. You need anywhere from ten to hundreds of videos per year.

RICK

Why is video so important? How important is video to a company's marketing, from a content standpoint, from marketing?

JEFF

That's a deep question. There's several things that have gone on, I think, in our world in the past ten years. Obviously, the cell phone, and the ability to transfer high-quality images be it picture and/or video, in a fast way. People are allowed to view high-end video from whenever and wherever, and ultimately create it themselves. Ultimately, they can now create very, very nice, well-done video, so, therefore, it's a new medium where people can see greater depth than a written word. I think that, along with 100 million millennials that have grown up around seeing themselves and seeing everything in real time and in high quality, that has changed the need to be ... *video to be not only a piece of your marketing, but it's got to be the breadth and the depth of your marketing.*

RICK

That's very well said. What made you start GoNetYourself?

JEFF

Again, we have streamlined the video production from start to end. There's a lot of companies out there that will do cheaper video. I get that, but what we have done is streamlined that process, because seven years ago, I saw in the market how expensive it was to do high-end, very nice quality video. We stepped into the market to create a different solution to that, because, at that point, when I talked to professionals, it was $1,000 a finished minute and up, and I'm like, no ... and, it's anywhere from thirty to sixty days to get that high-quality video back to them, and then there's all the back and forth between the editor and the end user. *We stepped in to try to create that process, which dropped* the *price by about ninety percent, but also not lose the high-end quality that people are looking for.*

RICK

I'm just going to give a personal endorsement. I happen to be a customer or client of yours and can vouch for everything you just said. I come from a huge background in video production, and I can say that you've really accomplished your goal of streamlining the production process, making it repeatable and also dramatically lowering the cost, which is the need for anyone to produce videos consistently. GoNetYourself is a fantastic solution.

I guess the biggest hurdle I see ... when I tell people they need to use video, the first thing that pops in their mind is, "I don't know how to do it. That's too expensive." How do you address those things, if somebody's like maybe making their first series of videos, or had a bad experience doing it the old expensive way?

JEFF

We always say, "There are times where you will make your own video, but then you need to figure out how you're going to scale that process." For us, it's all about process because of the many facets of video production that people don't see. For example, what happens when somebody has a bad day, and they have to repeat the process again? If you go out and hire high-end videographers, and you have a bad day, you now have to go pay that high-end videographer to come out again and again, because there are times when the person on camera just can't get it right.

Our whole thing is, how do you scale a process that is, I'll continue to say, affordable, repeatable, and executable? Ultimately, it's about learning how to build a process that can scale within your company. Everybody says, "Oh, I have a studio." Well, that's fine. You have a studio, but do you have a process behind that studio to scale the studio? Once you've built a studio, great. Now you could produce hundreds and hundreds and hundreds and hundreds of videos, but you have no process that stands behind that. What most people don't understand is the process from beginning to end, all the way from scheduling to script-writing to who's going to be on screen, how they're going to be onscreen, how they are going to act onscreen, who's going to help them through that process ... the more complicated piece of that puzzle is the editing of that process and the back and forth of each one of those videos.

The best way to create video is to understand the entire process from start to finish, every single piece of the puzzle that is in that process, and then putting a guideline for each one of those steps. That's what we've done at our company to scale that process.

RICK

Can you take us through the steps that you've systemized?

JEFF

In a very short way, we look at it as ... *Pre-production, pre-production, pre-production, as you've probably heard, in video production, is the key.* It's basically making sure that the person that is going to be onscreen, and/or the voiceover, and/or the talent, is well prepared. If you've done that piece of the puzzle up front, then that is basically having their script in place, having them practice that script, having the style of video that you are going to do in place prior to shooting. Those are just two of the major pieces of the puzzle.

Script and type of video being created, because a lot of times, if you go shoot a video and/or you get a script, but if everybody in the process hasn't checked off and said, "That's what we're doing, and that's what we're going for," then you could go spend a whole day or two days shooting video and end up with nothing, and it gets killed, and they've just spent $15,000, and nobody likes it.

That's what has to happen on the front end. So, script, practice, you know? What we always say ... Russell Wilson says, "Separation is in the preparation," and we say, "You got to prepare." So, preparation on the front end; then being well coached and well managed within the studio to make it in an efficient time and use. For us, if we've done a good job on the front end, the executive that walks into our studios is so well coached that oftentimes what is a half-day shoot or a full-day shoot for an executive is ... for one video, often takes less than thirty minutes.

Then, the third piece of the puzzle is the editing and the re-edit of that process. The difference between us and a lot of companies is, we're very agile in that process. We allow the client to see a lot of our rough drafts and say, "Hey, are we going right? Are we going forward? Yes? Then check the box and tell us to keep going in the right direction," versus where, in the old style of editing, a videographer and editor would go and create the full video without the client ever seeing it. That's a lot of how we have cleaned up the mess is, we're not scared to show them rough drafts.

RICK

That's awesome. I want to go back. You had mentioned a style of video or type of video. How would you describe the different types of videos that your clients do, or what you're seeing coming through your door? What are people producing? I'm asking this so that the people reading it will get ideas of the type of videos they need to produce.

JEFF

It's a broad range. We work with very, very small companies, startup companies, all the way to large Fortune 500 companies; you know, Microsoft, Amazon, Starbucks, all of those types of companies, so it's a wide range. I think the most effective video, in my understanding ... I always talk about, you've got to have the testimonials. *I would say you have to have the three F's: you have to have the Flirt, the Fix, and the Forward. Those three Fs are key.* The Flirt means the hook. You need to have the hook video. You need to have something anywhere from 30 seconds to a minute that catches somebody's attention, that says ... oh, and it's got a little bit of maybe an edge to it, or maybe something culturally that's out there that people understand and that says, "Hey, we're relevant, and oh, that's a little funny." *That's what your Flirt is. You're catching them in your hook, so you've got the hook video.*

You have the Fix. The Fix is the how-to video. Give me something of knowledge. Give me something of relevance, of how to fix whatever I'm looking for. It's the how-to video. It's short; it's probably two minutes, right? If you do this correctly, this type of video is ... we do it for two different reasons. You're teaching, and you're giving away information and knowledge for free, right? But you also have to understand how the millennials look for information nowadays. The millennials, they will never ask an older person for information; they'll just search it on the internet, find out how to do it, and then go do it themselves. That's why you have to be the authority on giving away information, and then they go, "Oh." That builds trust.

Now, there's the big thing: *you've hooked them, you've built trust because you have given them information that they find valuable, and you've given it for free. Now you've moved them forward, so then the third piece of that funnel of video production is the Forward, and that's where you can teach them longer pieces of information.* These are more, you know, 10- or 15-minute videos or the Forward might be where you move to longer story testimonials, where they will watch.

There's kind of like three different categories in there. You can teach them longer, you can tell them longer story form videos, and you can do a lot longer explainer videos. They want to know more about your product, and that's where you put that piece of the puzzle. So, you have the explainer, the educational, and the hook ... Anyway, you've got those three styles that move them forward in your funnel.

RICK

That's fantastic. I've never heard it explained that way, but it absolutely parallels everything I kind of say in the book. It's interesting, hearing it from a different perspective because it's also very much the direct response marketing model, which is, you have to catch their attention, which is what you said, the Flirt. A lot of times we do that with a problem solution, or we ask a question. Then you offer the solution, which is the Fix, but then the last part is, the longer part is, you really explain then exactly how they do that, or they're actually purchasing that part from you if it's a sales type of thing.

JEFF

I got in trouble with the Flirt piece because I sent that out in an email one time, and individuals gave me nasty emails back saying I was being sexist. I'm like, "No, no, no, you don't understand. The Flirt doesn't mean sexist, It's just a hook. It's just a hook." I think it hooks people, right?

RICK

It's an attention-getter, and that's important. I spend a whole chapter in the book talking about how important it is to grab people's attention and different ways of grabbing people's attention. We realize how important that is because if you don't get their attention, no one is going to watch your video.

JEFF

Right. You got to have some kind of purple cow.

RICK

We spent a lot of time talking about the open ... you know, scripting and pre-production, but didn't talk much about anything after that. As an overview, first, kind of take us through the steps of the production process, but just more of a bullet point "Here are the steps," and then maybe explain the steps in more detail?

JEFF

There are three steps to this process. There's the pre-production; there is the production, what happens in studio; and the post-production, what happens in the editing piece of the puzzle. Those three are essential. In the pre-production, it is absolutely critical for the client to have a clear understanding and they have to identify a style of video that's agreed upon prior to going into the project. I think that's probably the key right there. We all know what we're shooting at.

RICK

"If you aim at nothing, you'll surely hit it."

JEFF

Exactly! Once you've done that, determine the type of video you are producing, then you know how to price it; you know that you're not creating a nationwide, $100,000 commercial, and everybody has agreed upon that, right? Then the second piece that is so critical to that is that the script is agreed upon before you ever move forward. Once the script is agreed upon and you go, *"Okay, this is the script," ... because a lot of times, people don't know it's approximately 150 words a minute. If you're going to do a two-minute video, you're only looking at 300 words, but we'll get 1,000-word scripts.* You're going, "Well, you got a lot of cutting to do before we even get to any type of rough cut.

RICK

I've been doing production a long time, and I had never broken it down that way. That's really valuable information and will save people a lot of money. and it will save a lot of time. If someone has a 1,000-word script, it's going to cost that much more to shoot it when they really don't need all those words.

JEFF

Right, exactly. I think it's Abraham Lincoln who says, "It's very hard to write a 100-word script. It's easier to write a 1,000-word script." So, to force people at the front end to get to 150 words, or 300 words, and say, "That's all you get." Doing that on the front end will save a lot of time and money. Then they might say "Well, I've got an interview to do." Okay, I'll let you know, in an interview, you've probably got a two to three or four minutes, and you can only tell two stories. We've kind of narrowed that process that will clean up about 70, 80 percent of your problems right there. Your agreed-upon video style; how it's going to be shot; if it's going to be interview format, whatever it may be; and then people understanding how many words they have to hit their message. Then, from that piece of the puzzle, that they know where they're going to be, when to show up ... Is it going to be on a location shoot? Is it going to be ... and then what to wear? Now, it's really, really important that people understand what looks best on camera. We will have people come in with pastels and flowers or whatever, and you're going, "You know what, that just doesn't look good on camera." Well, a funny one was, one of our first T-Mobile videos ... and it's clear when we send out an invite that, "Please don't wear green," because we were shooting on a green background. The lady came in in a full green dress. A complete, head to toe, full green dress. We were just laughing going, "You didn't follow instructions," but you got to know what to wear. It's very, very important for people to understand simple stuff. Like, if you're shooting on green, you want solid, and you want ... solid probably reds or pinks, because that actually shows up best off of a green screen. It pops the best, right? People don't know those simple things. You don't really want to wear a lot of plaids. Those are the things that you've got to think through. *Then it's, practice, practice, practice that script. That person has to be so comfortable with the script that it seems natural, versus being read.* There's a lot of coaching that happens in that process. If they're going to be reading a teleprompter, are they comfortable at reading that prompter? Can they read it in such a way that people don't even know they're reading it? That takes practice.

All those things are preparations before you come into studio. When you're in studio, the nice part about GoNetYourself is we allow for practice time. We allow for practice hours for people to come in and practice in the studio. If they make a mistake, it's fine. Get them comfortable in front of camera, and that takes time. Then, once they've left the studio, then you have the editing process, that back and forth between us and the editors. The most important thing is that the client checks off on the content prior to going to editing. They say, "Yes, the content that was captured … yes, there's the two minutes that we all agree upon." Now we can move it to a final edit.

Here's another little trick: Make sure that the attorneys have looked at it. A lot of companies, if they're a financial firm, their attorneys don't really care about the assets that are put around it; what they care about is what is said onscreen. If you're working with a financial firm, you've got to make sure that, before you move to editing, you have the attorneys say, "Yes, what you said, that's okay."

RICK

You're doing a legal review and not just financial videos; a legal review is important if you are selling supplements or weight-loss products or fitness equipment, anything in which you are making claims.

JEFF

Yes, those are the things that you need to make sure the attorneys look for before you go to final edit. If not, you'll end up completing all of your re-edits and post-edits, and then the attorneys get it, and then you've got to start all over again. So, understanding and getting the content checkoff prior to going to edit is just one big tip on making sure that your process goes smoothly.

RICK

What are some other common mistakes you see people making when they come into the studio? I know we talked about wardrobe mistakes; we talked about practicing the script. Is there anything else, when you're in the studio, that you see people doing that maybe they shouldn't?

JEFF

Here's a big one you see with many companies, they have too many cooks in the kitchen. They might have eight people to sign off on their video. You might as well kill your video right there. We just roll our eyes and go, "Oh." That's number one.

RICK

Well, you know what they say. A camel was a horse that was designed by a committee.

JEFF

Exactly. That goes right alongside, is that the person who has the greatest financial stake in the process, or influence in the process, isn't part of the process. We have seen over and over, especially in large corporations, where we will get to the end, and the person who actually has the most authority has never been involved in the process, and kills it at the end, going, "No, that's not what I wanted." It's like, "No, you can't get to the end and have that happen." It is absolutely critical that whoever has the most influence and/or financial stake has to be a part of the process. If not, then your video is doomed to be in endless re-edit cycles, or ultimately just die and never gets to market.

RICK

That's really good advice. Everything you're talking about, I've run into at one time or another through my career doing video production so I can vouch for everything you're saying as absolutely 100 percent correct. Is there anything I didn't ask you about, Jeff, that you want to share before we conclude things?

JEFF

I think the key points then of the affordable, repeatable, executable model of video production, is that people need to focus on ... the three keys are focusing upon identified and agreed-upon style of video prior to getting started; the agreed-upon script, that is the right length ... we even say write out an interview. Do a phone recording and ask them the questions that you want to ask them. If you want to do a short video, keep those questions to a minimum. You're looking at three questions per minute. Probably lower, but let's go three questions per minute. *If you want a two-minute interview video, then you're looking at, we always say, five questions or less.* But have that scripted. They can get off-script; that's fine, but you want the narrow content that you know that you want them to say scripted prior to them coming in. It can still be authentic, it can still be non-prompter, but what you do is you know exactly the content that you want hit, in a very narrow soundbite; because remember, in video, you've got to speak in soundbites versus long text, right? But you have that narrowed down before.

So, agreed-upon script; agreed-upon video style; well-practiced ... you know, prepared before they get into the studio. Then the last piece of that puzzle: make sure that there are not too many cooks in the kitchen coming to edit, and the person with the highest influence and/or financial influence of that video is a part of that entire process along the way. If you do those things, you will be able to repeat that process over and over again.

RICK

That's really good information. One last thing: tell people where you're located, and your website address, so if they want to use your services, they can contact you.

JEFF

It's just, GoNetYourself.com is our website, and we have studios in Seattle, Bellevue, and Boise, Idaho, but we also can edit your videos and come to any location worldwide.

RICK

Well, I wanted to thank you for sharing so much great information about the ins and outs of video production, and a new model for doing it very inexpensively and a lot faster than the traditional way, so thank you.

JEFF

Thank you.

CHAPTER FOUR SUMMARY

- Creating a video has three distinct steps or phases, Pre-production, this is the planning phase. Production, this is the execution phase and Post-production, this is the editing phase and the place where the entire project comes together. Your focus should be on pre-production, good video can be expensive, so plan, plan, plan!

- Start with the end in mind. What type of video are your trying to produce? Once that is determined, create a script or outline that will guide your shoot. Aim for 150 words per minute of video.

- The best way to create video is to understand the entire process from start to finish, every single piece of the puzzle that is in that process and then putting together a guideline for each one of those steps.

- When getting started, take advantage of the many online resources and templates for creating a video.

CHAPTER FIVE
Make Your Video Content Compelling

*"Your purpose is to make your audience see what you
saw, hear what you heard, feel what you felt. Relevant
detail, couched in concrete, colorful language, is the best
way to recreate the incident as it happened and to
picture it for the audience."*
—Dale Carnegie

It was 1978, I had just graduated from college in Pennsylvania with a degree in Biology and moved back to my home at the time, Daytona Beach, Florida. Daytona is a tourist town and at the time not the best place to find a great paying job. I was working as a bartender and a lifeguard, fun jobs, but looking for something better to do. I decided to attend a seminar, that looking back on it now, really helped change my life. The course was called "How to Win Friends and Influence People" based on the book by Dale Carnegie. If you go online, they still offer these courses today. Some of what they taught was confidence in yourself, how to prepare a speech and one of the things people are afraid of most, the ability to get up in front of a group of people and speak.

One of the rules about speech-giving that we learned was that while preparing a speech always follow a very simple formula: *Tell them what you are going to say, say it, and tell them what you said.*

A SHORT SIMPLE FORMULA

The actual quote from Dale Carnegies book is: "Tell the audience what you're going to say, say it; then tell them what you've said."

This is a short, simple formula that not only works for giving speeches but will help all your videos perform better as well. I know it works because I've been using this formula for over thirty years to create videos that have sold billions of dollars of products direct to the consumer! I talk about many of these products and case studies in my previous two books, *BUY NOW* and *BUILDING BILLON DOLLAR BRANDS*, both available on Amazon.

I believe there are parallels between making interesting videos for your viewers and preparing a speech. Actually, if you study the components of what it takes to give an interesting speech, you can apply these same tactics to create interesting videos. A lot has to do with your target audience. When you are giving a speech in a room full of people who have come to hear you speak about a specific subject, these people are your target audience. Ask yourself, "What do I need to put into the power-point presentation (or video), so the people in my audience (or viewers) will be interested in what I'm saying?"

When it comes to video scripting/production, you should think the same way. Remember the old saying, *"If you try to appeal to everyone, you'll appeal to no one."*

CREATING A POWERFUL INTRODUCTION

Catch your prospect's attention. "On the average, five times as many people read the headline as read the body copy. When you have written your headline, you have spent eighty cents out of your dollar." —David Ogilvy

There is a great video on YouTube called "How to Start your Presentation, 4-Step Formula for a Killer Intro" video at http://bit.ly/Presentation4steps.

At the time of this writing, it had almost 450,000 views.

The video was created by Ann Ricketts, the founder of Lighthouse Communications, http://lighthousecommunicate.com/.

You should watch it two or three times at least. Every expert in video production, especially online video, says the same thing, you need to get people's attention quickly and get them hooked quickly, or you will lose people as they click away to something more interesting. From making Direct Response TV infomercials for the last thirty years, I have had to deal with this short attention span phenomenon on a continuing basis. If I didn't catch people's attention quickly, they just clicked to the next program with the remote control. If you don't get people's attention, the same thing will happen to your online videos even faster.

Another interesting thing I learned, was that once you grabbed the viewer's attention, they would stay until the end of the program, almost thirty minutes! So, if you can get someone interested in what your videos are talking about, they usually will stay engaged until the end, the total length of the video doesn't really matter. This holds true for every video format, from a TV commercial, to a video on your website, to a YouTube video. You need to grab the viewer's attention quickly and hold it. *The best way to do that is with a powerful introduction.*

Here is a summary of the four-step process Ann talks about in her video for creating a powerful introduction:

#1 Your hook: A story, a metaphor, an analogy, a shocking statistic, a question, or a combination of these things, something interesting and vivid right from the start.

#2 The Transition to your topic: I tell that story because…," "This story Illustrates…"

#3 Self-Introduction and a preview of your talk or video: What are the goals of your talk? What will you be covering?

#4 The Audience Benefit: What someone will gain from listening to your talk? Be specific.

THREE WAYS TO HOOK THE VIEWER

1. Start the video with a question. Would you like to spend less time in the kitchen? Would you like an easy way to lose ten pounds? Do you have trouble falling asleep? Asking a question at the beginning of your video is a sure-fire way to get the viewers interested in your topic to pay attention.

2. Start your video with a factoid. Here is a real example—In 1989, I used this factoid to start a 30-minute TV show about the benefits of fresh juice. This video hooked people immediately and went on to sell millions of dollars of Juiceman juice extractors.

   "Scientists have just discovered a naturally-occurring element in broccoli called indole-3-carbinol, or I3C, that has been shown to prevent breast cancer."

This factoid came from an actual news story on CNN and immediately caught people's attention. Our video went on to show how there were many other naturally-occurring plant substances that had remarkable health benefits and how drinking freshly-extracted juices was the easiest way to get many of these nutrients into your body.

3. Start your video with a story. We have been programmed through thousands of years of communication to listen to stories. Who can ignore a compelling story? This is also a great way to draw people into your video.

When I was creating and testing infomercials for products like Sonicare, OxiClean, and the George Foreman Grill, if we were not getting the viewer response we needed, the first thing I would look at changing was the introduction. A great example of this was the very first George Foreman infomercial. I thought it would be a good idea to start the video with boxing footage of George knocking out Michael Moorer to win the heavyweight crown at age forty-six, the oldest ever. We tested the show, and it didn't work, not even close. Because it was a new product, I made the basic mistake of not understanding our target audience, which at the time were mostly stay-at-home moms, who didn't like boxing. Once we took the boxing footage out and made the introduction of the show about the *benefits to the viewer of speed, convenience, and great taste,* the show took off and became one of the most successful infomercials ever produced.

THE SUCCESSFUL INFOMERCIAL FORMULA

You can learn a lot about creating successful sales videos from the formula for a successful infomercial. There are only a handful of people who were involved when TV infomercials first started in the mid-eighties, and I know them all. Most were from the real estate seminar business, like Albert Lowery, Robert Allen, Ed Beckley, and the guy I briefly worked for Tom Vu. These types of shows were all happening in the mid-eighties. Through LinkedIn recently, I had the good fortune to meet Kurt Wolfe, he started doing fitness infomercials even earlier, in the late seventies, before anyone else was doing these type shows. The reason I bring this up is that there is a very basic formula that I helped create that all successful infomercials follow. I'd like to share it with you. Again, if you study the steps, you can apply them to videos you are creating to make your videos more compelling.

First and foremost, any good infomercial must capture your attention. If it doesn't do that, it's very easy for the viewer to grab the remote and click to something more interesting. Think about online videos, people will click-away even faster if you do not engage them early.

FIRST—SET UP THE PROBLEM

Most products or services are a solution to an existing problem. You need to set up and explain this problem to the viewers. If they have this problem, they will be interested in watching more. Here are a few examples from actual TV ads and YouTube videos:

- Do you suffer from dry, chapped skin?
- Having trouble with your memory?

- Are you feeling sluggish and tired all the time?
- Would you like to lose weight?
- Would you like to be more fit?
- Tough to remove stains in your clothes?
- How do you get a wine stain out of your carpet?
- How would you like to spend less time in the Kitchen?

Visually show the viewer what these problems look like. The people who can relate to these questions will keep watching....to see if you are offering a solution to their problem.

NEXT—OFFER THE SOLUTION

Once it captures your attention, though, it has to keep it. So how do they keep you hooked? One word – *emotion*. Good infomercials and videos demonstrate why the product is a good value and why the customer would be making a smart, well-informed decision to buy it. Successful infomercials go into detail on exactly what the product can do for the viewer.

Offer your product or service as the best solution to the problem outlined above. Focus on the benefits your product will deliver to the viewer. Don't focus on being better than products offered by your competitors, but how your product is different and unique. What is your unique selling proposition (USP)?

THEN—THE CALL TO ACTION (CTA)

Most demonstration videos I see fail to ask for the order. Once you have presented all the benefits and the customer is practically dying to get their hands on it, you still have to ask for the order. This is known as the Call to Action or the CTA. Different offers, prices, and bonuses can be tested throughout the commercial and often are.

Now that the viewer knows the solution to their problem exists, make sure they know a way to get it. Offer an immediate call to action, a way the viewer can get your product now. Go to your website, buy it on Amazon, text for more details, call an 800#, et cetera.

MAKE AN IRRESISTIBLE OFFER

Make an offer that is better than they can find anywhere else. One way this is usually done by adding free bonuses…but only if they ORDER NOW!

With the Sonicare toothbrush, we had extra brush heads and information on how to get a better check-up.

With the Juiceman, we offered many different juice recipes, a knife, a cutting board, and a juice pitcher.

With the George Foreman Grill, we added many extra fat-free recipes.

Next, you need to induce scarcity, "only available for a limited time," or "not available in stores."

Always, always add a guarantee. A guarantee ensures that if for any reason viewers aren't satisfied, they can get a complete refund. There is no risk!

Different offer configurations, price points, and additional bonuses should be tested. The second thing, after the introduction, that I will change if an ad or video isn't working is the offer. A great example of this was when we were trying to sell the Rug Doctor carpet cleaners. This was a high price point item selling for almost $500 at the time. We tested a "soft" offer, no price given, just call or go online for more information. We tested different "hard" offers, like 4 monthly payments of $125 or 10 monthly payments of only $50, but it wasn't until we made an offer that said, "Find out how you can get your Rug Doctor for payments as low as $29.95" that sales really took off. So it is important to test. I go into more detail about structuring offers in Chapter 6.

ALWAYS ADD TESTIMONIALS

Everything works better with testimonials added. You need to prove that the solution really exists (social proof) and it's tried and tested to be effective. Nothing sells better than the word of a current user. Testimonials are a way for potential customers to see that other people "just like them" have purchased and benefitted from the product or service you are offering. (See Chapter 3 for much more detail.)

The most important aspect of a successful infomercial or video is to be absolutely authentic and genuine. The audience can tell when you are not and will tune out. All these factors combined will help you to make more interesting and better performing videos.

MORE WAYS TO MAKE VIDEOS THAT SELL: THE AIDA FORMULA

I love systems and formulas that work, they save you both time and money. Here is another simple formula for video success. It's called – AIDA.

- Catch your prospects **ATTENTION**
- Capture Their **INTEREST**
- Arouse their **DESIRE** for what you are selling
- Motivate them to take **ACTION**

This formula has been used in both the direct response industry and sales training for a long time, because it works. It's a good idea to follow this when you're creating your own videos. This formula is time-tested, and I use it because it works over and again, no matter what kind of media is involved.

I think something often gets lost in the noise of shiny new technological capabilities when people are trying to make videos that sell. That's why this simple formula remains so useful. Tried and true, it still works like gangbusters on any platform for your video marketing—Facebook, LinkedIn, Amazon—you name it. But even with this proven formula in hand, it's critical to "start with the end in mind."

What's your goal, what are you trying to accomplish with your video?

And I think then, once you realize that, you can understand exactly what action you want the viewer of your video to take.

Note that this doesn't apply to YouTube videos you're creating for pure entertainment – where people are tuning in to be entertained. This is all about creating videos that SELL.

Remember, *Video that entertains does not always sell, but video that sells can entertain!*

The AIDA formula empowers your video when you want the viewer to take some type of action that you've decided they need to do:

- Is it to go to a website?
- Is it to go to a landing page?
- Is it to call or text or walk or buy?

And really having THAT clear in your mind, as what the goal for the video is, is the FIRST step to putting AIDA to its most effective use.

Now let's go through the different elements of the formula: Attention, Interest, Desire, Action.

ATTENTION

When I wrote my first book "Buy Now," a number of very careful decisions went into the way it presented itself on the shelf.

First off, the title. "Buy Now" is a command. It demands attention. It doesn't suggest, it doesn't insinuate, it grabs you by the collar and tells you what to do.

We also chose the image of a hand with a GOLD credit card to give you

the notion that there was something in it for you financially. The letters were big, bold, stark, and distinct.

It grabs attention.

This is important. This is stuff that really works.

And it's especially critical to creating videos for use online, especially since we've discovered clear parallels to what drove our success on TV.

When you consider viewing habits online, it's much like TV where you're sitting there with a remote control in hand and at the ready. If you didn't capture their attention in the first ten seconds or sooner, they would flip to a different station. So you HAVE to focus on what you could use to capture a person's attention.

And I think with social media and online videos the attention span is even shorter. Which means in that first 5 to 10 seconds, you must attract a person's attention to get them to watch the entire video.

One approach is to raise a RED FLAG – as in "WARNING."

Note a clear distinction here...

You're NOT trying to get every single person that sees your video to watch it.

Instead, you're trying to capture the attention of the people who would be your absolute BEST customers, or your target demographic, or whatever. For example, if you're making an offer to pet owners, the first image they see could be:

This visual makes it clear the video speaks directly to people who love their pets.

Another good attention grabber tactic is PROBLEM-SOLUTION. Often times we'll do this with a question. "Do you have X problem?"

You can do this with words, with a voiceover, and especially with an image that clearly demonstrates the problem to be solved. For example, "Who wants to drink from a glass like this?"

Those are just a few ways to capture Attention right off the bat.

INTEREST

Now let's talk about the second step in the AIDA formula: INTEREST.

Your prospect's ears have perked up, and they're saying, "Okay. Well, this has got me." So how do you keep it? And how do you build on that interest? You keep asking questions, for instance: "Are you one of the thousands of people suffering from Macular Degeneration?"

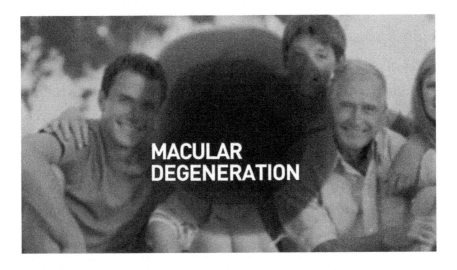

You can also build Interest with information that responds to a "Did you know that...?"

Or...

Because once you've captured the attention of the category of viewer you're after, you want to give them even more useful information at that point – especially how the problem could affect them personally.

Here's where you would go through the hassles of dealing with the problem they face – how their quality of life is negatively affected.

All these can drive and increase Interest.

DESIRE

Now that you've "twisted the knife" as copywriters like to say, you present the solution in a way that makes them desire the solution. You must lay out what it is you have to offer that is THE answer to their problem.

Again, use words, images, voiceover – all that makes the message of TRANSFORMATION clear.

You start here...

And wind up here… "It's that easy!"

Here's the place where you might also include powerful testimonials that reinforce the transformation that real people have experienced. "Hey! This really worked for me."

Then, once you've made clear that the transformation/solution they desire is out there just waiting for them…

ACTION

This brings us to the last step in the formula, which is Action or the Call to Action (CTA).

I think failing to include the CTA is one of the biggest mistakes people make in their videos.

They fail to tell people exactly where to go or what to do to take that final step… to have them visit your site, to have them download the information, or to have them click the *buy* button.

You can do the first three items in the formula perfectly – Capture ATTENTION, Drive INTEREST, Create DESIRE… But if you don't tell them to take ACTION, there's no way your video will deliver the results you intended.

So make sure you present the specific action you want the viewer to take. And just as important, offer some type of reason to take the action you want them to take – create a sense of urgency. Give them an incentive.

For example, with GoPro, at the end, the CTA stated, "Go to our website. Someone will win one of everything we make, every single day." So that was a contest. It gave a reason to go there, and it enabled them to capture the names and addresses of interested prospects.

The following pictures illustrate a clear CTA along with what exactly to do.

THE BOTTOM LINE

The bottom line to building your bottom line with video is to use the formulas I outlined in this chapter. I guarantee it WILL make your videos much better, engagement levels will be higher, and they will deliver the sales results you are looking for. Make sure to take action on what you learned. That is the key.

INTERVIEW WITH JACK TURK, COPYWRITER

I met Jack after giving the Keynote speech at The Dan Kennedy's GKIC Info-Marketing Conference in Denver several years ago. GKIC is the Glazer-Kennedy Insider's Circle, an entrepreneur network. I've since used Jack to help me write many successful direct response television (DRTV) scripts.

RICK

Hi, Jack. Today I want to talk to you about copywriting and more specifically direct response copywriting and how that can help in making videos more engaging and effective. How did you become a copywriter?

JACK

It goes way, way back. I've been a writer forever. I got into writing because I when I was in college there was a little ad in the student paper about, "Can you be funny? Here's a test." So, I took the little test on can I be funny, and I got a gig with the student radio station on writing comedy for a radio show we did. One of the guys in the group was Tim Allen. So, I knew Tim Allen back in 1976 and 1977. I actually appeared on a television show with him in 1977.

RICK

Wow, I didn't know that.

JACK

I'm still friends with Tim, and he's a great guy. Eventually, I wound up getting a job in the computer industry. I did a lot of technical writing and ended up at Microsoft in their multimedia group. I ran their documentation department, got involved with all the new media, I worked on Windows Media Player, all the video stuff. I wrote the first documentation for Windows Video. I wrote the software documentation for programmers. So, I have a background in writing, that goes back forever.

One thing I've always loved is magic. My sideline's magic. So I've always done magic. And I thought "Well, heck, I'd like to do some more shows." I got really good at marketing myself. I was doing two, 300 shows a year.

RICK

How did the direct response writing come in?

JACK

It was all direct response. I got really good at that. Other people started asking me, how can I do this? Could you write some copy for me? I started writing more copy for other people. And eventually, I just kept writing more and more copy, and that became more fun and more lucrative. I wound up at GKIC. They wound up hiring me as their head copywriter, and I was the head copywriter for GKIC for like three years.

RICK

Please tell people what GKIC is.

JACK

GKIC is a company founded by Dan Kennedy who wrote Magnetic Marketing and many other books on direct marketing. GKIC puts on seminars and offers courses and materials that help small businesses learn and implement direct response marketing to help generate more leads, more customers, and increase sales. Dan Kennedy is the Grandfather of direct response marketing and direct mail. I wound up getting a gig through them, and I kept doing more stuff for him, and he said, "Ah, we need a copywriter. Let's hire Jack," then I ran all their copywriting for three years. That's where I met you when you were the keynote speaker at one of the big info-marketing events that they put on.

RICK

That's amazing that you were the copywriter for the guy who's the guru of direct response copywriters.

JACK

I did a lot of stuff in Dan's voice. Dan has said that I write in his voice better than anybody else has ever done. I came the closest to be able to write in Dan's voice. And I'm actually proud of that.

RICK

In all talks and presentations I do I recommend Dan's books because people always want to know how they can get started in direct response marketing, and I said, well, the first book I ever read was *The No BS Guide to Direct Response Marketing* by Dan Kennedy. It's a great place for people to start to learn more about how to do direct response marketing and to start making those strategies part of their videos.

JACK

In 2015, I decided I wanted to go off on my own. And so, I've been freelancing since then on a variety of projects. I've really enjoyed all the projects you and I have worked on together. I've grown in terms of understanding more about launches, and the whole big picture of marketing and copywriting is a piece of it. But overall, thinking through offers, thinking through campaigns, thinking through funnels, how to actually pull everything together I've gotten reasonably good at that sort of thing.

RICK

One of the things I'm trying to help people with in this book—in this chapter specifically—is to think about when they are producing a video that they should learn some basic copywriting because copywriters know how to capture a person's attention quickly and get them engaged, starting at Point A and ending up at Point B. The more you can learn about how to do that, the more that will help you when you are producing a video.

JACK

I think you make a really good point. A lot of mistakes I see over and over again with people is that they try to do too much with their offers and their script copy for videos. *They are just not clear as to what they want the customer to do.* Or they say, "Well, you can do this or that, or do you ... " And the customer goes, "I don't know which I should do." And you have always been really good about that. One thing, one action. Simple.

RICK

Yes. It's important to keep one clear, simple action that you want the viewer to take and stay focused on that. I want to get a little bit more into this for people that don't understand direct response. You can take your skill set of copywriting, and you said you can use it for magicians, you use it for doctors, dentists, gunsmithing. You and I have worked on several television commercials. What's the one common thread in the writing you have done for these?

JACK

I think the common thread is that every one of these has a specific offer that has a specific call to action that you can assess at the end. Did it work or did it not work? It's very measurable. This is about putting something out in front of someone and saying, "Hey, I think this has real value to you. Here's why you need to act on this right now." Every one of these offers has that same underlying principle.

RICK

If you want to give someone advice on how to be a better copywriter what would you tell them to do? I know it's taken years and years for you to get to where you are, but if somebody wants to learn some basic skills, what would be some good advice?

JACK

I think the first great advice is to start saving your junk mail. Some of the best ones I think come from political parties, organizations like the NRA, organizations like AAA. The ones that send you not just a letter, a very simple letter, you want to save the junk mail that is packed with stuff. Those are the packages you want to save because those packages cost them a lot of money to put together. It might cost them two bucks, $2.45 to send each one, but they know after sending 100,000 of them what their responses will be and how they can monetize that response. They wouldn't be doing it unless it was worthwhile to them and they're generating the response they want. That means the copy works! So that's the first thing, save your junk mail. Go through it and really read and try to understand what they're doing with their headlines and their offers.

And honestly, I think what makes for good copy, is having empathy for your customer or viewer, really trying to get inside their heads. And I think that's something that, again, I'm going back to when I said the junk mail, the political parties, are really good about understanding your hot buttons, really understanding where your head is at and where your emotions are at, where your heart is at. And they pushed those hot buttons, and they're getting into the conversation going inside your head, and they try to be thematic, like up to date with current events, et cetera, et cetera. So that's really important that you can get inside your customer's head. And really, *if you want to be a better copywriter, really get to know your customer or viewer.* The better you know your customer, the better copywriter you can be, even if you're not eloquent in terms of being a great writer if you can sit down and write a note to them where you really know where they're coming from and you really empathize with them, that has power. It's got a lot of power.

RICK

That's fantastic information. Facebook advertising has really taken off and is a very lucrative platform for video ads, but if you don't know who your customer is and who you're targeting, you will just waste money ... And that holds true for any advertising medium, whether it's direct mail or radio or TV or Facebook, Instagram or whatever. So, the more you understand who you're addressing from the standpoint of copywriting or producing a video, really makes a huge difference.

JACK

Absolutely. *The four things I focus on are the viewer's hopes, their fears, their dreams, their pain, those four things.* If you can just write those out and think about it, and try to be inside their shoes, you will have a real advantage right there.

RICK

If we're talking about making videos that are more engaging, more interesting, that's a perfect starting place, know who your customer is and then try and address one of those four things you just mentioned.

JACK

Yes, you see it a lot with really good direct response videos. Many times, it's a pain point. I've seen this over and over again. It's sure a lot easier to sell a cure than a preventive action.

RICK

Right. So it sounds also like you're talking about problem-solution.

JACK

Exactly. Problem-solution.

RICK

You're identifying the problem, and then you're offering a specific solution.

JACK

Well, there is one more step in there. That's state the problem, then agitate the problem, then offer the solution. The classic copywriting formula.

RICK

Tell us more about that.

JACK

Let me give you an example. One of the commercials that we did together had to do with a product that will protect you from blue light from digital display screens. But you want to make sure you don't just want to talk about the problem-solution, you want to take the knife, you want to twist it and really want to agitate, you want to drive home the point, this really is bothering you, isn't it? This is really causing problems so you can't sleep at night. Your day's ruined because you've got this thing going on. You want to beat the drum much more before you offer the solution.

RICK

So, problem, agitate, solution, are the three steps.

JACK

Yes, and don't shy away from agitating. Don't be reluctant to do that because people are, as you well know, they're very reluctant to take that next step. It's very hard. I've heard it said, imagine you're talking to Homer Simpson who was sitting on the couch. He doesn't want to do a darn thing. You got to slap him upside the head about fifteen times. Look how annoying his kid is. Bart's gotta beat him upside the head fifteen times before he'll get Homer off the couch. You're basically being Bart. You're Bart Simpson as a copywriter.

RICK

You're hitting people over the head and just making them take notice.

JACK

Yes, how many thousands of messages do we get in a day? The same old stuff over and over again. Do something different. Be creative ... try to say it in a different way ... One of the best lines, this is a Dan Kennedy quote, he said, *"Say interesting things, in interesting ways."*

RICK

That's awesome.

JACK

I think every time I write something, I stop and that's the only edit I do. Did I say something interesting in an interesting way? And not just rattle it off in the same way you've seen it before.

RICK

This chapter is how to make videos more engaging, more interesting, and right there is a short formula for exactly how to do it. Say something more interesting, in an interesting way, that's a great, great nugget of information.

Let's talk a little bit about offers ... so we state the problem, agitate, then offer the solution. You have to give people a way to order or go to the website or respond to what your product or service or whatever action you're trying to get them to do. I want to talk about different types of offers or how do you start thinking about offers?

JACK

I actually know a guy who's working on a book of offers, which I think is brilliant. I think there's a lot of things you can tweak in your offer. I have a general principle, and I really believe you should make your best offer; however you configure it, with like payment plans, pricing, bonuses, all you can toss in. You should make it so good that it actually, literally makes you squirm a little bit to present it, and that it hurts. It hurts that I have to give you this good an offer. And that's the way you are almost certain to get it accepted or people will take the action you want them to. I think that actually comes through honestly in the copy, you know what? I am really giving you a good deal here. And you feel it. I'm giving you a really a good deal. You should take this.

RICK

I heard a term for that, it's called the irresistible offer.

JACK

Right. I think a lot of people go, "Well, this is my price, and this is my thing, and that's what I do. And they can take it or leave it." Okay. That's fair, but I think they're thinking short-sighted. A) because you should not think of the offer in a vacuum that this is my one shot, this one customer and this is it for eternity, and I think that's a mistake people make. You should think of your offer, I think, in the context of the long-term relationship you expect to build with that customer, with that client. This is sales 101 I got from my dad, actually, who sold cars. My dad was a wonderful car salesman, very successful in a little town in Michigan back in the 70s. He was selling 300 to 500 cars a year in a town of 2,000 people, and he did that for ten solid years. And he told me the way you do this. That's pretty impressive. He said, "Yeah, well, you just give him the best deal you can. They'll just keep coming back."

RICK

Very simple. What I find is always that really, really simple advice works the best.

JACK

Give them the best deal you can, just do that....and that's strategic thinking.

RICK

Let's stay on offers, how important is a guarantee?

JACK

I think a guarantee is extremely important. Let's look at it this way, you have to address that, when I was doing birthday parties, I guaranteed the parties. I guaranteed if I don't knock your socks off and the walls aren't ringing with laughter, shaking with laughter at the end of this, hey, don't pay me. People need that extra security to help them take the final step.

RICK

I just finished reading your book, tell people the name of your book and where they can get it and some of the information that's in there.

JACK

My book is called *101 Fast, Good, Cheap Hacks for Writing a KILL-ER Sales Letter* and, it's available on Amazon. It's pretty simple in terms of it's got 101 different hacks to writing sales letters. I am a big fan of systems. I'm a huge fan of short cuts. A lot of little tips that I've learned and I'm very, very quick at writing. I think I'm one of the world's experts in writing copy fast because I've been writing like I said, I've been writing for forty years. I've learned a lot of things, and there's just lots of little things you can do to make your copy work better. For example, one of my tips, and it's a very simple one, is never start from a blank page. I believe so strongly you never start from a blank page.

RICK

Like those direct mail pieces you told people to save?

JACK

Exactly. Go take the headline for one, just copy it and then start messing with it, start changing words around or whatever. Change it to fit your market, your customers.

RICK

That's a really great idea because even when it comes to writing a video script or something like that, I know from doing this for a long time, the hardest thing in the world to do is starting with a blank piece of paper. If you send me a rough draft of something, all of a sudden, I become very creative, and it's easy to make changes and make it great. But the hardest thing in the world is to start from a blank piece of paper. So that's really, really good advice is for somebody to start with some type of copy or something or another idea they found somewhere else and then mold it into their own script.

JACK

Absolutely! Another good hack—and this is actually illustrated by our conversation right here—is work from questions. Come up with the questions you have about your copy, about the letter you are working on and respond to them. For example, I didn't have an outline of what I was going to say to you today, but you gave me good questions, and I can respond to your questions. We all respond to questions. So instead of saying, "Here are the five reasons you should take this offer." You could also just do something like, "What are the pain points you're going to experience if they don't take this offer?" And you can answer that kind of thing. So filling your copy with questions that you can answer and respond to is another hack that will get you off the fence and off and running quickly. I think that's a really good hack. Another really good one, we talked about offers earlier, I think this is a really good principle. Write your offer first before you write your sales letter or video script, that way you've thought it through, and you know people are going to be chomping at the bit to get this thing you are offering.

RICK

There's an old saying, "Start with the end in mind." So you know where you want to get to, and you're really clear on that. Then it makes writing to get to that point much easier.

JACK

Absolutely. Because then you're making your case, everything, everything leads up to that, you're basically setting all the criteria, setting the buying criteria for why you want to have, you're laying the foundation for why, oh, but here's all the pain points. And *boom* here's the answer.

RICK

If you are reading this right now, one of the many reasons I'm interviewing Jack, is that I read his book and I felt like almost 95 percent of the content about writing sales letters that you could take and transfer that information and use it to make successful videos. That's what's really important here and why I think it's such a great book because there is such a parallel between writing a good sales letter and creating a good video that's going to persuade someone to do what you want them to do. The more you understand that foundation, the better you're going to be when you go to produce a video to try and get people to take a specific action.

JACK

Thanks, there's a lot of commonalities. There is also some templates you can use, like we talk about the problem, agitate, solve. I have some other little templates for a very simple sequence to fill in the blanks. I really believe in using templates as much as you can. Once you learn them, you should follow them. Know the basics then you play it and then you riff on it.

RICK

This is good advice for someone that's thinking about creating a video. One of the things that was really helpful on the scripts you did for me is you had the written word, but then you put some pictures in, which enables you to visualize and it almost makes it come alive. You created some rough storyboards.

JACK

When I get stuck in terms of a project, sometimes I'll just go off and look at pictures. I'll go Google something, and I just see what pictures come up. Images are extremely powerful. You really want to write visually. You want to write emotively. And a picture's worth a thousand words. What helped me in writing those scripts is

I actually tried to come up with the pictures first. What image do I want to have first and then find something and then go and write some copy for that image and then I go onto the next scene and think what image do I want to show in here? I really did try to think in terms of the scripts I did for you, image-wise first before I actually wrote any of the words.

RICK

That's good advice. So, if somebody is thinking about making a video, they could go find some pictures first to help them visualize what they want.

JACK

Absolutely. Hey again, even if you're writing just copy, I put a lot of pictures ... People don't think about Dan Kennedy, but he used a lot of images in his copy. He's always tossing in pictures in his copy and different stuff. Again, saying interesting things, in interesting ways.

RICK

Anything you want to talk about that I didn't ask you?

JACK

This is I think the biggest obstacles for writing that people have, and I hear it over and over again, and I think I've finally managed to get over it myself is, is just write. Just write it. To play off Nike, just write it. We all have this editor inside our heads that's constantly critiquing every single word you type. And it's going, "No, that's not the right word. No, there's probably a better. No, no, no. This is right. You said that blah, blah, blah." Shut off the wise guy. He's a wise guy. He's always criticizing you. Learn to shut off the wise guy. Just write it. The wise guy is not your friend. The editor inside your head is not your friend. You just need to ... And just write like you talk, as you and I are sitting here talking to one another. Write just like that. Like you're talking. When you're writing a letter, you're doing a video, you are talking to the person on the other side one-on-one. "Hey, I know you had some problems. I know it really hurts and let me tell you, I got something that could really help. I really think it's the right thing for you to do this. Check this out."

If you got a friend who is hurting, and you got something to help them, wouldn't you just sit down and talk to them and say, "Hey, do this, this will help." That's what you're doing in writing. That's what you're doing right there.

RICK

Jack, if someone wanted to reach out to hire you, what's your email address?

JACK

It's jack@jackturk.com.

RICK

Great. I wanted to thank you for taking your time today and thanks for sharing some of your great experience.

CHAPTER FIVE SUMMARY

- You need to create a powerful open to your videos to hold viewer attention.
- Hook the reader with a question, a factoid, or a story.
- Use the AIDA Formula, Attention, Interest, Desire, Action.
- Tell the viewer what they're going to see, then show them; then tell them what they just saw.
- In your demonstration videos always include a clear Call to Action (CTA).
- Have your CTA be an Irresistible Offer.
- Always include testimonials.

CHAPTER SIX
Make Me an Offer:
The Key to Higher Conversions

"Persuasion is a science-how you can say something in
one particular way to increase the likely-hood of ascent."
—Robert Cialdini Ph.D., professor of marketing,
business, and psychology

In chapter three I showed you the three most popular types of online video, based on viewing habits. They are **Tutorials**, which are primarily used to educate and for customer service. Then there are **Testimonial** and **Demonstration** videos that are used primarily for selling and marketing your product or service. In this chapter, we are going to take a deeper dive into demonstration videos and what makes them work, some direct response strategies that will help make your demonstration videos convert or sell better, and we will also look at the most important step in of a demonstration video the Call to Action or CTA. But first, we are going to learn about some basic human psychology and underlining principles about why offers work.

WHY OFFERS WORK

I love to play golf, and I belong to a golf club near where I live called The Club at Snoqualmie Ridge. Besides having a beautiful golf course, the club offers many social activities for its members. One of the events that they offer are wine-tastings from various vineyards from Washington state. The club sets up several tables in one of their meeting rooms, and various winemakers bring their wines, and you go from table to table tasting the wine. If you like any of the wines, they have both bottles or cases available usually at a small discount to what you would pay at a retail store. These events are hugely successful for the wineries as they sell many cases of wine. Why is that? I know when I'm standing at one of the tables tasting the different varieties of wine there is a strong internal pull to purchase from that vendor and a feeling of guilt if I walk away after tasting the wine and don't purchase anything. Why does this happen? There is a powerful psychological rule at work here when it comes to persuasion. This one is called the *Rule of Reciprocity, and it prompts us to repay what someone has given us.*

Think of some other examples of the rule of reciprocity that you might have run into.

- How about when manufacturers set up little stands in Costco and give you free samples of food or drink—do you feel compelled to purchase their products?
- Have you ever received a piece of mail from a non-profit organization that included free mailing labels or included a

penny or a nickel in the request letter—have you felt compelled to donate?

- How about the dreaded time-share sales pitch? Usually, you feel obligated to at least listen to the sales pitch, because of a free gift that the hotel or resort has given you.

Many infomercials trying to sell you a product will use a "Free Trial Offer." These offers are proven time and again to out-perform a "hard offer" where the product price is listed. A consumer ends up paying the same price, but because of the rule of reciprocity, conversion rates are usually much higher for the free offer.

There are real human psychological reasons that these offers work. As a video producer who is trying to get people to respond to your videos by purchasing your products, visiting your website, leaving an email address, or clicking the *buy* button on Amazon, the more you know and understand these rules the more success you will have in getting people to take the action you want.

In his book *INFLUENCE, The Psychology of Persuasion*, Dr. Robert Cialdini lays out these rules of persuasion and the science behind why they work. I highly recommend you buy, read, and study his book. http://bit.ly/InfluencePPRC

Recently we had several huge snow storms in the Seattle area, lasting over two weeks. We received more than two feet of new snow that wouldn't go away. This is very unusual for Seattle, as it might snow a little, but soon melts within a day or two. On top of that, the local media over-hyped the storms, even calling it "snow-mageddon" or "snow-pocalypse" creating a lot of fear in people. This in turn, caused a huge rush to the local Home Depot or Lowes stores for snow shovels, de-icer, and salt. The stores were out of stock for all these items very quickly. I was interested in getting some de-icer so I called my local Lowes store and they said that a truck delivery was coming in at midnight and I could come in the morning to get some, but there was a huge demand, so I better get there early. The next morning, I went online and found out Lowes opened at 7 a.m. I got there at about 7:45 a.m. and as I was pulling into the parking lot, I saw a stream of people, almost like ants in formation, coming out of the store exit pushing shopping carts laden down with multiple bags of de-icer. I parked and went inside and one of the employees was sweeping up a small pile of de-icer from a broken bag next to an empty pallet. I asked if they had any de-icer left. He said they were all sold out. I asked how much they had gotten in and he said 18 pallets with 56 bags per pallet or 1008 bags…gone in less than forty-five minutes!

I had just witnessed another form of persuasion, *The Rule of Scarcity, opportunities seem more valuable to us when their availability is limited.* The thought of losing something motivates us more than the thought of gaining something of similar value.

Another great example of scarcity marketing is the "Black Friday" deal. Think about the stampede of people you've seen in person or on the news as they try to buy the limited quantities of the product being offered at a discount. I remember seeing on the news last holiday season a mob of people at a major department store were trying to get the few remaining large screen TVs before they were sold out. Several people were hurt in the mayhem that followed. This is all because of the scarcity principle.

We use the scarcity concept in our video offers all the time. Have you ever heard statements like these?

- Only available for a limited time!
- Supplies are limited, order now!

- Supplies are limited, and when they are gone, they are gone!
- Not available in retail stores!
- Only available through this special TV offer!

The key is to increase the urgency of your offer by being as specific as possible. If you are offering a limited quantity, give the exact number because *specifics are always more persuasive than generalities.* If your offer has a time limit, don't say "offer ends soon," instead say "this offer is good only for the next 24 hours."

THE SIX UNIVERSAL PERSUASION PRINCIPLES

Dr. Cialdini says there are six universal principles that can persuade people to buy. Let's examine these principles to see how to apply them when we are creating the offers or CTAs in our videos.

Rule #1 The Rule of Reciprocity—the desire to give back.

Rule #2 The Rule of Scarcity—the desire to have those things we have less of. "Dwindling in Availability" rare, uncommon, limited time or quantity.

Rule #3 The Rule of Commitment and Consistency—our desire to be consistent in what we have already done. Start with a small request first. Stubborn consistency allows us to avoid thinking too much before making a choice.

Rule #4 The Rule of Social Proof or Consensus—people want to do what everyone else is doing. People want to follow the lead of others, just like them. When in doubt, follow the crowd. In chapter three I present the importance of using authentic testimonials in your marketing. These can be the best form of social proof.

Rule #5 The Rule of Authority—people tend to follow authority figures, third-party experts. We are taught from a young age obedience is right, disobedience is wrong. In chapter seven, we learn about how to be your own spokesperson in your videos, establishing your authority which will lead viewers to take the action you want.

Rule #6 The Rule of Liking—people prefer to say yes to those they know and like. Use aspirational people, physical attractiveness, that will come across just like your viewers and people will respond.

These rules should act as foundational principles to think about every time you make a demonstration video. Which rule or rules can you combine to help make your videos more effective? Now that we know and understand these rules and the psychology be-hind them, the next step in the process is to understand some basic direct response strategies and techniques that will help your call to actions (CTAs) work better.

UNDERSTANDING DIRECT RESPONSE

"Advertising is fundamentally persuasion and persuasion happens to be not a science, but an art."
—William Bernbach, Founder of Ad Agency Doyle Dane Bernbach

It might seem that the quotes from Dr. Robert Cialdini at the beginning of this chapter and the one from William Bernbach above directly contradict each other, but actually, they work togeth-er. Once you understand the underlying human psychological principles and can apply them in your videos, then you can start experimenting, testing, and fine-tuning your offers so they will continue to work at higher and higher levels. This is where the "art" comes in. Many times, you will not know how well a new offer will work until it is tested in the marketplace.

START WITH THE BASICS

The objective of a direct response ad is to trigger an action that leads to a sale, or request for more information. There are many direct response techniques to accomplish that objective, but by far the most important is the offer.

Direct response marketing is a highly ethical way of selling. It's focused on the specific problems of the prospect and aims to solve these problems with education and specific solutions. It is also the only real way for many small businesses to affordably reach their prospects. The goal is to always have your marketing campaigns deliver a positive ROI leading to profitable results. It is important to know what a customer is worth to you, and then decide what you are reasonably willing to invest to acquire a new one. That is your target. Direct response is an accountable way to run marketing for any small business, as it is highly focused on return on investment.

Direct response marketing with video is designed to evoke an immediate response and compel your viewers to take a specific action, such as opting in to your email list, picking up the phone and calling for more information, placing an order for your product or service, being directed to a web page or ordering on Amazon, etc. *Direct response is all about triggering an action that results in a sale, and a compelling offer is the best way to trigger that action.* Direct response allows you to understand the performance of your offer, usually without waiting, as a response is nearly instantaneous. Other attributes of a good direct response ad are that they are trackable and measurable allowing you to accurately figure out your return on investment (ROI) on each ad spend that you do.

Direct response marketing is the fastest way for most companies to get clicks, calls, and customers. These techniques are powerful, and I have used them to help build many iconic brands, like Sonicare, the George Foreman Grill, OxiClean, and GoPro. These case studies and more are explained in detail in my previous book *Building Billion Dollar Brands*.

http://bit.ly/BuildingBDBrands

An infomercial or direct response TV commercial is a great example of video direct response marketing in its purest form. It combines all aspects of creating an effective video marketing tool, demonstrations, testimonials, spokesperson, and effective offers. Then, if interested, viewers can respond via phone or going to a product landing page or company website. These same direct response creative techniques drive digital advertising on Facebook and Instagram, on Amazon, in email newsletters, and all across the Internet.

I just finished making a series of short sales videos to launch two European products into the US market via Facebook and Instagram. They are a Ginseng based Skincare line called GinJo and a Ginseng based men's energy & stamina drink called G5.

The basic structure of these videos is similar to what I used in my successful TV infomercial campaigns, but they are shorter in length. All the steps I used to create these videos are outlined in the chapters of this book. I'm hoping one of these products will be the next Billion Dollar Brand!

MORE ASPECTS OF VIDEO DIRECT RESPONSE

The Video Uses a Strong Opening. Direct response video marketing has a compelling message of strong interest to your chosen viewers. It uses attention-grabbing copy paired with interesting visuals to support what is being said. One popular way is to ask a question or use the problem-solution technique. I go into great detail on ways to capture people's attention quickly, in Chapter Five.

The Video is Aimed at a Specific Audience or Viewer. Who is your target audience? Who do you want to watch your videos? Who are you creating them for? When I was first working with GoPro, we had a very clear target market—extreme athletes—and the videos that were produced were targeted at this niche group of people. Once we had built a good base and strong following, we expanded our videos to reach parents, families, and pet owners by making videos that appealed to those demographics.

Video Direct Response Asks for a Response. Direct response advertising has a "call to action" using a value-packed offer compelling the viewer to do something specific. Sometimes the aim is not necessarily to sell anything from the initial CTA but to get the viewer to take the next action, such as requesting a free e-book or white paper in return for leaving their contact information so that they can be contacted beyond the initial response. This is normally referred to as lead generation. Most people try to hide the offer until the final few seconds of a video. You will have much great success if you make your offer clear, prominent, and easy for the viewer to respond to.

Multi-step, short-term follow-up. In exchange for capturing the viewer's contact details, valuable education and information on the prospect's problem is offered, usually for free. The information should carry with it a second irresistible offer tied to whatever next step you want the prospect to take, such as ordering your product, service or course. Then a series of follow-ups via different media such as mail, e-mail, fax, and phone are made. Often there is a time or quantity limit on the offer, (The Scarcity Rule).

Maintenance follow-up of unconverted leads. People who do not respond within the short-term follow-up period may have many reasons for not buying at that time. There is solid future value in creating names for your database. They should continue hearing from you once to several times a month via email or other means.

YOUR CALL TO ACTION TYPES OF OFFERS

The most important part of any video direct response ad is the offer or CTA. You should spend time brainstorming the best possible offer for your product or service. A clear call to action is vital and something I see many people not doing correctly.

I also feel that *crafting offers is where the art and science of persuasion is combined*. Once you understand the basis of direct response and the types of offers that have been proven to work, you are free to create new and different approaches.

There are always new and effective offers to be found, even in seemingly tired product categories.

- Capital One invented the balance transfer offer in credit cards, which helped propel them into the Fortune 100.
- General Motors invented the "employee discount for everyone" offer, which was so successful that it was copied by all the other major car makers.

THE TWO MOST EFFECTIVE TYPES OF DIRECT RESPONSE OFFERS

#1-Saving Money

This type of offer always works well, in almost every product category and at all times of the year. It can be presented in many different ways:

- Pay half now, nothing later.
- 50% off.
- Get two for the price of one.
- A BOGO offer—buy one, get one free.

If you want an unlimited supply of money-saving offers, just check your mailbox. I am–thanks to my wife–constantly bombarded by these types of offers. Here are just a few I got over the last week.

- Bed, Bath and Beyond, 20% off coupon for anything in their store.
- DSW shoes, 20% off plus two free gifts.
- Wayfair, 10% plus free shipping for orders over $49.

#2-FREE

Free is the most powerful word in direct response marketing. We will talk about other powerful words later in this chapter, but let's focus on the word FREE. There are many things you can offer for free. Free shipping, Free gifts, Free bonuses, Free trials, Try it for Free, a Free product sample or Your first order is Free, are excellent ways to overcome buyer hesitation, objections, or concerns.

Offering Free information can work especially well with expensive products like fitness equipment or expensive services such as insurance services. Offering free information is also a great way to get sales leads and to build your database of prospects.

Note that free information is important for search engine optimization (SEO) and content marketing. And besides website content, you can offer free information via a variety of mediums, YouTube video, DVD or flash drive, brochure, or .PDF download, workshop or seminar, online or in-person, blog or social media platforms such as Facebook, Instagram, or Twitter.

Another type of product offer you can make is what's called a **Hard Offer.** This is where the purchase price is shown in the video. You will get fewer people responding, but they will be more qualified prospects. Or you could use a **Soft Offer,** which does not reveal the product price but might say something like "payments as low as $14.95/month." You will get many more people to respond to this type of offer, but they will be less qualified, and an additional step will be needed to close them. Offering No Price at all and asking people to just call or go online to receive Free information is going to get the largest total response of people, but with the highest number of least qualified people. I often test a variation of these three offers to see which one ends up producing the greatest amount of revenue and then that is the offer we can use to scale the business quickly.

A good example of this type of testing was the campaign I did for the Rug Doctor. They make the best carpet cleaners on the market. Until I started working with them, the units were only available for rent at over 30,000 locations across the country. You have probably seen their red rental stands inside of your local grocery store. My agency started a campaign to sell the units direct to the consumer. The cost of the basic unit was $495 and went as high as $800, so I was working with a very expensive product. We must have tested over a dozen different offers, Hard offers, Multi-pays, Soft offers, and the one that finally worked was a simple offer that said, "payments as low as $29.95" along with $50 worth of FREE cleaning products. We sold $12 million worth of cleaners the first year! Always try combining different aspects into your offer and always test to see which offers work the best.

OTHER TYPES OF VIDEO DIRECT RESPONSE OFFERS

Lead generation offers

Lead generation offers are typically free offers designed to get respondents to raise their hands and say, "I'm interested!" The most common lead generation offers are white papers, special reports, information kits, brochures, booklets, catalogs, newsletters, videos, CDs, DVDs, webinars, and seminars.

Order generation offers

Order generation offers are paid offers. When people respond to these offers, they are using their credit card, writing a check, or committing to pay at a later date.

Continuity offers

Continuity offers are for companies that sell products on a monthly basis. Common examples are magazine subscriptions, supplements, membership clubs. The offers used for these types of companies are usually free trials for a period followed by an agreed-upon monthly billing.

Traffic building offers

Traffic building offers are most often used by retailers who want to see their stores filled with customers. The most common traffic building offers are discount coupons or free event promotions.

Fundraising offers

(See Chapter 10.) Fundraising offers don't sound like offers at all because it seems like a one-sided proposition. You are asking for a donation. In return, the donors enjoy a feeling of satisfaction for donating to a cause that is important to them. How you structure your "ask" amounts would be considered the offer. To provide additional incentives, fundraising promotions can benefit from premiums or free gifts.

MAGIC POWER WORDS AND PHRASES OF VIDEO DIRECT RESPONSE

Here is a short list of many of the words and phrases that I use in crafting my video offers. Experiment with different ways you can combine them to create an irresistible offer for your target prospects.

The most powerful word
YOU. You're seeking a personal connection with your customers, so always use the dependable second person narrative in all your

video marketing. I have a good friend who is a top copywriter and he gives a simple suggestion on how you can get any website to be more engaging and convert better. He says that everywhere on your site that uses the word I, we, or ours, replace it with You and Yours and the results will be dramatic!

The second most powerful word

FREE. We already know about the word Free. Say a free brochure. Not brochure. Say a free consultation. Not initial consultation. Say a free gift. Not gift.

Complimentary. This word puts a more valuable twist on Free. If you're graciously providing something of value without monetary exchange, your audience may feel compelled to take the action required to learn more about it.

Easy. "Only 3 EASY payments of $19.95." People like things simple and easy.

Safe. Safety is among the most basic human needs, so it's inherently powerful. A great phrase to use is, "Easy, Safe, and Effective."

New. "New" People tend to be interested in the latest and greatest.

Now. There's no time like the present to consider your offer and take action. The name of my first book is *Buy Now*. You can order it on Amazon.
http://bit.ly/BuyNowebook

Instant. Similar to now, this word communicates immediate gratification.

Save. People always like to save money.

Introducing. This says, "Look here at what's new, different, and worth sending this message about!"

Attention. Here's a word that gets the viewer's attention! I've started many of my direct response TV (DRTV) commercials with this one word.

Powerful. This persuasive word is tied to the ability to quickly impart the dramatic efficacy of the product, service, or solution they're used to describe.

Because. This gets right down to the "why." Why should you take advantage of this offer right now? *Because...*and the ultimate reason your prospects will take action.

Guarantee. There is no risk, you have nothing to lose so why not order? Here is an example of a powerful guarantee, "We guarantee the quality of the diamonds we sell." To increase the power of this guarantee, you must close the loophole that exists in the customer's mind. "If the Gemological Institute of America doesn't confirm our diamond's color, clarity, and carat weight to be at least as good as we promised you, we'll buy back that diamond for the price you paid, reimburse you for the cost of grading, and pay you an additional five thousand dollars. If other jewelers aren't willing to match this offer, you've got to wonder why."

Coming up with a powerful guarantee is one of my favorite parts in creating offers. Here is another one I used, "Here is our better than money-back guarantee, Try our widget for 30 days, If you do not look and feel better than you ever have, simply return it and we will refund your purchase price, no questions asked, and the free bonus is yours to keep just for trying our product today!"

Exclusive. This word tells the recipient of the message that they're not just part of the crowd—they're among the lucky ones to receive this offer. As in "Try this exclusive TV offer."

Risk-Free, No Obligation or No Risk. Important when you are offering anything free. People want to be reassured that there are no strings attached. You're basically saying, "It's unconditional: we won't bother you or make you talk to us or give us money" in exchange for trying something they may actually end up liking and wanting to buy. It puts the customer in the power position. I know that using the terms *Risk-Free* and *No Risk* make the offers perform better.

Limited time only. The underlying reason that this works is because of the scarcity principle that we discussed earlier. You want to generate a response *now*. One way to do it is with a *specific* time-limited offer, such as "This offer expires 11/29/19." Buy now!

Here are some other forms of Scarcity statements,

Act now. Basically, take the call to action at this moment…a pretty clear-cut directive.

Don't miss out. This phrase can strike a nerve associated with wanting to be a part of something valuable, whether that's a tangible experience or a savings opportunity.

Hurry/Time is running out. These put the "act now!" pedal to the metal and support the offer expiration date!

Last chance/Limited time. If the valuable offer isn't going to pass this way again, it's literally now or never.

Announcing/At last. People like to think they are getting in on the ground floor of a new thing.

Everything you need. Telling your audience that your solution or offer is going to cover all the bases makes their life or a particular process easier—and can make it easier to give it a try.

Tips/How-to. These are content marketing words that repeatedly drive clicks and leads for direct response marketers. Content promising to provide actionable ideas, best practices, and tutorials are valuable to prospects in the sales funnel. Adding numbers to these phrases make them even more powerful – **11 Timeless marketing Tips** – using a number or statistic not only stands out from all the letters, but it also makes people stop and take notice.

Here are a few of my most successful video offers:

The JUICEMAN

My company, Trillium Health Products was the first to sell a juice extractor as a health machine and not as a kitchen appliance. We wanted to provide everything people needed to get started juicing right away.

Price = $297 or 3 easy payments of only $99.

Free Bonuses—Cutting board, knife and cleaning brush, plus three educational pamphlets: 1) Immune Strengthening with fresh juice, 2) The Juicing Weight-loss Diet, and 3) The Anti-aging juice diet.

Guarantee—A No Risk 100% 60-day money-back guarantee; "Try it for 60 days, if you don't feel better than you ever have before simply return it, and we will refund your purchase price no questions asked.

Upsell—for $49.95, an 8 (cassette) tape course on all aspects of juicing.

This offer generated millions of dollars in sales. A few years later, after Salton Housewares purchased the company, the DRTV show was not working as well. Salton had an excess inventory of bread machines they could not sell. I changed the show opening to announce, "stay tuned and find out how you can get a FREE bread machine worth $200 when you purchase a Juiceman juicer from today's show." There were limited quantities of the bread machines so besides creating great initial value there was the scarcity principle at work as well.

SONICARE

When the Sonicare toothbrush was first launched the price was $150, they were having difficulty getting traction in the marketplace. The DRTV show that I made created millions in sales and huge consumer awareness helping launch the Sonicare brand.

Price = $150 or 3 easy payments of only $49.95.

Free Bonuses—3 extra brush heads worth $14.95 each, plus a video on how to reverse gum disease and get better dental check-ups.

Guarantee—A No Risk 90-day better check-up 100% money-back guarantee. "Try Sonicare for 90 days, if you don't get a better dental check-up, simply return it, and we will refund your purchase price no questions asked.

Upsell—A second unit, (or as many as a person wanted) at a 20% discount.

OXICLEAN

Price = $39.95 or 2 easy payments of only $19.95.

Free Bonuses—A micro-fiber cleaning cloth. We would super-size the OxiClean tub from 16 oz. to 24 oz., we included samples of Orange Glo furniture polish and Kaboom tub and tile cleaner.

Guarantee—A No Risk 30 day better clean guarantee. "Try OxiClean for 30 days, if it doesn't clean your toughest messes and stains, simply return the unused portion, and we will refund your purchase price, but the free gifts are yours to keep."

Upsell—We offered a 20% discount for people to go on a 30-day auto-ship program. People stayed on this program an average of 4 months creating a much larger initial sale value of almost $150.

RUG DOCTOR

Price = $495. This was a "soft" offer, and we did not reveal the price. Instead, we said, "find out how you can get payments as low as $29.99/month."

Free Bonuses—**Over** $80 dollars of Rug Doctor cleaning products like Pet stain remover, Red wine remover, special Oxi-Cleaner, and spot and stain remover.

Guarantee—A No Risk 100% 60-day money-back guarantee. "Try Rug Doctor in your home for 60 days, if it isn't the best carpet cleaner you have ever tried simply return for a full refund, and the $80 worth of cleaning products are yours to keep for Free."

Upsell—An offer to upgrade to the Rug Doctor Wide-track unit for $700.

GoPro

Price = $300.

We ran a series of 30 second TV lead generation spots with this offer at the end of each commercial; "Go to our website, and someone will win one of everything we make every single day."

The effect was to drive massive traffic to the GoPro website. Three things happened.

1. People would register for the contest allowing them to build their database and to follow up by email.
2. People would get to the website, see and watch all the great video content and then share the videos with their friends creating a viral effect.
3. People would purchase the product, generating revenue, which could be used to buy more advertising helping to create more brand awareness.

Please notice the structure of each of these product offers. They all have payment plans, valuable Free bonuses, a strong and unique guarantee to eliminate risk, and a good upsell to increase average order value. There are no limits to structuring offers as long as it works financially, so let your creative juices start flowing and see what you can come up with.

INTERVIEW WITH KEVIN DONLIN, DIRECT RESPONSE COPYWRITER

Please note:

there is a free offer checklist at the end.

RICK

Please tell me your name, the name of your company and a little bit about what you do.

KEVIN

Sure, I'm Kevin Donlin, and my company is Client Cloning Systems, and I do copywriting and marketing strategy for businesses, doing $2 to $20 million in revenue. As a copywriter, I write words that sell in print, online, and in video.

I have a fortunate background, I've done a lot of different jobs. And I remember one of my idols, Jay Abraham, talked about how he held a bunch of different jobs, and this gave him a lot of insights into the human condition. I think if I have one advantage as a copywriter, it's that I've done a lot of things and I can talk to anyone.

I've been a teacher, a musician, a warehouse worker, cashier, stock boy, record store manager, webmaster, and lifeguard, to name a few. I used to drive a tractor and line baseball fields with chalk in the summer, I've worked in Tokyo for a Japanese company, and I had a paper route as a kid.

So, I've been fortunate to have a lot of different jobs in my life. And, I guess, that's one thing I'm very grateful for, is that *I have a lot of different insights into the human condition. You really have to understand the human condition because there's people selling to people; it's never a video selling to a person. There's no such thing as B2B sales, it's always P2P, person to person, at the end of the day.*

John Carlton is one of the best copywriters living; he had a psychology major in college, and so he's very good at the psychological insights that help you push the right buttons with folks. So that was a very long-winded answer; I hope you can make some sense of that, but that's been my background.

RICK

There was a lot of great information in there, and I find it interesting because I made my whole career in marketing. And I never formally studied marketing in school; I have a degree in biology and just like your background, held many different jobs and just kind of learned selling and direct response by going out in the marketplace and doing it and seeing what works and what doesn't work. I agree with what you said in your answer that a well-rounded background with lots of experience and understanding human psychology is really a great foundation for marketing and direct response marketing.

KEVIN

Yes, if you look at David Ogilvy, one of the forerunners of modern advertising, he sold kitchen stoves door to door. He was a farmer, and he tried tobacco farming—very labor intensive—before founded Ogilvy & Mather; and he was a research guy for Gallup, I believe, so again, a lot of different jobs in the background. And some of the best copywriters I know didn't even go to college. I think if you have a marketing degree, you might be at a disadvantage. I don't mean to insult any of your readers, of course!

RICK

You're not. I just heard a commonality when you were talking about David Ogilvy and selling door to door, and you've had a job where you were selling door to door, and you mentioned that you have to sell on the phone. It's the same thing for me after I graduated from college with a BS in Biology, I sold suntan lotion on the pool decks in Daytona Beach Florida. It was commissioned only. If I didn't sell, I didn't eat. I found that if you learned to sell, it's a good foundation for all types of marketing.

KEVIN

Right, I agree.

RICK

Sometimes, I think people get too caught up in technology and they forget about the basic principles of selling and persuasion. Anyway, what I wanted to ask you, you mentioned working with companies doing $2 to $20 million in revenue, what are some of the things that do you help those companies do?

KEVIN

Sure, one quick bit of foundation then I'll move on to that. I think it's important to note that I was a webmaster for FedEx.com from 1995 to 1998. There were only about 100 useful websites online at that time, and so I have a long background in writing online copy; whether it's emails or web pages, but also videos and webinars.

And so, I've been in this space for very long time, just an accidental pioneer; kind of a Forrest Gump of online marketing. I just stumbled into it, so that's been my background, a very long time doing online marketing. As far as what else I do with my clients, *if I have a secret, it's to find one thing that's working for them and then to multiply it.*

If you've got a person to person sales message that's working, let's make it instead of one to one let's make it one to many. Let's do a webinar. Let's do a video. So, I'm very good about ferreting out something that's working for you and multiplying that. A lot of my best wins have come with people who already wrote a really good sales letter. I just came in and made it a little bit better since that's what I do all day every day, I can see things differently.

I don't work with startups, you notice it's $2 to $20 million; you got to be profitable, I'm not a miracle worker, I can't multiply zeros. I can't teach you marketing. If you don't understand marketing in general, and direct response marketing in particular, we're probably not a good match. So I'm very good at finding a message that works, improving it, and then rolling it out to different mediums; direct mail, phone scripts, video scripts, platform sales scripts, email promotions webpages. *There's an almost infinite number of ways you can roll one message out to multiple media,* and that's what I try to do for my clients.

RICK

That's a fantastic answer, and I feel like I'm listening to a mirror of myself because I do the same thing. I don't work with startups, but if you have something that's proven in the marketplace, even at a small level and $2 million's a good threshold, then you can come in, and we see how you can multiply that. I've given that same talk to many, many clients before; exactly what you said. Kevin, what is copy that sells?

KEVIN

It's going be copy that persuades you to take action now. That's what I do. Meaning that you're not just going to hear about it and remember the name the next time you go shopping. You're going to pick up the phone and call, you're going to click the order button, you're going to download some information, you're going to take an action.

I found that copy that sells best is copy that kind of bypasses logic and goes right to the emotions. This is going to help you make more money.

One of the best promotions I did for a client in recent years had the headline, "Mom, Dad, I Got Rejected Again!" And it was to help you increase your sales test scores, SAC and ACT, test scores so you can get them into the right college. The client's previous headline was, "Results Obsessed Test Prep." I still remember it because you can't even say it; "Results Obsessed Test Prep." It did okay, I don't know how he sold anything with that, but I changed it to "Mom, Dad, I Got Rejected Again!" It was about a kid who got a rejection letter from college. Why? Because their test scores were bad. The result was a 139% increase in sales in 30 days for my client. Total extra revenue was over $1 million.

Because that new headline immediately cuts to the core of any parent. And I happen to be a parent whose daughter got rejected from her first choice of colleges, so this is from my own experience. Very easy to write that headline; didn't change a whole lot with the rest of the copy, but it was just finding that one good idea.

And if you can find one good idea that just pushes an emotional hot button, you can bypass logic, you can bypass sales resistance, resistance of any kind. So, you can push an emotional hot button in your prospect and just make them move in the directions you want;

it's not too hard to guide them once you've got them moving. And so, that's what I try to do. *If there's a principle to best projects, it's always been finding an emotion that bypasses logic that just requires action, and then we kind of guide that action.*

RICK

You mentioned that you changed the headline and you had some pretty dramatic results. How important is the headline or, in the case for my readers, the opening to a video to capture attention to get people hooked in? How important is that and are there any tips you can give us?

KEVIN

The answer is it's all important. It's everything. *Without attention you have nothing.* For my client, who more than doubled sales in 30 days and got an extra million dollars in annual revenue, that headline was literally a million-dollar idea.

If you're doing a video, attention is everything, especially online video. You've got to not only get attention but keep it and you've got to keep it throughout the entire video; so you really have to work hard to get attention. The first 5, 10, 15 seconds are all important in the video. Now the bad news is you've got to work really hard, and you've got to get their attention, and you've got to keep their attention. The good news is when you're crafting your video presentation, a lot of people struggle at doing it in order. And they take days, and weeks, and months to come up with that first 30 seconds. The good news is you don't have to do it in order, just like a movie; no movie is shot from A to Z, from start to finish; they do the scenes in a different order.

What I will counsel people that I'm mentoring in copywriting is just start anywhere, just start writing with what is the easiest and come back to the beginning later. You can just put a placeholder in your outline—big intro, a resting introduction—fine, come back and do that later and oftentimes you'll find something during the process that just jumps out at you, "Wow, this is cool. This belongs at the front, I can hint at it at the front and get back to it later." But *you'll often find that the attention-getting device, the attention-getting idea that you need, it can often come as you're writing the rest of the piece.* So, the good news is you don't have to do it in order, just start writing and find that thing that's going to get attention and put it at the beginning.

RICK

That's really good advice because I know sometimes the hardest thing to do is start with a blank piece of paper and write a good script or sales letter. Is there any other advice you'd give someone to help them write better, more effective copy?

KEVIN

If you want to write better copy, look at what you've written already; especially something if it's working and just go through the language and look for all the instances of 'I, me, my, our'. The 'we,' the 'me,' the 'I centered' stuff. Just change all of those words to 'you, you, you, yours, yours, yours' and, of course, it won't make sense when you do that, you're going to have to go back and rewrite all the copy; that's the point. If you can rewrite all your copy and make it 'you centered' it's going to improve immediately, without exception.

The place where most people get into trouble is their copy, their videos, whatever; they make it all about them. And they're excited about their product or service; they should be. But it doesn't matter at all to the prospect, to the viewer, to the reader. We're all selfish, we've all got a monologue in our heads about "How do I fix my problem?" *If you can use 'you, you, you' you've got attention which goes back to something I said earlier, 'Without attention you have nothing.'" And so when people see a letter or a video that's all about 'you, you, you', it's going to get their attention* if, for no other reason, that most the stuff that we read, most of the stuff that we see, it's about 'our company's stuff' and 'our company's story'; no one cares about that.

RICK

That's a great answer. Why do you think it's so effective when you talk about the other person?

KEVIN

Well I think it's related to the Dale Carnegie idea, I believe. He was the guy that said, "A person's name is to that person the sweetest and most important sound in any language." So, if I say "Rick, Rick, Rick." I have your attention. You know you're talking to a sales pro when they drop your name into the conversation. "So, Rick, how was your day this morning?" They immediately have your attention.

So, if I don't know the name of the person, and I can't scatter it throughout the email or the video, the next best word is 'you'. And so "You, what was your opinion, what do you think?" *Everyone loves to talk about themselves and so if they think this communication is about themselves, you've got their interest, nine times out of ten.*

RICK

You mentioned Dale Carnegie; that's one of the books I always recommend to people, trying to learn persuasion. I took a Dale Carnegie course, "How to Win Friends and Influence People," and I use his simple formula for giving a speech sometimes to structure a video, "Tell them what you're going to say, say it, and then tell them what you said." As simple as that is, I use that formula sometimes in making videos, and it's effective.

KEVIN

Yes, that is a master's degree in psychology and how to deal with people.

RICK

As long as we're talking about changing some words, do you have any other power words or power phrases that you use when you're trying to write persuasion pieces?

KEVIN

I'll give you a general answer and a specific answer. *Generally, 'new' and 'now,' those are great words; everyone's looking for new, it's in our DNA.* We're always scanning the horizon; it's caveman and women for something new. "Is that a new cloud over there? Is that a tail sticking out of the bush that's attached to a predator?" We're always looking for new stuff so. And, of course, you have to back it up; it's got to really be new.

I've found that news items, the calendar, that's often a really good draw. Of course, it can make your promotion dated. But if you can tie something to the calendar about something that just happened ... Back in the day, I used to work in job placement, and I worked with a new recruiter, and we were doing videos. We did a number of very, very lucrative webinars, and we would always throw in the latest unemployment statistics very early on. And I would always ... Here, I'm going to tie this together with you. The news is "Rick, did you know the latest national unemployment rate is 4.3 percent?" And the audience would say "Okay." I'd go, "Guess what your unemployment rate is, Rick? It's 100 percent because you don't have a job." I have their attention. I've thrown the name in because it's about you, and we would do that early on in the presentation. And it's kind of funny. and so that's how you kind of tie things together with news; it would change every month.

RICK

That was a good answer.

KEVIN

Using the idea of news and what's new. Now as far as a specific answer that works just as well, it takes a bit of research. But Eugene Schwartz, one of the best copywriters who ever lived, he used to say that "You don't need to have great ideas if you can hear great ideas." And he maintained that if you're a really good listener, you don't have to be the very best copywriter; because your client, or your product, or your service, or your market they're going to tell you things that work.

I believe he wrote the sales letter that launched Boardroom Publications, "Now Read 300 Business Magazines in 30 Minutes." I may be butchering it. But he heard Marty Edelstein, the CEO of Boardroom, say that pretty much while he was interviewing him for that piece. and so, he uses the client's idea, repackages it as a headline; and it was a huge winner.

So, *one of my secrets is to just interview clients for 45, 60 minutes sometimes twice, and just let them talk and sell me the product or the service, and then just talk about why they got into the business they're in; just questions that may seem kind of meandering. But I will listen to the client, and they will almost always have really good ideas that I can just polish and bring out and put in the presentation.*

And related to that, *the corollary is, listen to the customers, listen to what the people who are buying the thing are saying. And so, testimonials have an additional use, not just as social proof for your piece. But why do people buy, what are they saying, and what problems were they trying to solve? And if you read enough testimonials, you'll find commonalities, you'll see themes.*

One *of the best secrets I give the people to write better copy faster, go to Amazon.com, read the book reviews; maybe you've heard this before. But read what people are saying about something that they paid money for as a solution to their problems.* And that's just invaluable market research; forget focus groups, because that's just people on a Saturday morning wanted you to pay 100 bucks. A focus group has a purpose, I suppose. But go to Amazon, it's a paid focus group. All these people spent money and their reviews ... And they're not all real, of course; that's a fact of life. *But when you can find a review that's really emotional in nature, that's your market talking and I've taken language directly from book review., I've taken language from blog postings, and I've taken language from comments on the blog postings. That's a really valuable source of market language, people who are posting their reaction to a story.*

If there's a blog post about a story and it's got 500 comments, go through all 500 comments and probably on number 493 you're going to find a headline, or in number 360, you're going to find just a remarkable reason for why people buy something. And so that's the kind of market research you want to do and, again, it's the idea that *you don't have to have great ideas if you can hear or find other people's great ideas.*

RICK

... I'm just sitting here chuckling because, again, you're saying everything that I do in my consulting practice. One of the very first things we do on a video project is interview actual paying customers. We find 15 to 20 people from the client's database, sit down, videotape these testimonials which, like you said, we can use them later in our marketing campaign. But really what we're listening for is exactly what you just explained, the answers and why they bought the product, what they liked about it, what they didn't like, and all the time the answers to the best marketing campaign are right there. It's kind of a template that we've used over and over again, and here you are repeating the same thing; it's really amazing. I always tell people that you can never write lines as well as what someone that is actually a testimonial says.

KEVIN

Bingo. And I think as proof of that, I mean, people may know this, they may not. But there's an old advertising phrase "I'd walk a mile to smoke a camel." It's for Camel cigarettes. It was written by a copywriter who overheard one guy say it to another guy. The copywriter got the credit, but it was some guy smoking a Camel who said that. That copywriter didn't need to invent a great idea because he heard it.

RICK

If you listen, there are good ideas are everywhere. That's a great tip about reading the Amazon reviews. It's a great place to find some great copy. I looked at some research from Tubular labs, and they talked about the most viewed types of online videos fell into three categories, and they were: Tutorial videos, which are good for education and customer service, Testimonial and Demonstration videos, which are great for selling your product or marketing the product if done correctly. An important part of a demonstration video is making an offer. Or once someone sees the demonstration, you have to let them know how they can buy the product. So how important are offers in what you do?

KEVIN

They are all important, and I'm just looking at a checklist that I'm going to refer to you in a minute...because I want to be thorough. Gary Halbert, and probably others have said *the order of importance in any promotion: Number one is the list. Who are you promoting to? Is it past clients, is it total strangers? The list. Number two is the offer. What are you giving them in exchange for their time or their money? And third, in importance, is the creative, the copy, the video.* So really, if you don't have the right list, forget it; nothing else matters. If you're trying to sell bacon to vegans, your offer and creativity don't matter. So next in importance is the offer. This afternoon, I'm writing the order form for a client, and then I'm doing about a six to eight-page sales letter probably later this week. The order form comes first. What's on the order form? The offer. So, *if you don't know what your offer is, and it's not clear, and it's not irresistible, then you're building a highway to nowhere, and nothing else is going to line up correctly.* So, the offer, like attention, it's incredibly important.

As far as the kinds of offers I do, they're *typically two kinds. There's lead generation, which is people giving you their time. Then there's a sale, which is people giving you their money.* So those are the two kinds that I write. And so, this is maybe helpful for readers, or viewers or whoever, *but I refer to a checklist to make sure I don't miss anything. So, if there's another principle that will improve all your stuff is have a checklist for what you're doing.* Especially video production or if you're new to copywriting, but every surgeon worth his or her salt has a checklist; and if they don't you kind of want to leave the operatory if it's not too late, because they're going—

RICK

Airline pilots have a checklist.

KEVIN

Exactly. Everyone who's doing a complex job follows a checklist and so, you don't want to wing it here so I have a checklist I can refer to it. I can go as much depth as you want. I can give you the overall broad strokes here. *But for lead generation, you want to have a clear call to action.* I see so many promotions that just have a phone number at the bottom. Well, do you want me to call it, when should I call, who's going to answer? So it's got to say "Grab your phone and call now 777-555-1212." A clear call to action.

You'd have an intriguing title, give it not just for more information, "There's going to be a free DVD." So, give what you're offering an intriguing, attractive title. *Number three is—have credible value.* You can't say that ... Because people have a highly sensitive BS detector these days. So, you can't say this is a $15,000 value unless you can seriously show this is worth fifteen grand. You've got to give it a credible value.

Number four is scarcity, of course. So back to the idea of a calendar. If it's at the end of the month or it's 24 hours, in the case of a video, "When this timer expires the offer ends." Scarcity is incredibly important for your offer.

And then, *fifth, for lead generation offers have multiple response options: phone, fax, email; the more, the merrier.* I just did a promotion for a Facebook marketer and three of our orders came in by fax; now figure this one out, from people who wanted help with their Facebook advertising, three responses came in by fax. And it's because I pushed him to include a fax option; without that maybe we don't get the response.

RICK

Kevin, can we share your Offer Checklist with my readers?

KEVIN

Yes, this is selling by demonstration, right? I'd be happy to do that.

RICK

That would be awesome. I will share it at the end of this interview.

KEVIN

I just gave you five ways to make a lead generation offer stronger. So, to add to that, if we're doing a sales offer, I would add three other elements; I have the previous five in place. But I also will include free gifts, or bonuses, or premiums because it's never just enough to say, "Give me your money and I'll give you this widget." It's the stuff that you throw in along with the sale that can often drive the sales, especially if the perceived value is greater than the price for the thing itself. And it can be really, really trivial stuff too. And it could be stuff that's totally unrelated to what you're selling. In my example, "Contact me for a Free Marketing Skull Session, and I have a copy of this book on my desk, Wealth Secrets of Warren Buffett, it's a $30 value, and I'll ship you a copy for free if you're one of the first three to respond." So that's a gift, it's called gift with appointment or gift with the sale; but the premiums are a critical part if you're offering something for a sale, the bonuses. Second really important, often overlooked, payment plans. If something is priced over 100 bucks, consider offering payment plans and don't call them payments, call them installments, payment implies money, but installment means you're being smart with your money and making it easy on your budget.

I can't tell you how many times that I've been able to sell very expensive coaching and consulting, where the first response was "No I can't afford it." And I say, "Well if you could afford it, would you go forward?" And they say "Sure." "So now, we'll break it into three installments and make it interest-free. How's that?" And they have to say "Yes." Because they've just said, "If it were affordable, I would say yes." This goes into some Robert Cialdini stuff about consistency, I suppose.

RICK

Yes, getting to a small yes first before asking for a larger yes.

KEVIN

But payment plans always, always, always, always increase sales without exception. If you can offer interest-free payments, so much the better. So, payment plans, installment plans, often overlooked, with sales but always effective. And then, of course, *the guarantee, you can Google guarantees, and they're critical; you have to remove the risk.*

FedEx, which was an employer of mine many years ago, they launched an entire industry in 1973—express distribution—based on the promise that it will absolutely, positively be there overnight or your money back; that was part of it as well. You don't hear the money-back part so much anymore; they make you jump through hoops. But FedEx launched a multi-billion-dollar industry based on a money-back guarantee. So, guarantees are critical, because they work. *Anything to remove the risk is going to increase your sales by improving your offers.*

RICK

Another great example of using a guarantee is Domino's pizza. They launched their business with a "30 minutes, or it's free" delivery guarantee. I have to say, the information you are sharing is almost like getting a master's degree in putting together offers.

KEVIN

Exactly.

RICK

What do you look for when a client brings you something, and the offer isn't working? What are some of the first places that you check?

KEVIN

I will look for guarantees, I will look for payment plans; those are often missing. I will look for premiums, and gifts with purchase or bonuses, they're almost always missing. Giving the product or service a sexy title, free consultation has been done to death, for example, so I'll always come up with a unique name for a consultation for almost every client, like "Marketing Skull Session." Or "29-Minute Brainstorming Session." The name that you give your consultation ... Just look for language that's not commodity language. For example, in my business, I offer a Free Client Cloning Kit. I don't offer a free download, I don't offer a free report, it's a free client cloning kit. If you Google "free client cloning kit", all search results lead to me. There's no one else on earth who offers that. So, find language that's unique to you; make it up if you have to. That's often a good place to start is if you can be the first person with the name of your thing, that is very important.

RICK

You've touched on a couple of the concepts from Dr. Cialdini's book, *Influence, The Psychology of Persuasion*. You mentioned scarcity, you mentioned social proof, I think you mentioned consistency ...Are you familiar with his work, and do you use it in your copywriting?

KEVIN

It's on my short list of books that every marketer should read. I can go grab my copy, it's very dog-eared. Yes, so the answer is yes. Everything you're talking about, of course, is absolutely true.

RICK

What I did in this chapter, about offers is, I started out talking about what motivates people from a psychological standpoint and understanding that, before crafting an offer.

KEVIN

It's back to emotions, and I'll talk about Cialdini's book, but you've got to push these hot buttons, I mean, you're really playing with fire here if you can get people whipped up. And that's why, by the way, if you look at political fundraising sales letters, they will get you angry within the first two or three paragraphs. The reason for that, you become irrational, and you become susceptible to suggestion, and you want to do something to relieve this feeling that you have. "I've got to stop Nancy Pelosi" or "I've got to Stop Trump," and so I'm going to donate. It makes me feel better.

RICK

They've been doing a really good job lately with those political ads because people are really angry.

KEVIN

Twitter is an outrage machine, that's all it is. But, this proves our point here, basically, which is that people ... I don't know if we're addicted to emotions, we're addicted to the adrenaline rush of outrage, or anger. But some of my most ... but all of my most effective promotions ever have pushed emotional hot buttons.

That's why the web is so effective really because it's a lot of pictures, a lot of videos. People would rather look at videos than read anything. That's why YouTube is so big, that's why video selling is such a rich field of endeavor, because we've only been reading words for about 5,000 years, and we've been humans for over 100,000; so that's like a 95 to 5 ratio, and we'd rather look at pictures. Cave drawings were around for many, many more years than words so we'd rather look at pictures. We'd rather watch and just imbibe information. So, your pictures, your emotional underpinnings, your emotional hot buttons, *anything you can do to bypass logic, bypass thinking and get right to the heart of the person—that's going to improve your results.*

I can talk about Dr. Cialdini now. We've got six big ideas from him, the six universal persuasion principles. I think the rule of scarcity is one of my favorites, as long as it's believable. Well *if you see a countdown clock on a web page, for example, that's believable, it's like a bomb ticking. What's going to happen at the end? I don't know, and I don't want to find out. And so, at this point, when you see that countdown clock, it's a mechanism, sure, but it's bypassing logic because your eyes are riveted to the thing.*

RICK

We use that same thing on our TV commercials; you have to order in the next five minutes, and the clock will be ticking down.

KEVIN

There's a reason for that.

RICK

Yeah, the underlying principle is the scarcity.

KEVIN

Of course, you know this and if you can go to QVC at any hour of the day and watch something that's going to stop; there's a clock there, that's a mechanism. And so, by the way, QVC is a great learning place for emotional language. You'll hear words like 'anniversary' and words like 'family' on QVC; they go right to their female audience. This is not being sexist, it's just research shows that women, perhaps, are more attuned to the ideas of anniversary and family and nurturing and so the hosts on QVC see are really, really good at what they do, and they're throwing in these emotional words to get the attention and to get the action from people.

RICK

I just want to build on your statement. When people are trying to make demonstration videos, don't reinvent the wheel, go look at what they do on *Home shopping and QVC. They demonstrate products every day. Copy what they do, take the best of what they do and use it in your videos; there's a reason they use close up shots, there's a reason that they do the things they do because it's proven to work.* I'm a big believer in learning from other peoples' experiences.

KEVIN

Yes, and I'm sure they were learning from you, by the way, Rick, your stuff. You don't build billion-dollar brands one after the other by accident, so If anyone's following a checklist for success, it's you. So, it's late in the interview for me to give you credit, but your stuff is phenomenal, and it's not by accident.

RICK

Thank you, that's why I enjoy talking to you so much. We have a lot of common threads underlying what we do and just building on the QVC example, one thing that's going to come up that I think is going to be a game changer for people who market products is, Amazon is starting to do live streaming so you can actually demonstrate your products in a live stream; which is really a miniature QVC channel. The people who know the persuasion principles and how to sell and structure offers, how to do this correctly, they're going to be far ahead of the people that don't, sales-wise. That's what this book is all about, is showing you what to do in your offers, including bonuses, including a guarantee, taking the risk out; all the things you mentioned. If people do that in their presentations, they're going to be head and shoulders above everybody else, generating much more revenue.

KEVIN

Yes, The whole idea of selling on QVC or wherever—selling suntan lotion by the pool-by demonstration—I'm guessing at some point you would maybe take some out and maybe spread on your fingers and say, "It just glides on, it stays on when you are in the water, you can dip your hand in the pool and look, it doesn't wash off." Selling by demonstration.

RICK

Well the other part of that is, living down there, obviously I had a great tan and when people would come down from Minnesota, where you live, people who haven't seen the sun in six months, and they say ... "I want to be like that guy." And I say, "Well here's how I did it." That's an authentic testimonial, social proof. Then because I'm the lifeguard, that's authority selling. I always talk about upsells too; it takes just as much time to sell one bottle of suntan lotion for $8 as you do to sell an entire system of products for $99. You need the pre-tanner, the bottle for the base tan, the advanced tanning oil, and then the aloe for after sun, the whole thing.

KEVIN

That's what separates the one-offs, the one hit wonders from the billionaire makers is that you were selling systems, you weren't selling a bottle of lotion; you were selling something for $99. So, back to the idea of demonstrations... I have a free giveaway. We can talk about it before we finish, it's called a *Client Cloning Kit*. And it's the idea I try to give people ... Not everyone can write copy, not that I'm a wonder-worker; but it is what I do all day every day. So, *if you have better tools, you can do better work. What I try to do for people is to give them tools to improve what they're doing with their marketing.*

RICK

What was the name of your giveaway again?

KEVIN

It's called a *Client Cloning Kit*, and you can get one free one at my website, www.ClientCloningSystems.com. And one of the tools in there that almost everybody loves is what I call The Paper Email. And it's based on the premise that if you've ever written an email that worked once, you can print the thing, put it in an envelope and it'll work again because you're delivering it in a different medium ... and, yes, this is a sales letter by another name! But the idea of printing and sending a Paper Email is far less intimidating than writing and mailing a sales letter, which gets far more people to actually do it. It's the easiest thing in the world when you demonstrate it like that. The challenge is to find a way to demonstrate what you are selling. I'm a copywriter, how do you demonstrate copywriting? That took a bit of work to come up with that, but it's been worth it to me. So, find a way to visually demonstrate what you're selling; show the results. In your case, show me your tan. Tada! It works, look at me; so that's an example. *Find a way to demonstrate it, visually, and you have a huge edge in videos that sell.*

RICK

That's awesome. Sometimes people can get overwhelmed with all the new technology, and I tell them, that they need to really understand the foundational things which we've been talking about in this interview, on what makes people take a specific action. Can you comment on that?

KEVIN

Let's talk about online video ... What makes people take action? There are a couple of things. The longer you can keep people engaged, the better your chances of getting the sale. So that's why the really, really long-running video sales letters, the things that sell millions and hundreds of millions of dollars ... There's one called The End of America, from 2011, that sold financial products. It was 77 minutes long, an hour and seventeen minutes. The longer you can keep people engaged with your video, the better the chances of you're getting the action you want it, and this is because people hate to feel like their time was wasted. This goes back to multilevel marketing, I suppose, or in person seminars. If you had people driving to an event, and they spent two hours listening to you, they really didn't want to go home empty-handed; because their whole evening would have been wasted. The longer you can keep people engaged with your message, your video, the better your chances of converting them at the end. This goes back to attention, earning it, getting it, and keeping it; it's hard, it's hard. But if you can get ... If you can give people a message that's endlessly interesting, and then you keep promising in the next five minutes, and if you stay tuned, there's language you can use, "In just a moment I'll tell you." "If you stay to the end, you'll get this." If you can keep people engaged in your video, longer is better. *The longer they stay with you, the better your conversions; and that's probably the most important principle I can think of.*

The other thing would be to, of course, deliver value. If you're delivering information that people can actually use, they're going to appreciate you. This touches on the idea of reciprocity from Cialdini; if people feel like they're really getting value, they're going to stick with your video, and they're going to favor you with a good response. So that's kind of a way of keeping attention, it's giving value; so I guess the two go together, attention and value.

RICK

It's really enjoyable listening to your answers because it's confirming principles that I've noticed successful companies do over the years. In my book *Building Billion Dollar Brands*, one of the steps in building a brand is, always *deliver more value and then the second, you mentioned earlier in this interview, was always listen to your customer;* and so, just some basic brand-building steps.

I wanted to see if you had any additional thoughts on anything we didn't talk about? This has been really, really informative, I mean, it's just a lot of great information in here, and if there was some area that we didn't cover that you wanted to comment on, I'd like to give you the opportunity to do that.

KEVIN

Well thank you. If I were to pin it down to just a few areas, what you just said earlier just made me remember one of my heroes in copywriting, Gary Bencivenga, he's retired now, but he wrote some of the best sales letters ever. *Two of his principles where "Make your advertising itself valuable." And also related to that was "Longer is better."* And if you can deliver value in a longer promotion, a longer piece that involves the reader, so it's got to be about him or her, and not about you or your product; you're going to win.

RICK

Now that's very well said. Like I said, there's a lot of great information here, and I want to thank you for taking the time to do this. Tell us how people can get in contact with you and also the name of your giveaway; because I think that that would be important if people want to build on the things they read here.

KEVIN

It's called a *Client Cloning Kit.* It's a very real Kit that I send out by U.S. Mail, with 5 little tools inside to build your business. You can get one free one at my website, www.ClientCloningSystems.com. And if you like what you see there, you and I can have a conversation about your marketing if you mention this book. You're invited to call me at 612-567-6642 or visit www.ClientCloningSystems.com.

RICK

That's awesome. Kevin, I wanted to thank you for taking your time and sharing so much great information. It was really fun for me, I've learned some new things too.

KEVIN

You learned stuff that you forgot you knew. I really enjoyed this as well, we'll talk again very soon, I look forward to it.

RICK

Bye Now.

THE OFFER CHECKLIST

Here's how to Make better offers.

Let me explain...

The late, great copywriting legend Gary Halbert once said words to this effect: The 3 most important elements in any promotion are, in order:

1. **List** (the people you're selling to)
2. **Offer** (what you are giving them in exchange for their time and/or money), and
3. **Creative** (the clever words and images you use to sell your offer).

Okay. I can't help you with #1, the list. Not today anyhow. But I can help you with the second element, your offer. Which is nice. Because, by making better offers, you convert more prospects into paying clients—with NO additional effort on your part. This gives you an almost infinite return on your investment here because you won't need more new prospects to get more new clients. You'll simply be selling more to the prospects you already have. Pretty neat, huh?

Think about it. Why make lukewarm offers to 100 prospects and get only 5 new clients, when you can make fantastic offers to the same 100 prospects ... and get 10 new clients? Or 20? Or more? In fact, I've seen evidence from Bob Bly and other top copywriters that—simply by making better offers—*you can improve the response rate to your promotions from 10% to as much as **900%**.*

First, a definition. What is an offer? Simply put, it's what your prospects *get* when they respond, combined with what they have to *do*. Here's a simple example: "Call toll-free 1-800-888-5555 for your Free Information Kit." The kit is what prospects *get*. Calling is what they have to *do*.

Now, let's talk about two kinds of offers you can make: Lead Generation and Sales.

THE OFFER CHECKLIST

1) Lead-Generation Offers

These are what you make when you want prospects to raise their hands and say, "Yes, I'm interested. Please tell me more." If you want to pull in more leads who are qualified for what you sell, make sure your offer checks most or all of these boxes:

- ☐ **Clear Call to Action.** Tell people what to do – call, download, et cetera. And do so clearly. If you read it to a 10-year-old, will they get it? Example: *Call 555-555-1212 today for your Free DVD.*
- ☐ **Intriguing Title.** Give the "thing" in your offer an attention-getting title. Example: *Call 555-555-1212 today for your Free DVD "7 Ways to End Back Pain Without Surgery."*
- ☐ **Credible Value.** Does your offer have a real value? It should. And that value should be within the bounds of reason because your prospects' BS detector is highly sensitive. Example: *Call 555-555-1212 today for your Free DVD "7 Ways to End Back Pain Without Surgery." A $39.00 value, it's yours at no cost or obligation.*
- ☐ **Scarcity.** More people will respond if they think they're in danger of missing out on your offer. So, inject believable

scarcity. Two ways to do this are to limit the supply or use a deadline or both. Example: *Call 555-555-1212 today for your Free DVD "7 Ways to End Back Pain Without Surgery." A $39.00 value, it's yours at no cost or obligation. While supplies last. Offer ends April 30, 2016.*

☐ **Multiple Response Options.** The more ways you let people respond, the more people will respond. People who fear being sold on the phone will happily respond online, for example. Example options: web page, email, phone, fax, text, reply envelope.

2) Sales Offers

If you're selling something in your offer, add these elements for higher response:

☐ **Free Gifts/Bonuses.** How many free gifts or bonuses? Two is usually better than one, according to direct-mail authority Dick Benson. Example: *Enroll today to claim your Free Marketing Skull Session ($395 value). Plus, if you're one of the first 3 people to respond, you get an EXTRA 5th Coaching Session ($495 value) FREE.*

☐ **Payment Plan.** In my 21 years of marketing, I've never seen a payment plan fail to increase response. Ever. Include one if you can! And, NEVER call payments by that name; call them installments. Example: *Your investment today is 3 monthly installments of only $999.*

☐ **Guarantee.** Finally, remove the risk of buying from you by offering the strongest guarantee you can. Not only will your sales surge as a result (more than paying for any refunds, in all likelihood), but, if you take credit cards ... you already have a money-back guarantee. Any unhappy client can request a chargeback from the credit card provider, who sides with the consumer most of the time. Which means you'll give a refund anyway. So just offer a guarantee, okay? The longer, the better. Example: *You can't make a mistake, thanks to our One-Year Money-Back Guarantee. If you don't LOVE your results, you pay nothing.*

CHAPTER SIX SUMMARY

- Always include an offer. A compelling offer is the best way to trigger action.
- Know and understand the 6 principles of persuasion: Reciprocity, Commitment and Consistency, Social Proof, Liking, Authority, and Scarcity.
- To get your videos to perform better, try to use as many of the Power words and phrases of video direct response.
- You don't need to have great ideas if you can hear or read great ideas.
- Payment plans, always, always, always increase sales without exception.
- Always offer a guarantee—anything to remove the risk is going to increase your sales.

CHAPTER SEVEN
Authority and Credibility:
Who Is Your Spokesperson?

*"Speakers who talk about what life has taught them
never fail to keep the attention of their listeners."*
—Dale Carnegie

You have your own business, product or service and you want to tell the world about it using video persuasion marketing. Having a good authentic spokesperson is a powerful, proven way to get viewers to pay attention to what is being said and having those viewers respond to your message. It's been proven over and over again that having a person on screen delivering a message increases engagement and the effectiveness of the message as compared to using just images alone or images and voiceover.

You might be thinking, "Who can be that authentic spokesperson?" Many people and businesses when they are first starting up don't have the extra money to pay a celebrity or influencer to be the spokesperson. You should consider being your own spokesperson.

DISCOVERING THE SPOKESPERSON CONCEPT

I first discovered this concept almost thirty years ago, in the very first marketing campaign I did, that became successful on a national level. I was investing in real estate at the time and went to a seminar teaching how to buy a distressed property. There were eight people in that first seminar I attended. The person teaching the seminar was a Vietnamese immigrant named, Tom Vu, who didn't speak English very well. I did what I was taught and was able to "flip" a house in two weeks and made $12,000, which was a LOT of money for me at the time. I was so grateful that I called a local business magazine and was able to get him an article and then later created my very first infomercial, "Secrets of Success," using Tom as the spokesperson. Over the next three years, we went from seeing eight people a week to thousands using Tom as the spokesperson. He was hesitant to do this at first because he felt his English wasn't good enough to do the job. But people will always respond to authenticity over a highly polished message from a hired gun. I knew I was onto to something.

After that, the founder/spokesperson successes continued. I used Dr. Jeffery Bland to promote his own weight loss product, The Perfect Diet, which produced $20 million in sales. Later, using Jay Kordich, a.k.a. The Juiceman, helped create the whole fresh juice movement in the early 90s, which led to over $75 million in sales. Jim Sorensen as founder/spokesperson followed with Momentus Golf at $30 million in sales for a golf swing training device. Then, the George Foreman Grill with George as the spokesperson. People loved and really responded to George to the tune of over 100 million units sold! The next founder/spokesperson was Nick Woodman and the GoPro camera, reaching a $1 Billion in sales in only eight years.

Some other examples, ones that I didn't work on, are the old TV commercial with Victor Kiam for Remington razors, "I liked the product so much I bought the Company!" There is currently a highly visible and successful campaign running on TV called My Pillow, and the spokesperson is the founder, Mike Lindell. There are many more examples I can point to, but just know this—the concept of the founder as spokesperson really works!

WHY IT WORKS—THE AUTHORITY PRINCIPLE

People tend to follow authority figures. Most of us are raised thinking that obedience to authority is correct behavior and disobedience is wrong behavior. Many-times we obey authority mindlessly. In the landmark book, *INFLUENCE, The Psychology of Persuasion*, Dr. Robert Cialdini talks about a series of experiments done at Yale which validated this point. Based on the results of the experiments, the researchers concluded that we all carry within us a basic sense of duty to authority. "It is the extreme willingness of adults to go to almost any lengths on the command of an authority figure."

Establishing yourself as the authority figure in your videos will lead to higher engagement and trust in the message you are trying to deliver to your viewers.

WHAT DOES A SPOKESPERSON DO?

As the spokesperson, you are the face of your company and or the products you are trying to sell. The best part of being your own spokesperson is that you automatically bring authenticity, credibility, passion, and expertise to any video you make. As the founder of the company you better have these traits, or your business is going nowhere!

As the spokesperson, your tasks are to take the company from being an "it" to a "we." You are now the face of the company, and people will relate more to an actual person than just an image, voice, building, or logo. If you want people to respond to your message you need to build trust and credibility. If you are the founder, you automatically are granted these. The next step in the process is regular communication with your followers, customers or clients to keep your face, the face of the company in front of them, raising the awareness of your company's goals, services, and products. This will help remove any psychological purchasing barriers that might exist.

BE YOUR OWN SPOKESPERSON

If being your own spokesperson is so effective, then what's stopping most people? I truly believe it starts with confidence and a belief in yourself. Believing in yourself is the first step to success.

There is a saying that "success comes from within." Here are three steps you can take to develop that confidence to be in front of the camera and start being your own spokesperson.

1. Visualize yourself as you want to be

There is a great quote from Napoleon Hill, author of *Think and Grow Rich*:

"What the mind can conceive and believe it can achieve."

Confidence comes naturally to those who are successful, but success comes only to those who are confident. Start acting and picturing yourself as a highly successful person. This will come across on camera and people will respond positively to you.

2. Affirm yourself, use "I Am" statements about yourself

"I am the best spokesperson ever," "I am successful," "I am good on camera," et cetera. Here is another great quote from a famous self-help author, Louise Hay.

"You have been criticizing yourself for years, and it hasn't worked. Try approving of yourself and see what happens."

3. Do one thing every week that scares you

Try making your next video with "You" as the spokesperson or how about doing your first Facebook Live video?

One last quote from T. Harv Eker, author of *Secrets of the Millionaire Mind: Mastering the Inner Game of Wealth*:

"If you are insecure, guess what? The rest of the world is too. Do not overestimate the competition and underestimate yourself. You are better than you think."

Many people let fear get in the way of being in front of the camera. Fear of not doing it correctly. Do not worry about trying to create the perfect video. People will respond better to you if you are just genuine. A badly produced low-quality video is much better than no video at all! The advice I give people is to pretend that you are at a tradeshow and at your booth telling someone about your product or service. If you just capture that conversation on video and use it, people will respond positively.

USING A CELEBRITY SPOKESPERSON

As some companies start growing and have more resources to work with, they may choose to work with a celebrity, an influencer, or a pitchman, to help sell their products or services. Personally, I have had both, a lot of success and some very expensive failures using celebrities. Here is what I learned:

WHAT YOU NEED TO LOOK FOR

Using a celebrity in your videos or TV ads can be very expensive. It's important you find the correct person, or you will lose a lot of money very quickly, and you can even hurt your brand. So, what do you look for in a celebrity spokesperson? Authenticity, credibility, passion, and expertise! If this sounds like the same traits you need as your own spokesperson, it's because they are. The closer you can match a celebrity's personality, interests, and what they are known for, the better match for your brand. Let's look at a few examples from some DRTV ad campaigns I did.

Sonicare: Richard Dysart. Ok, you need to be a little bit older to understand this one. When we were looking for a spokesperson for the Original Sonicare infomercial in 1996, after a lot of research we had it down to two candidates, Vanna White and Richard Dysart. We were marketing a Sonic toothbrush, you would think that Vanna White might be the more logical choice as she has beautiful white teeth and a perfect smile. She was and is very popular as the host of "Wheel of Fortune." I chose Richard Dysart instead.

Richard did not have pretty white teeth, in fact, he did not smile during the whole commercial. Instead, he was deadly serious in his deliveries. What did he bring to the project? *Trust & Credibility.* At the time of the Sonicare campaign, Richard was in the #1 rated show on TV called "LA Law." His character was Leland McKenzie, the head of the law firm. First, he was a great authority figure and in the role as head of the firm other lawyers from the firm would come to him with their problems to resolve. He always made the right decision, and people trusted him. In the Sonicare ad, he was able to deliver a serious message about gum disease. People believed him and purchased the product, even though it was the most expensive toothbrush on the market at the time.

Hunter Fan Air Purifier: Peggy Fleming. Perhaps, *the most trusted* people are Olympic gold medal female figure skaters. You see big pharma companies using them in their commercials all the time. When we were engaged in marketing a new Air Purifier from The Hunter Fan Company, we choose Peggy Fleming as the spokesperson. She was believable and sincere when she talked about how this product could protect her and her family from air-borne germs and viruses.

eMedia Guitar lessons: Peter Frampton. Who better to be a spokesperson for a product teaching people to play the guitar than one of the greatest guitar players ever? Peter brought authenticity and passion to this project. An added benefit was that he cared about the product so much that we were able to hire him very inexpensively.

Some other examples are Linda Evans for an anti-aging beauty product, **Robert Wagner** for a home safety device, and **Hulk Hogan,** for the Thunder Mixer. For Rug Doctor, we used **Lou Manfredini,** Home improvement expert and the national spokesperson for Ace Hardware stores.

What resonates through all these examples—Authenticity, Trust, Passion, and Credibility!

WHAT CAN HAPPEN WITH THE WRONG SPOKESPERSON

I think it is important to talk about one of the biggest and most expensive flops in using a celebrity. We were working on a campaign for Johnson & Johnson. They were introducing a new line of skin-care products. They picked out a very famous actress and model to be the spokesperson, who was starring a popular TV show at the time. Even though she was paid hundreds of thousands of dollars upfront, from the very beginning her attitude was horrible. She acted like what she was doing was beneath her level of celebrity. This lack of passion and interest came across on the screen. The campaign was a total failure, not to mention the tension on the set of dealing with a prima donna. The lesson goes back to finding a spokesperson who cares about your product or company enough to get excited about what they are doing. Otherwise, you should move on.

UNDERSTANDING WHAT THE RIGHT CELEBRITY SPOKESPERSON CAN DO FOR YOUR MARKETING EFFORTS

- **Helps Build Credibility** – By bringing in the right celebrity you are adding immediate credibility (https://content-marketinginstitute.com/2015/05/trust-credibility-website/) to your product and brand. I've always maintained that establishing credibility with your followers is the fastest way to sales success.

- **Helps Build Awareness**-Brand awareness is all about letting people know that your product exists and is available to purchase. The right celebrity will accelerate this process.
- **Helps Draw more traffic to your site.** A well-known and respected celebrity will serve as a draw to your website, the products on your site, and the videos you have there. People will have more of a tendency to share those videos as well.
- **Helps Attract the media.** The right celebrity spokesperson will naturally attract additional media coverage. It is easier to get a celebrity booked on both national and local PR appearances, this is also a great way to drive more traffic to your website and increase sales and awareness for your brand.
- **Helps Inform and influence.** Celebrities with a connection to a health issue or illness help educate and inform the public. When we were marketing a breast cancer testing kit, we used Olivia Newton-John as a spokesperson because she suffered through this terrible disease and her battle with it was very public. She was extremely passionate about the subject.
- **Helps Influence People to Buy.** Many will buy an item just because a celebrity told them to. It's due to the concept of authority described above as well as the fact that people want to emulate celebrities that they follow and care about.

INTERVIEW: BERNIE THOMPSON, FOUNDER/CEO, PLUGABLE.COM

I'd like to leave you with one last example of the effectiveness of being your own spokesperson as it works in today's market place. Several years ago, I gave the keynote speech at The Prosper Show in

Las Vegas for Amazon sellers. I met a fellow Seattleite there named Bernie Thompson, and we now get together frequently for breakfast. Bernie is a computer engineer who owns a very successful business called Plugable, https://plugable.com/, which sells computer peripherals like docking stations on Amazon and other online market platforms. Plugable is a Top 200 seller on Amazon. Bernie has built his business from day one by creating video content to explain and showcase his products on his own website and on his YouTube channel. Bernie is his own very effective spokesperson. His interview will show you both the power of being your own spokesperson and the power of using video to build and grow your business.

RICK

Hi, Bernie. Please tell us what Plugable does, when you started it and why you started it.

BERNIE

Plugable Technologies was started in 2009. I had worked in the computer industry for almost twenty years at that point. I'd worked at IBM and Microsoft. I've worked at chip companies, and there were some things that I wished the device companies would do better in terms of their products and their support and their information. And so I thought, well what if we could build a better device company that kind of tackled those things? And rather than having a call center in some foreign country, actually setting up a support system where we would have US-based customer support. I kind of saw the opportunity in 2009 to kind of put that all together and that was the genesis of Plugable.

RICK

What does Plugable do?

BERNIE

We connect this with that. So, it's a nice broad brand. We're here in this space of things that are compatible or not with each other and you're trying to make this monitor work with this PC, or this device work with that device. So, Plugable ... *We connect this with that.*

RICK

Where do you sell your products?

BERNIE

We knew we wanted to do an e-commerce focus because we didn't want to have to build a sales team from day one. And in 2009 the world was kind of split between eBay and Amazon, but we saw some things that Amazon was doing and in particular fulfillment by Amazon, where Amazon would take care of warehousing and fulfillment of orders. They're going to handle marketing, sales, logistics and leaving us to really focus on the product and the customer. And so that's what we did. We kind of had an Amazon focus. Now today, fast forward nine years, we're one of the top companies on Amazon for this type of electronics. We have grown every single year, very successful.

RICK

You also have a great website, Plugable.com. https://plugable.com/.

Why do you have a website and what kind of information is on Plugable?

BERNIE

As we're selling on other platforms, we're always very limited in how much information we can get out, and part of the *whole value proposition of Plugable is that we provide a lot more information about our products.* From the things you'd expect, like features, but also some of the more interesting things, like, okay well for this scenario, how would you use these products to kind of tie it all together and achieve this interesting thing? Or troubleshooting type information. If we see an issue that's recurring, we'll put up a blog post and really not be afraid to air our dirty laundry and just kind of say, well okay, there's this thing that's happening, where this set of people are experiencing this problem and here's our best advice on what to do about it, or how we're going to handle it. Plugable is our one place where we kind of have complete control and complete permission to put out content, but then is both immediately read by kind of our fans, our people who've chosen to follow us and also available as people are searching the Internet for solutions that do this, or that solve this problem that were found right there.

RICK

When did you start using video on Plugable.com and what prompted you to do that?

BERNIE

I actually started using video almost immediately, *video has been kind of central to our content strategy* almost from day one, and I think that first video that we put up was ... I had gone to a technical conference to talk about kind of the technical, gory details of our first product that we had put out and just this opportunity, which had been around for a few years at that point, but this opportunity to just kind of put that content out there and for our most savvy or the technical influencer type audience, that would be a really interesting video for them to watch about this technology and they might ... exactly the kind of person who would watch that deep dive video on the technology might be the one who would turn into a brand advocate or a fan of our company. And then, later on, we just continued doing video where we ... It's a different kind of video where it really is focused on the information content. It'll be *a video where ... like that example of there's some kind of interesting thing that you can do by combining a few of our products. Well, that's much better shown than being told in text or even photos.* So we would just set up a camera ... I would just set up a camera and hit the record button myself and kind of run through this cool thing that could be done with our products and then post that on YouTube and a lot of those ... We would never know exactly what videos would take off, but some of those videos really took off to *hundreds of thousands of views,* and in the end, that collection of video content has really turned into one of our best marketing assets.

RICK

What's your YouTube channel?

BERNIE

It's just YouTube.com/Plugable. Plugable is spelled with one G, by the way.

RICK

In the last nine years, how many videos do you think you've made?

BERNIE

It's maybe around 200 or so. We have 15,000 subscribers to our YouTube Channel but probably we accumulated that through about 200 videos.

RICK

I know that Amazon limits the communication you can have with your customers. It's just the way their model works, so do you look at having 15,000 followers on YouTube as a valuable resource for your company?

BERNIE

Yeah, it's hugely valuable. I mean one of the challenges on Amazon is, basically ... They give you a window of time when you first launch a product, to kind of establish the initial run rate of your product. Amazon basically ranks a product based on its historical sales, it creates this effect where you have this opportunity when a product first launches to kind of demonstrate to Amazon that there's a lot of interest in this product. And so, there's a number of ways to kind of prove to Amazon or to create this traffic which proves to Amazon that a product is interesting and has an excited audience. But really the best method, if you can do it, is just to get people excited about your product right at launch and have them legitimately feel like, wow, this is interesting. This is exactly what I needed and come and buy it. So those 15,000 YouTube subscribers who are watching ... When we launch a product, we'll do a video. We'll show all the things it does. We'll kind of educate about what it's good for and what it's not good for so that we get the right kind of buyers who this is the right product for them and they're likely to really understand the product, and if they buy it, they're likely to have a good experience and write a good review. *We've got 15,000 potential people that we can just kind of turn that fire hose towards our new product launch and get them excited about going to Amazon to buy the product. So yeah, it's a huge asset.*

RICK

As far as making the videos, a lot of people are tentative. They get scared. And you mentioned you just picked up your iPhone and started shooting some stuff. Can you give any advice to somebody that might be thinking about making some videos and from your own experience?

BERNIE

I mean I think it is scary and there's that initial barrier of just kind of putting yourself out there. I think if you love your products and you've created these products for reasons, it's really just a matter of kind of letting that through in video, talking about the product, why did you do this product, what's exciting about this, what are the things to think about related to that product? All of those things are things that I just try to capture really in a conversation. *Every video is just a conversation between me and some people who might be interested in what I've just done.*

The other interesting kind of advice in a sense I would give is, especially as the years have gone on, we've gotten more professionals involved with our video, and there's this concern that we're damaging our brand by putting out this kind of slapdash video, the iPhone type quality video or whatever. And I say, *it is better to just get some content out there and kind of talk with your audience rather than being perfectionist* and we still ... Where we are right now as a brand, we're trying to get more professional, but I'm also trying to tell our team, at the same time, it's okay to have different levels and different targets for video and to continue doing the kind of quick videos with lower production quality even while we're trying to deliver some other videos with a very high production quality and I don't think that damages the brand as long as we're careful about kind of what channels we use and YouTube is just this great channel that's very accommodating of a stream of videos, which might not all look alike or might not all speak to the same audience. YouTube is a good channel to have that content get out.

RICK

I really agree with that. I think people are looking to be too perfect before they put out the videos and to me, *good content trumps good video production every time,* and so you're doing it exactly the right way. Let's switch gears a little bit. You're in quite a few of your own videos. I could say you are a spokesperson for your own company. Tell me a little bit about the reason you're on camera explaining things and what your thought process is behind that?

BERNIE

This company, for the first two years of its life was just me, and we were doing video. I was doing video already. So there's a little bit of that but behind that is also recognition that the authenticity of knowing that the person who kind of owns the company—who's really putting their reputation at stake—does love the product and does know about the product and is able to explain the product and is willing to kind of spend the time to have a conversation with the potential people who are interested with the product and put that on film. *I do think it's a powerful method of establishing trust.* It's interesting in this space, with these sorts of electronic devices, especially the ones Plugable does, which are really often utilitarian.

Our customers come to us because they're trying to achieve something. They want to connect this with that and maybe it's a type of product where, unlike a piece of clothing or other things, there's maybe a slightly less of an emotional connection, but I think that it's one of the reasons why we've been successful is that even though you might not think that electronics are something where you care about your connection with the company or the owner of the company. It's how—I guess the way I'd put it is at least your biggest fans, your enthusiast customers, they care. And you care about them because they're the ones who, in their organizations, and in their sphere of friends, when somebody comes to them and asks, well I've got this problem, how do I solve it? How do I do this? They go, yeah. You just need to buy this Plugable product, and that'll take care of it and even if we can't kind of create a connection with our whole customer base, we always can at least create a connection with our enthusiasts and *having that kind of owner of the company speaking for the brand, authentically telling the story of what we're doing, makes that connection stronger.*

RICK

I'm a big believer in the founder, regardless of how good they are on camera or think they are, to do that because of the authenticity which you mentioned and the passion and who's going to have more passion for their products and company than the founder? And so I'm a really big advocate for exactly what you're doing. I mean there's a lot of reasons for your success. This is one of them because I believe, since the beginning, you've been doing things the right way, but you're not completely like other companies in that a lot of people don't do that and they are afraid to get out in front of the camera, and that's why I go *back to any communication is better than no communication,* especially from the founder. Anyway, I think it's attributing to some of the success you're having.

One last question, Amazon is opening up to video. Have you started doing any video on Amazon? Do you plan to do that and if you have started doing it, have you seen any initial results? Like any kind of lift or conversion increase or anything like that?

BERNIE

Amazon actually is really enthusiastic about video. They have a lot of plans inside Amazon to use more and more video. Yeah, we basically have a number of different places where we can place video right on Amazon.com. One place is our brand store, and we can do high level, kind of brand corporate ... company brand level videos there. And then the other place is on each product. We have a single slot for a product video on each product and Amazon may expand that opportunity over time to different types of video and different lengths of video.

Yeah, and I think it definitely makes a difference. I mean it won't turn an unsuccessful product into a successful one, but it will magnify the success of a product that would be successful anyway. We've definitely seen with our products that have had video the longest that they tend to do better. The video is going to help you, especially for that research-oriented buyer who wants to compare products or actually for the more novice buyer who just wants the reassurance and may get lost in the product details, especially in our area but watching a video, kind of just seeing it work, seeing it do and having that validate that, oh yeah, that's exactly what I want. That does increase conversion rates.

Our intent is really to have a video for every product and have that video kind of serve those different audiences of buyers in answering their questions and giving them confidence in us as a company and confidence in the product—that if it is actually the thing they're looking for that they're going to have a good experience with us.

RICK

Thanks Bernie, you are doing a great job!

CHAPTER SEVEN SUMMARY

- Using a spokesperson is a powerful way to engage your video viewers.
- People like to hear from the company founder or product inventor.
- You can use a Celebrity as a spokesperson if they are the right fit.
- People will respond positively if you are your own spokesperson. Both sales and conversions will go up. Start getting in front of the camera—not just behind it and watch your views and sales start to skyrocket!

CHAPTER EIGHT
Video Persuasion on Amazon

"Our point of view is we will sell more if we help people make purchasing decisions."
—Jeff Bezos

DO THE SAME THING, BUT USE A DIFFERENT DISTRIBUTION PLATFORM

By this point in the book, I have shared enough information for you to produce more engaging videos that will also help you convert better. You have many choices on where to use the videos you produce. The people at Amazon are no dummies, they are interested in selling more product, and they know the power of a good video demonstration and how that will help them do that.

If you are currently selling on Amazon, the sooner that you incorporate video into your listings the better you are going to do sales-wise. I've had many sellers I know tell me that a good demonstration video about their product can increase sales by 20% or more. Use the techniques that I have taught you in the previous chapters of this book, and you will start to see better results immediately.

A GREAT EXAMPLE TO FOLLOW

If you want a really good example of a company and product line that is using video to its highest and best use on Amazon, then please check out FitLife.tv, http://fitlife.tv/. My friend Drew Canole has built a hugely successful business in the supplement category using several of the video persuasion techniques we have discussed in this book. First, he is the founder and company spokesperson and is in most of the information-oriented videos that his company produces. Second, they have done a remarkable job of building a passionate community of followers. Third, he uses hundreds of powerful before-and-after transformation testimonials, as personal endorsements that his products work. On the Amazon listing for his flagship product, Organifi green juice powder, he uses an awesome testimonial of a woman talking about how the Organifi helped reverse a serious health condition she was having as well as how much weight she lost. During the testimonial video, they show a before-and-after picture that supports what is being said. I suggest you watch the video right as it appears on the product listing. Go to the link listed here, scroll down towards the bottom of the page, and the video I am referring to is called: Organic Superfood Power – Organifi Green Juice Superfood Supplement. http://bit.ly/SuperfoodVideoExample

I'm sure Drew and his company will be early adopters of what Amazon is introducing next.

A GAME-CHANGER—LIVE STREAM ON AMAZON

As of the time I am writing this book Amazon had just introduced a new service, live streaming. This will bring interactive live video to the consumer's shopping experience. Think of it as a mini-version of QVC or Home-shopping, but it's your very own channel!

Using the Amazon Live Creator, a mobile application, you can create interactive and shoppable live streams on Amazon.com on desktop, mobile, and through the Amazon mobile app. By creating a live stream, you can chat with Amazon shoppers in real time and let them see your products up close.

Creating your first live stream is easy. In just a few taps, select which products you will feature and go live. Once live, your stream will appear on prominent places such as product detail pages, your Store on Amazon and on Amazon.com/live.

To reach even more shoppers, you can also pay to promote your live stream.

WHY LIVE STREAM?

To Drive Sales. During your live stream, shoppers can purchase your featured products in the carousel displayed next to your stream.

To Interact with your Viewers. Chat and interact directly with shoppers as they watch your live stream.

To Get Discovered. Reach more shoppers on Amazon.com and build your brand through interactive live streams.

Here is what one early adopter says about the experience with Live streaming:

"Live Streaming has helped increase daily visits to our product page by a multiple of five and significantly grew our sales."

WHERE DO LIVE STREAMS APPEAR?

Your live streams appear on Amazon.com on desktop, mobile, and Amazon's mobile app in prominent places such as product detail pages, your store, and on Amazon.com/live. You can also pay to promote your live stream to reach even more customers.

LIVE STREAMING IS EASY

Creating a live stream is easy. First, download the Amazon Live Creator iOS mobile app. Once you have installed the app, you can stream your video content on Amazon.com on desktop, mobile, and Amazon's mobile app. You can stream directly from your phone camera or through an encoder using a professional camera. Follow these steps and live stream today.

1. Download the Amazon Live Creator app on your iOS device.
2. Log in with the email address tied to your Seller Central account.
3. Follow the in-app prompts to select the products you will feature.
4. Schedule your live stream for a future time or go live instantly.

If you can't tell, I'm really excited about this new service and the opportunity it provides for using your Video Persuasion principles. I'm currently working with two very large Amazon sellers, and we are already seeing a lot of success!

INTERVIEW WITH JASON BOYCE, FOUNDER/CEO OF AVENUE 7 MEDIA, AN AMAZON MARKETING AGENCY

I met Jason after I gave the keynote speech at the Prosper Show in Las Vegas. After the show, we started getting together every Friday morning for coffee and conversation at the Issaquah coffee house. Jason was educating me about all things Amazon, and I was educating him on how best to use video to help his business grow both on and off Amazon.

RICK

Hi, Jason. Tell me the name of your company, and what your company does.

JASON

Hi, Rick. I'm co-founder and CEO of a company called Avenue 7 Media. We are an Amazon marketing agency, and we help sellers be successful on the Amazon.com platform. I learned how to be successful on Amazon with my first company, Dazadi.com, where we became an eight-figure seller. We made a lot of mistakes and built a lot of systems and processes based on our experience at Dazadi.com. We've built these processes, and we now offer this service to other folks who are trying to be successful on the Amazon platform.

RICK

Let's just talk about your background first, and then we'll get into Avenue 7. Tell me more about Dazadi. How long have you been selling on Amazon?

JASON

Sure. We've been selling on Amazon for over sixteen years now. Before we were Dazadi, our business was called SuperDuper-Hoops.com, and we were selling basketball hoops online. We were drop-shipping them. Amazon actually called us and asked us if we'd sell our basketball hoops on their platform, Amazon.com. We were really surprised, because at that time, all the way back in 2003/2004, Amazon was really still just a bookseller, and they were selling DVDs and those types of things. So, it was a real surprise to us that they actually picked up the telephone and called us. I don't think they do that anymore, by the way!

RICK

Not unless you're Nike. Right?

JASON

Exactly! They will call if you're a big brand. We were actually selling basketball hoops on Amazon before Amazon Retail was selling basketball hoops on Amazon. We've gone through several iterations on the Amazon platform and grown with them on that platform. We're pretty good at what we do. We're a Top 50 seller in the sports and outdoors category, and we're better than a Top 200 seller on Amazon as well, largely because we've been on that platform for so long. We just learned a lot of lessons and applied them.

RICK

Just to be clear, that means of all the people in the world selling on Amazon, your company, Dazadi, is in the Top 200?

JASON

That's right. There are 5 million Amazon sellers at the end of 2017. Two and a half million of those sellers actually have an active listing, and of those two and a half million sellers, we are Top 200, which is mind-boggling, but yeah.

RICK

That's really impressive. Congratulations.

JASON

Thank you.

RICK

Just so I can share with the people that are reading this, from an experience standpoint, from both the longevity of doing it and the sheer volume of working with Amazon, you have a lot of experience in this area.

JASON

We really do. Again, we learned it the hard way, trial and error. We made a lot of mistakes. We've probably made just about every mistake that you can make selling on the Amazon platform, and we have learned from it and built some repeatable processes as a result of those lessons learned.

RICK

That's awesome. I don't call them mistakes. I call them learning experiences. Some are more expensive than others.

JASON

Some have been very expensive. We've had some million-dollar mistakes on Amazon for sure and learning experiences. I like that better than mistakes.

RICK

Tell me a little bit about Avenue 7 and what that company does. You mentioned it's an agency to help other people sell on Amazon.

JASON

A few years ago, because of our success on Amazon, we started getting asked to be on seller panels and speak at internet retailer events. The Prosper Show for Amazon sellers comes to mind, and it's one of our favorite shows. Every time I would speak at those conferences, a group of folks would come up and ask a million questions about how we were being successful on Amazon. As a result of those conversations, we kind of started informally helping a small group of sellers be successful on Amazon. I really enjoyed that process. I almost enjoyed doing that more than selling my own products. I can't really describe why, but it's always very meaningful for me whenever we're able to help solve somebody else's problems.

So, this year, 2019, I wanted to make it a more formal process, and I started Avenue 7 to help sellers navigate and become successful on the Amazon.com platform. We help them do everything from listing optimization to managing their advertising campaigns, which has become a big and necessary thing on Amazon. We help them both from an objective level, with their search engine optimization, as well as the subjective level, helping them, from your school of thought, pulling out features and benefits and putting their brand in the best light possible on the Amazon.com platform. You know, we've found it very meaningful, and we're really enjoying it. We've got a nice slate of clients, and it's growing very rapidly. We've had some great early successes.

RICK

That's awesome! You mentioned that Dazadi is in the sporting goods category. Tell me some of the products they do and then some of the different product categories, not necessarily just specific products, but some of the categories you are working in with Avenue 7.

JASON

Sports and outdoors is a very big category, and some of the subcategories that we've been successful on lately with Dazadi is the home fitness category. So, specifically, we have some exercise bikes and some rowing machines that we've been very successful with. We also do home rec, so think air hockey tables, billiard tables. We also do outdoor games, like bocce ball, ladder toss, and bean bag toss. So, the product mix is really about making your home awesome and having fun in and around the home. Now, as it relates to Avenue 7, it's a broad spectrum of categories. We've done everything from the supplements category to home and appliance, home and kitchen category, sports and outdoors, of course, and several others. The jewelry category is another one that we've been involved with, and we're also currently work in in the golf sub-category.

RICK

So, really a broad range. You can take your knowledge base and really apply it to any of the categories that somebody might want to come to you with.

JASON

Absolutely, all of the systems and things that we use also apply to all of the other categories, we're expanding into other categories pretty rapidly. They're very similar across the multitude of categories on Amazon.

RICK

When someone comes to you with a product, how do you determine that it's a good product or something that you want to work with?

JASON

That's a great question. Amazon is the best place to go online in order to find what competitors or what top sellers in a given subcategory are doing. It's one of the first things that I do whenever we're approached by a new client. We find out what their subcategory is, and our team does a full background and research on their category to identify how the client is doing currently, but also how the best sellers with similar products to the clients are doing on Amazon. You just have to know where to look. We've built our own software to identify how many units are being sold in a given month, in a given year, it's really great information.

An inventor may have an idea for a product that's a great idea, but what we have found on Amazon, if there's not a market that already exists on Amazon, it's really hard to create a new one. It's always amazing to see the reaction of clients when we tell them, "Okay. This product is not something that is already selling on Amazon in any big way, so we need to talk to guys like Rick and help create some educational video to be successful," or we'll tell them, "Yeah. This product is doing $10 million a year. Your competitor's doing $10 million a year on Amazon." Their jaw usually drops whenever we have that conversation.

RICK

I've heard some of the numbers for some products. You would never expect them to be up in the millions of dollars, and it just blows your mind away. But I just wanted to come back to something you mentioned. One of the products or product categories you mentioned was stationary bikes. I know they have been around for a while, but I'm going to tie that into some of Amazon advertising that is happening. Other stationary bikes are getting the benefit of the huge advertising campaign that the product Peloton does. So, you have a product out there blasting the TV airwaves. What I've found when that happens is when someone's doing advertising like that, it not only raises the sales of your own product in all the different distribution channels, it also raises the sales of everyone else's products... Just another example of how powerful advertising can be and the halo effect that it can have.

JASON

I absolutely agree. I think we're absolutely getting a benefit from that huge TV campaign that Peloton has been running and they continue to run. Now, they're expanding into other categories, like treadmills and some other products as well, so we expect to see a lift from that marketing as well. One of the other things that we do at

Avenue7 is something that you perfected frankly two decades ago, which is we have a system we call Launch and Learn. We launch the product on Amazon, and then we listen. Before we launch a product, we do a full analysis of the top competitors, the top-selling items, and we read every product review, especially the negative ones. We review the questions that the Amazon customers are asking and what those answers are, and we try to identify what's wrong with the product before we even launch it.

Once we identify what's wrong, we share that with the client, and we say, "Hey. Take this to your engineers. Take this to your factory. Ask them if they could solve this problem before it lands." Whenever they do that, whenever they improve their product before it lands, we call it out in the infographics and explain why our client's product is better. So, in other words, we're launching differentiated already, based on great Amazon intel that we're getting directly from customers who buy similar products. Then after we launch, we're continually listening and continually reading all those product reviews as well and providing that great product intelligence, customer-driven innovation to the client, so that they can improve their product and get to that four-star review.

Once you get four stars Product Reviews or better on Amazon, you really can gain pricing power, so you can actually start to increase your price when your product is reviewed better than the competitor. It's a process that we kind of perfected when we were with Dazadi products, and it works really, really well. It's something that a lot of folks don't think about, but that information is readily available, and when you can take action and improve on the product, you can really grow your sales exponentially.

RICK

I have an example of a client that brought a product to us. You've heard of the Vitamix Blenders. They're like the Mercedes of blenders, you know, very high quality, but also very highly priced. I think they're $300 and above. So, these guys were big into making smoothies, and they wanted a powerful blender, but they didn't want to pay that much. They went to China, sourced out blenders that had almost all of the basic qualities of a Vitamix from a power standpoint, but they were able to price it like $150, and they were shocked. They brought in a half a container and sold out very quickly. Then they just started a business just by finding a little niche, and finding what someone was doing well, and then differentiating or improving on it. It doesn't always have to be from a price standpoint, just something that can differentiate from the competition.

JASON

Well, that's a perfect example of what Jeff Bezos always says, *"Your margin is my opportunity."* When some competitors out there that are big and well-financed, if they've got super fat margins, it definitely spells an opportunity, especially on Amazon, because Amazon is about product reviews. An Amazon customer will buy a brand that they've never heard of if it's priced right, if the features are there, but more important, if it's got great product reviews. Really optimizing a product in your listing to drive those product reviews, and we're not talking about black hat reviews, because that's no longer a thing on Amazon. Those are really helpful, and you can really build a business by doing that.

RICK

I'm going to come back to what makes a good listing. I just want to go off on a little bit of a tangent. You'll appreciate this, I'm doing some consulting work with a company, another Top 200 Amazon seller, called Plugable, https://plugable.com/.

They make anything USB related, computer peripherals, and they recently hired an external PR firm, and they just did their first product launch, and pre-launch they have sent out the product to get reviewed by all the industry tech magazines, and probably had half a dozen articles, and they basically started with their normal amount of inventory, and they sold out in the first day, which normally that would take weeks, according to the old way of doing it. So, it just, again, shows you *how off Amazon or external advertising, PR, if done correctly, can have a huge effect on the Amazon listing.*

Speaking of that, when you talk about optimizing listings, someone brings you a new product, what are the things that you tell them to do or the assets that they need to make a good listing that's going to help sell that product?

JASON

Well, nowadays, because private label is such a successful way to go on Amazon, the very first question we ask after the presentation is, do you have a registered trademark for your brand? It's really important. What you get when you get that USPTO or Canada or Mexico, trademark registration certificate, is what's called Brand Registry on Amazon. Brand Registry comes with a number of additional features that allow you to put your brand in the best possible light. For example, *if you are a brand registered brand on Amazon, you can upload video. I highly recommend great video before launching.*

It helps with the organic search rank. It helps with conversion rates. Amazon is really becoming a product video platform. Having good video is important. Brand registry also gives you more of an opportunity to talk about your brand on what's called Enhanced Brand Content (EBC) pages on a product details page, and it allows you to have a website within Amazon basically *called Brand Pages, where you can really put additional video talking about your origin story, your brand story.*

I think that that's really important. I think aside from good product reviews, today's customer also wants to know your background story, how the company was founded, why they're different, why they're special. With Brand Registry, with that registered trademark certificate, you can get all of those features. When you do that in a successful way, in a smart way on Amazon, your brand really grows and takes off.

RICK

Do you recommend people use video, and why?

JASON

Video has become so important. You know, they say a picture's worth a thousand words? So, what does that make video? It's that much more important. *So much of the traffic now on Amazon, and they don't release these numbers, is coming from their Amazon app and from mobile. Amazon has a new program where you can actually advertise your video on the Amazon app, and it's been hugely successful. So, video is really important. You know, not only video that's posted on the Amazon platform, but if you have a growing YouTube channel that's driving traffic from video to your Amazon listing, that can have a huge positive benefit.*

You know, we were just talking about off Amazon traffic. Amazon's algorithms really love off Amazon traffic. They know when it comes, and they really give preferential real estate and ranking to folks that do this in a good way, like you had mentioned with Plugable. Having a successful off Amazon campaign really helped them sell out in one day. I mean, that's astounding. That's really great information. *But having video, advertising on the YouTube channel, putting it and posting it on the Amazon channel is really, really important, not just any video, good video that calls out features and benefits, testimonials about the product. What makes your product better than the rest of the crowd? We've just seen so many positive metrics when you have video, compared to listings that don't have it. It's really important.*

RICK

It sounds like you've been listening to me when we get together for coffee, because you just listed all the components of an effective video. Let's dive into that because sometimes you see just really not very good video. I don't mean production quality. I'm more focusing on the content. Video Persuasion is about the content of a video that's going to help a product sell better. You just mentioned some of the main ones, which were focusing on not only calling out the features, but more important, the benefits, and then adding testimonials to them. Talk about testimonials for a minute. Are they a good selling tool for your products?

JASON

You know, first of all, I have to go all the way back ... Our videos at the time on Dazadi were just assembly videos showing people how to put the product together. I will never forget you saying, "That looks like work. Why are you showing work on your videos?"

RICK

Well, you know, it's funny. The name of those types of videos ... and we covered this category in an earlier chapter in this book, *those are called tutorial videos, and they're very popular, and there's a place for them, but they're more for customer service and not for marketing and selling. The demonstration videos are for selling.*

JASON

Sure. I've learned so much from you, in terms of the importance of video and what's important. You taught me this. Having human beings interacting with the product, happy, smiling, aspirational, it makes this unconscious connection in the customer's mind that makes it okay for them to order, that makes it real for them and more tangible. Good video that calls out the features and benefits, I love it when they can talk about a snippet about why the company started. People love to know how you came about, how you started your company. Back to your original question, the testimonials. The testimonials are so important. I mean, we just finished talking about how important product reviews are on Amazon. In my mind a testimonial. Those are a form of testimonials. I think the video testimonials are that much more impactful and that much more powerful. Another thing that you taught me many years ago was when you go, and you record these testimonials for a client's customer, not only do you get great information about what's great about the product, but it's that same process, that customer-driven innovation. You also find out what customers would like to have as an added feature or benefit in the product, and you share that information with the client to help them make a better mousetrap, if you will. The process of shooting those testimonials is important, because it helps you highlight what's good, but it also helps you educate the engineers and the owners of the product on how to make it better. It's a win/win situation as far as I'm concerned. When a customer—

RICK

It's a constant feedback loop.

JASON

A constant feedback loop. That's the name of the game. That's how you beat the big boys with the big brands and all the big budgets.

RICK

Okay. Let's go back. I'm jumping around a little bit, but talk about YouTube again, how if you're taping a product video, and you create this nice demonstration video, and there's some testimonials in there, you should put it on YouTube, but then you said you possibly can link it back to Amazon as well?

JASON

Absolutely. Our designers can embed a link directly to your Amazon listing or to your own website if you prefer. But I just think that there are huge benefits to getting a higher rank on Amazon. Why is that? It's because of the algorithm on Amazon, and they really love that off Amazon traffic, but more importantly, Amazon in the United States has the most eyeballs, the most customers. You know, *55% of all product searches start on Amazon. They have become the internet of products.* It's where people go where they want to buy physical goods and have them delivered to their home. Thirty percent of product searches start on Google, but guess what? On Google, there are a dozen Amazon links directing you from Google to Amazon.com. Even though half of all product searches start on Amazon, I believe even more are ending there. So, you're going to be really hard pressed to get the same amount of eyeballs and traffic on your own site as you can on Amazon. So, it's a dual strategy. I'm not saying don't waste your time, because it's really important that you build your own customer list but, *being able to drive traffic from a YouTube video by embedding a link on that video, sending you to your Amazon listing helps you move up the rank, gives you better real estate. It gives you that Main Street real estate on Amazon, and you're going to see much more sales volume on that channel.*

RICK

That's awesome. It really confirms ... One of the things I talk about people is repurposing video. You shoot this product video, and it might be ... You know, it could be five minutes. It could be thirty minutes, whatever. That would be good in its full length to put onto YouTube because length isn't as important, but you might only take a small chunk of that and put it on Amazon. Is there any specific length you shoot for, for Amazon videos that you like to see?

JASON

Well, on the metrics that we see, people are dropping off after 90 seconds so I would say no longer than two minutes, but you're absolutely right. *If you can do a one or two-day video shoot, you can get video that you can use on YouTube, on Amazon, on Instagram, on Facebook.* There's no limit to what you can re-edit it after the shoot. ... In some cases, *we've been reusing video for years, and it looks fresh to the customer, and we format it for the given sales channel. It's hugely beneficial.*

RICK

Let's go back. If someone doesn't have a brand page, can they still use video?

JASON

On the Amazon listing you cannot upload video as a third-party seller unless you are Brand Registered, which is what we're a proponent of. As a third-party seller, you're selling on Amazon, not to Amazon. Without brand registry, you cannot upload video, which is why getting your trademark registered officially and getting that certificate is so important.

RICK

Have you heard about Amazon doing live streaming? If you have, what do you know about that?

JASON

I don't know a lot about it. I know that they are doing it, and I remember seeing a lot of live feeds during the holiday season. So, I have not seen any metrics yet, and Amazon is very tight-lipped when it comes to sharing those kinds of metrics. It's really sort of a black box.

RICK

I'm really fortunate, again, in working with my client, Plugable. I don't know if they have people beta-testing the live streaming, but they're doing it with Plugable. They haven't actually done their first one yet. They were getting set up. Then there was a glitch at Amazon, and they couldn't do it, but immediately *a light bulb went off in my head and said this is basically a home shopping channel within Amazon. You're basically doing product demos live on camera, and if you do that live streaming correctly, to me, it's going to really, really boost product sales and conversions, because live demos work on QVC. They work on The Home Shopping Network. It's gotta work on Amazon as well!*

JASON

I agree. I would love to hear the results once Plugable goes live.

RICK

I'll let you know.

JASON

That'd be great. I think that the live stream video, when I think about my purchasing habits, and I'm an Amazon customer, I don't usually like to watch on my mobile device, which we believe the majority of traffic is coming from now, on a mobile device. I don't like to listen to sound, unless I'm in the privacy of my own home, because it's annoying. If you're on a train or you're in the public, you know how it is when you have to hear somebody else's video on their mobile phone. That being said, I think that it's the next big thing, and I'll explain.

When 5G cellular data becomes readily available to everyone in the United States, and you can use your phone to stream video onto your television from your phone, and it's as fast as any high-speed broadband right now, I think what you just described is going to happen in a big way. It's very much like the Home Shopping Network. There's a huge subset of customers that love to see those sorts of interactions. They like to be sold. They like to be shown what the features and benefits are in a live feed. I think that once 5G gets fully implemented in the United States, that live streaming is going to take off. That's not to say that there won't be benefits now short term, but I really think that the promise of that is yet to come, and when it does, it's going to be big. I agree with you.

RICK

I agree 100% with you, and again, that's why I spend a lot of time in this book talking about what you should be doing in a video to get a viewer to take a specific action, because I can see a lot of people doing what you did early, before we met, doing live streaming and doing a tutorial video, and here's how a product works. That's not what's going to sell the product. Basically, just a simple fact of basically asking people to order is going increase conversions at least by 20%. Asking them if they should maybe check out one of your other products, it's known as an upsell, is also going to increase orders. So, really *the knowledge of what to do in a video when you're trying to get a viewer to take a specific action is hugely important,* and again, one of the reasons I'm writing the book.

JASON

I completely agree with you. If you think about the old Home Shopping Network, you had to pick up the telephone, and call, and maybe wait on hold, and give your credit card information over the phone. Imagine if you're streaming from your phone onto your TV, you really like this product, and you just hit a button. It's a one-click purchase, and your item arrives in two days or less to your door. That is such a better experience with much less friction. I think you're right. I think it will increase lift by 20%, if not more, just because of the pure convenience of it.

RICK

So, getting a little bit more specific on the videos, are titles and graphics important? Is it important to call out certain features and benefits by putting graphic titles up on the videos?

JASON

Yes, absolutely! As we're talking about Amazon listings, the copy is really important. Do most customers read all of the copy? No. But there's a couple of things that we like to achieve in the written copy on a product listing. Number one, we do a ton of research upfront to find out what the most relevant, highest volume keywords are on Amazon that customers are searching for that most relate to our product. We make sure we're not keyword stuffing, but we put a reasonable, rational, well-written explanation and representation of those keywords in the copy. In that respect, it's really important for organic search and for sponsored search as well. But we also like to call out those features and benefits in written form.

The second part about that product listing and why we spend a lot of time on what we call infographics, which is an image of someone, either the product or someone interacting with the product because it's above the fold ... If you think of the old newspapers, right, all the most important headlines are above the fold. The rest are below. The infographics, even if you have brand registry, are the top left of your screen, and in your mobile device you can thumb through and see all of them.

So, we spend a lot of time, our designers spend a lot of time calling out in images features and benefits, dimensions, the best features, and the reasons why a customer would choose our product over a competitor's... the differentiating factors as well. We put them in the image and point to it directly. We find tremendous success when we maximize those additional images, and we do a good job with infographics. Again, it's just because it's all above the fold.

RICK

I just want to emphasize that it's important to mention what the features of the products are, but equally as important to then tie that feature to what's the benefit to the end user, because that's what's going to help really get people excited about a product. "It's got this feature. Well, what does that mean to me, the end user?" And always making that connection.

JASON

So true. I remember when we first started on Amazon. We would take these specification sheets on other people's product that was created for engineers, and we would just take it, and copy it, and put it right on the listing as if the customer even cared about a lot of these specifications. It was not user-friendly. It didn't get to why I, as a customer, would benefit if I were to purchase this product, and it was awful. There are probably hundreds of thousands of folks that still do that. They just take that copy from the manufacturer and list it while hoping for the best, but that's not the way to do good copy that sells. The way to do copy is what you just described. It's calling out why your product is different, why your product is better, and what am I, as the consumer, going to gain after I hit the buy button?

RICK

You talk about good copy. Even though this is a book about video and the content of the video, two of the interviews in this book ... are with two of the top copywriters in the country about what are their secrets to persuading people to purchase? Because if you know that, then that information translates directly to video as well.

JASON

Rick, that is such a great point. I can remember a specific example on Dazadi where we worked with somebody, someone I think you recommended, a copywriter. We had a landing page, and we tried our best to do the copy originally. Then we hired the copywriter you recommended to help us, using direct marketing tactics. We found that those direct marketing tactics are still very relevant ... When we upgraded the copy, we saw an 800% increase in engagement on that landing page.

RICK

It's amazing. Say that again. I don't think people will believe you. An 800% increase?

JASON

We launched it for two weeks with our own copy, there was terrible engagement. We updated the copy with one of your experts—that you probably recommend in the book—and *using direct marketing sales tactics, I call it the science of selling,* we incorporated that copy. We ran it for another two weeks, and we saw an 800% increase in engagement, time on site, click-throughs, et cetera. It works. It just works.

RICK

It's amazing, but not surprising. You called them old direct marketing techniques, which they are because people were doing some of these things back in the catalog days, back in the 1930s and 40s, and the direct mail days in the 70s and 80s. Human psychology doesn't change. The things that motivate people don't change. Really, just the delivery systems have changed. So, basically, it used to be snail mail. Then it was email. Then it was direct response television, and now it's Amazon. If you can understand, again, I preach this all the time, the basic direct response principles, you can put them to work, even though technology has changed significantly.

JASON

Not only do I believe you, I've seen the results, and I agree with you.

RICK

Jason, anything else Amazon related that you want to share with the readers? Then maybe or even more specific, anything video related from your experience, or any last tips you want to give somebody?

JASON

I think I'd like to address one misconception or misnomer when it comes to Amazon. There was a public case recently with Birkenstock, where the Birkenstock CEO decided, "I can't control my channel on Amazon, so I'm pulling all of my products from Amazon." I really felt—at the time I read that article—that it was a bad decision. It's because if you want to protect your brand, there is a way to do it. There's a way to protect your pricing integrity and control the channel, but the worst thing that you can do is cede that ground on

Amazon, because what happened the next day when Birkenstock pulled all their inventory off of Amazon? Sellers that they had never heard of started listing and selling Birkenstocks on Amazon.

Of course, Birkenstock now has no control over what those listings look like. They can't control the video, nor any of the copy. We just talked about how important that is. I would like to tell your readers that there is a way to protect brand on Amazon, and the worst thing that you can do is to NOT sell on Amazon because if you have a brand that's growing in popularity, somebody else will sell it. If you do this the right way, you can control who sells on Amazon, make sure that your price integrity is maintained and that your brand is being presented in the best possible light. I'm a real believer in this, and I really hate to see it when public companies make this decision to pull off of Amazon, because if they're not there, they're still going to be there, and they're not going to have any control over it.

RICK

That's great information. Jason, I wanted to thank you for taking the time today. This has been really informative and a lot of great tips that the reader can take away and start to use immediately if they're selling on Amazon. So, thank you.

JASON

Thank you, Rick. Always a pleasure.

CHAPTER EIGHT SUMMARY

- Start incorporating video into your Amazon listings.
- What has worked on other sales platforms will usually work on new platforms. Observe what is working and how they are doing it and then integrate that into your videos.
- Use your video persuasion knowledge to create powerful demonstration videos for your Amazon listings.
- Live streaming on Amazon is a game changer. Start using it now to get ahead of the competition.

CHAPTER NINE
Social Media and Video: The Big Three

"Not brute force but only persuasion and faith are
the kings of this world."
—Thomas Carlyle

When it comes to video and social media, I like to break it down to what I call the Big Three, Facebook, Instagram, and YouTube. In this chapter, I will discuss all three, but because there is so much good information to cover, I include two different interviews, the first will focus on Facebook and Instagram and the second will be more about YouTube and Facebook Live.

FACEBOOK & INSTAGRAM

I do a lot of speaking and consulting with many businesses that are in their early stages and most are trying to grow quickly. What I find is that many of them are getting their highest *return on invest-ment* (ROI), from running video ads on Facebook and Instagram.

Some of the results are pretty astounding. I'm currently working with a German agency on the launch of several products in the US that is considered one of the top in the world at creating and placing Facebook and Instagram ads. They are just coming off a campaign where they helped grow a US Skincare line to $100 million in revenue using these types of video ads. I've worked with another company that had similar success with a hair styling product. There is a lot of opportunity here.

To me, Facebook and Instagram are currently the most powerful social platforms for business growth. This is great news if you are a marketer because as we've discussed in previous chapters, people will respond in higher numbers and buy more from video ads than other formats. These two platforms allow you to specifically target the prospects you are looking for and get your video ads and brand content placed where they are searching. A good analogy is that these platforms are like interstate highways and your ads become the billboards that drivers see along the way.

There are two parts to running video ads regardless of the platform, First, is the creation or production of the ads or content you are running and then, second, is the media buying component or placement of those ads. For placement I suggest you work with a very good agency or buyer that has a track record of success in placing ads. See the list at the end of the chapter.

One of the early lessons I learned in TV advertising was that the *video content is more important than video production quality.* What do I mean by that? A video with low production value, usually done cheaply, but has content that resonates with the viewer will *ALWAYS* outperform a video with high production values that is more expensive to produce, as long as the content is more interesting to the end viewer. I have witnessed this time and time again. A great example of this is in the creation of consumer testimonials. Testimonials that I will pick up on the fly at a trade show booth with a hand-held camera always work better than a nicely produced talking head with a slick background.

This statement is even truer when it comes to online video. I believe people shy away from videos that are too well produced and too slick, inherently they know they are watching an ad or an over-produced segment. Compare that to one that is done on your smartphone. People are used to watching this kind of inexpensive self-produced video day in and day out on their own social media channels. Just like the testimonial example above, there is an *authenticity* to them that people will respond to.

CREATING AN AD FOR FACEBOOK

Facebook makes it really simple for you to create video ads with step-by-step instructions for the different types of ads you see on Facebook every day, such as:

Vertical Videos – These will get scrollers to pause and pay attention with edge-to-edge, full-screen video ads. In a recent study, 65% of respondents said that brands using vertical video for their advertising are more innovative.

Short Carousel Videos – These allow you to showcase up to ten images or videos within a single ad, each with its own link. You can highlight different products, showcase specific details about one product, service or promotion, or tell a story about your brand that develops across each carousel card.

Collection Videos – These allow you to pair video ads with product images to let people explore and buy. Collection is an ad format that lets people move from discovery to purchase in a smooth and immersive way. Each collection ad features a primary video or image with four smaller accompanying images below in a grid-like layout. Customers who tap on your collection ad to browse or learn more will be seamlessly taken to a fast-loading visual post-click experience powered by Instant Experience—all without leaving Facebook or Instagram.

Long In-Stream Video Ads – These let you reach people who are engaging with longer video content on Facebook by placing ads inside of that content.

I could write an entire book about the steps involved in creating video ads for Facebook, but great information already exists from Facebook itself. Anytime you can get information directly from the source, that is always best. To get complete step-by-step instructions on how to create these types of ads and more just visit: https://www.facebook.com/business/ads/video-ad-format

If you want to move on from producing simple videos on your smartphone, there's more great news for you in that you do not need expensive production equipment to create a video that will work on Facebook or Instagram. Two of the best resources I've found that cover the basic video equipment needed are from:

1. Dominate Web Media

https://s3-us-west-2.amazonaws.com/dwmfiles/
Video+Equipment+Guide.pdf

2. Digital Marketer

https://www.digitalmarketer.com/blog/video-marketing-tools/

And if you want even more in-depth resource for everything you need to know about video advertising on Facebook, check out "The Ultimate Guide to Facebook Video Ads" also from Digital Marketer. https://www.digitalmarketer.com/blog/facebook-video-ads/

And for more information on Instagram ads: https://www.agorapulse.com/blog/instagram-ad-features

WHO ARE YOU TARGETING?

Facebook has a targeting system that is second to none. Do you want to target parents of healthy eating young children who live in Seattle? Or people over fifty interested in life extension living in Florida? Or men over forty interested in Auto-racing? Because of the amount of data that Facebook collects, you can accurately target just about any group. The targeting and retargeting options available through Facebook Ads are exceptional. Facebook ads are also connected to Instagram ads so you can run both in a single campaign, connecting you to audiences on both platforms. Since the biggest goal of Facebook Ads is to put your content in front of users—without waiting for them to come find you this is a great advantage if you are a marketer looking for the right audience to buy your products.

If your content is going to be interesting to your end viewer you have to know who your viewer is and who you are trying to reach. You cannot be all things to all people, but your content can be extremely interesting to a certain number of people. Remember, *If you try to appeal to everybody, you'll end up appealing to nobody.*

There is an important lesson you can draw from the direct mail business and writing sales letters from the famous copywriter Jim Rutz. He says, *"Never write to a crowd. Crowds don't write checks or even read. Individuals do. Write to your brother, sister, or best friend, never to a targeted prospect."*

Your videos should do the same. Always ask—Who is it for?

On Facebook, potential buying audiences can be placed into three categories as follows:

Cold Audience:

They are unaware of their problem, but they fit your target demographic. They need to realize their problem fully before being open to your solution. They are called a cold audience because they usually are not ready to make a purchase. Right now, they do not know or care about your brand. Cold audiences will usually respond to direct response video ads that offer links to more information, demos, videos online brochures, free e-books, video links, and so on.

Warm Audience:

They are aware of their problem, and they want to make an informed decision about whether to purchase a solution or not. They are warm because they are seeking knowledge and information about the solution your product or brand offers. If you can deliver more information about your brand's solution, your brand will become an authoritative figure and trustworthy for this audience. Warm audiences will respond to your direct response videos that offer more information, promotions, e-books, tools, and such.

Hot Audience:

They are highly aware of their problem, and they need a solution. They are hot because they are ready to find a solution, but they do not know if it will be your product or your brand's particular solution. They'll choose your brand's solution if you ensure that their particular concerns are addressed, and their desired specific solution is visualized. Hot audiences will be most susceptible to your direct response videos that call for direct sales and/or leads.

While doing DRTV advertising, I worked with trying to get cold audiences to purchase expensive gym equipment like a Nordic Track or Bowflex. One of the most effective things we did was first run the ad reaching as many people as possible for the least amount of money. This type of advertising was a shotgun blast to a cold audience. We then offered a free video and brochure to anyone who wanted to learn more. Anyone who wanted these things became a warm audience. We then followed that up with a phone call to close the sale for our product. Anyone who bought was obviously a hot audience that could be marketed to again.

INTERVIEW WITH KURT BULLOCK, FOUNDER AND CEO OF PRODUCE DEPARTMENT, A FACEBOOK AD AGENCY

RICK

Hi, Kurt. Please tell me the name of your company and a little bit about what you do.

KURT

So, my company's name is Produce Department, https://www.producedept.co/, and we are an e-commerce marketing agency. We primarily work with Shopify stores, and we work with both new and established brands, primarily in the channels of email automation and paid traffic.

RICK

Tell me a little bit about your background. How did you evolve into Produce Department?

KURT

How I took steps to coming into creating the agency was through running my own brands. I had created a brand, we took it up to a run rate of a couple million dollars a year, and I sold it to my younger brother, and he still runs that. I'm still a part of that company, but that was how I really got introduced to using paid traffic to take a new brand from zero...to a couple million in sales. It took us three months to really get the business to the point where we had to bring on a bunch of staff and everything. So that really showed me the power of paid ads, and it really was trial by fire. That was how I learned enough so I can now help others with their paid ads.

RICK

Absolutely. I tell you that's probably the best way to learn ... There's a lot of parallels, I learned everything that I know about direct response marketing from marketing my own products initially before I opened an agency to help other people. I learned very similar to the way you did, and I feel like it gives you better experience that you can pass on to the clients that you work with. So when you say paid traffic, tell me a little bit about what platforms you're using.

KURT

So I am specifically using Instagram and Facebook. I've team members that do YouTube, and we're dabbling in Pinterest. But, really I would say for the majority of our Shopify clients, we're doing Facebook and Instagram.

RICK

One of the reasons I wanted to interview you was that I read a really good email you sent out about using video on Facebook. But, before we get specific to Facebook, how do you use video in your marketing? You talk about Facebook, Instagram, e-commerce sites, just maybe a more of a global view of how you look at video in helping e-commerce sales.

KURT

One of the great things about video is the way that it can help people progress through sort of the different layers of awareness, right? Of getting to know you and your brand. So I really like video for that reason, especially top of funnel because *it helps prospects connect with your brand, build trust, learn about the products that you offer or the problems that you solve, and it can kind of do that sometimes in one piece of content where it can be hard to make all those things happen with maybe a single image ad and some texts.* Because a lot of times people are just skimming the text or not reading it at all. They're just looking at the headlines. So that's one great use, or I guess reason that we use video.

RICK

So when you come across someone that has a Shopify site and they're trying to market their product, and they don't have any video on their site, do you recommend that they start to use video to help build brand awareness and sales on their site?

KURT

Yes, A lot of the video that I create is really ad-oriented, so it's for a specific purpose. So I look at my funnel as sort of broadly speaking, hot, warm or inserting at the top, cold, warm, and hot, and then I'll use different videos at different parts of the funnel depending on the problem that I'm trying to solve. But in general, I highly recommend that Shopify store owners dip their toes into video. I definitely recommend just kind of getting into that rhythm of video content creation for all our Shopify store owners and then we use that in our advertising a ton, especially top of funnel.

RICK

So it's a good idea for people to create video for content on their site and then you can repurpose that video and re-edit it and use it for advertising as well.

KURT

Definitely, yes.

RICK

Let's take someone that has a product, and they have a Shopify site, take me through the steps that lead up to what you do to do the online marketing for them, like building the funnel. And then where does video take place in that?

KURT

The way that I look at funnels is that we break it down into three tiers, our cold audiences, our warm audiences, and our hot audiences. Then, as a separate layer, loyalty audiences, past customers where we're looking to get repeat purchases. So, at the top of the funnel, that's going to be our cold traffic. These are people that have made it to your website, and they have probably never engaged with you on social media. These are fresh audiences. And this is where a lot of the experimentation is happening, is at the very top of the funnel.

In the middle of the funnel, our warm audiences is where I would include our engagement audiences. These are audiences that know who you are, they may have seen your content on social media, they may have been to your blog, your website, but not necessarily pulled the product pages and added things to their cart. These are people that are just kind of engaging with your content. That's what I would consider warm audiences. If I'm going to break that down a little bit farther, that would be fans of your page. There are actual engagement audiences for Facebook and Instagram that you can target, that would be people that view your videos. You can target those people based on how much they look at. So those are all my middle of funnel audiences, my warm audiences.

Then at the very bottom of the funnel is my hot audiences and those are people that, at this point, they know who you are, they know the products that you offer, and they probably just need maybe the right deal or for your ad to come along at the right time. At the bottom of the funnel, I'm targeting people that have added to cart, people that have actually pulled up specific product pages. And in those ads, that's usually where I might introduce a discount code, if anywhere, in the funnel, but that's where I usually find discount codes work the best.

So that's broadly how I would set up a funnel for my clients. Then at the very bottom is going to be our past customers. And so, to those people, we're making offers of new product launches whenever something new comes out, promotions, and re-engagement campaigns. So periodic campaigns that go out. Let's say that we have a 90-day timer after your most recent purchase or 60 days, then you start seeing ads with top-selling products and other interesting things that would bring you back into the mix, into the funnel.

RICK

First of all, it makes all the sense in the world what you said about the hot leads, and you're trying to get them to just take that final step, so that makes sense using the discount code to get them to make that first purchase. Now going back to trying to tie this back into video, are you producing different videos for different segments of the audience in the funnel?

KURT

I am. Sort of my overall thinking on this, which just ties into the whole idea of a funnel, is that when I'm looking at the functions of the marketing I create, a lot of it breaks down into these four categories. I would say to grow the audience, so just kind of building an audience, to generate traffic from that audience. That would be the second sort of phase or function. The third would be to nurture those relationships and then finally to generate sales. And so I think that helps illustrate the point that it's hard to do all of those things with the same copy or the same content, right? All the way top to bottom. I like to have messaging videos, images, offers that match where they are in that process and what we're trying to do.

So to tie that back to video, I bring it in, typically it's a phased approach, so I'll do top of funnel. I will have different video for top of funnel and then usually for middle of funnel. So that would be— *let's say top of funnel—could be talking about your brand story, it could be a walkthrough of your product, it could be unboxing videos.* Those are a few ideas of what we'll do at the top or even *just talking about the benefits of your product.*

And recently I've actually had a lot of luck, top of funnel, with getting for some of these products where there's a shop or some sort of process that they can show off, *I'll get the owner to turn the camera on himself* and just say, "Hey, this is the business that I run. Let me show you a little bit about what we do and how we make these products." *Those have been some of my highest performing ads,* surprisingly, for some of these brands where they're actually making their own products at a local facility or something.

RICK

People love to hear from the founder/inventor of the product. It's very authentic and they know it might be advertising, but it's also a message directly from the founder, the inventor, and it's more believable than a lot of ads. And so I'm not surprised that you have found that they work better.

KURT

Right, exactly. It has authenticity to it. And also, it fits in well with the other content that you would see on your feed because people are always sitting on their cameras on themselves and showing you what they're doing, it doesn't stand out. For middle funnel or bottom funnel, and sometimes I'll use the same videos for both of those, *I've been having a lot of luck with social proof ads.* For instance, it could be as simple as a slide show, let's say five to six slides with maybe a product image, or a lifestyle image, and maybe five stars, and then a review and we'll kind of go through a series of maybe five or six slides with those reviews. Those have been working really well for me, for middle of funnel.

And then as I mentioned, unboxing videos or user-generated content. So that's been awesome for me, middle of funnel. For people that have engaged with your brand, but they haven't taken steps to actually make a purchase or really go down to the product level, I think that just...We're sort of manufacturing touch points here, so they can get more familiar with your brand, and we don't want to be showing the same content in the same angle every time because different angles speak to different people and are more or less effective with different people.

RICK

I hear you loud and clear and it's interesting what you mentioned about social proof. I am a big advocate of using testimonials as social proof. You talked about using the images with a five-star review, and that's social proof, but in a way, it's a testimonial. And we find testimonials to be really, really powerful if they're authentic. I'm not talking about hiring an actor to make up a story. A lot of times we'll go into a company and reach out to their database and set up a day where we film testimonials, and if we film 10 to 12 people in a day, we'll get some really, really powerful testimonials that they can use for content, but then also turn that into advertising as well.

KURT

Love that! And then just along that sort of thread, and this is a bit of a tangent, but it's something that's been very powerful, we call it social proofing our ads where we'll take an ad that we're going to run somewhere in the funnel, and we will run a certain type of campaign. It's a like an engagement campaign where Facebook's actually trying to get people to like, comment. And so we'll use those ads, get lots of comments on them, and then we'll switch them from engagement ads to conversion ads, ones where we're trying to actually get the sale, and that helps the relevant score go up, and then that actually has some social proof with comments from...Oftentimes we'll target those to past customers. You get a lot of people on there that say, "I love it." Or, "I just got mine." Or whatever it might be. So that works great.

RICK

That's awesome. One of the big obstacles I find with people using video is video production. How do you make your videos? I know there's not just one way you probably use but, talk a little bit about how you create your videos.

KURT

That's an obstacle for us as well. I'll be totally frank, what we typically do is we'll try different approaches. We'll see if we can get the owner to do something himself or herself and turn the camera right this way and do that sort of walkthrough video. Oftentimes we will make videos using product shots. Not product shots, but lifestyle shots. Still images is what I should say, we'll cobble together still images and that works well. There's a lot of web apps now that will add movement, so they'll pan your still images around.

Going back to the brand that I started, one of my most powerful ads that ... it was kind of responsible for my company taking off was just a video that I took of my wife. It didn't show her, it was just neck down because this was for a pendant and we just filmed her with the pendant, and she took her hands and opened and closed the pendant, almost like boomerang style, if you're familiar with that, it goes forward and backward. We did that video, and there was a little bit of music behind it and then some simple copy. It wasn't anything fancy. It was with my iPhone, but it was responsible for ... I don't know, it was responsible for launching the company and creating hundreds of thousands of dollars in sales.

RICK

I'm not surprised, those kind of close up shots are the way they have been selling jewelry on QVC and HSN for years, so you know it must work. It's also interesting that you're mentioning a lot of online parallels to what I've experienced in the past on direct response television. That is that you'll search for the right video or the offer, you do a lot of testing to figure it out, and then you find the one that works, and that's the one you can ride for a long time. It's amazing how much growth and sales that one particular video ad can have ... I always say it's like finding the key that unlocks the safe to the marketing sales when you find the one that works. That's what's fun about it, it's kind of like an art and a science put together of figuring out that one video that you can do that will really help grow a business and create more sales.

KURT

Yes, I've definitely found that to be the case.

RICK

Are there any online apps or platforms that you use for video production that you would recommend to people that you've had some success with?

KURT

They're introducing new ones all the time, but what I'm using right now is one called Waymark. So it's, https://waymark.com/ and that's been working great. Another one that I use is ... It's a real simple name. It's called Over. It's an iPhone app called Over, and they create new templates for you that you can go in and kind of just plug your content into and adjust the size and maybe add some animation and stuff like that. So those are two that I use a lot.

RICK

That's great because, like you said, there are probably dozens of them out there. Thank you for sharing those two with us. Is there anything I didn't ask you about that you want to mention when it comes to using video in your online marketing?

KURT

I'll mention that when it comes to Facebook and video, I've been having a lot of luck with vertical video because vertical video takes up when you're looking at it, essentially the whole screen on your phone, it captures a lot of attention. *Vertical video has been doing really well for me, particularly in Instagram story format, that has been working great for warm audiences.* So that's been working really well middle of funnel. Then for top of funnel and middle of funnel Square has been working awesome. And that's a new placement that Facebook just introduced in the last couple months. But square videos have been awesome, and they also play on Facebook and Instagram. *If you're going to create one video size, Square is a good one because you can use it across both platforms.*

RICK

That's valuable information because if someone's trying to do this on their own, there's a lot of trial and error to find out the information that really works. I know being in an agency like yours, you get the opportunity to work with many clients and try lots of different videos. So that input is really, really good. Earlier in the chapter, I included a link to step-by-step instructions on how to make those kinds of videos.

KURT

One other anecdote, I've got this brand that I'm working with right now, it's an interesting brand, and we're using content. They create these really wild videos ... they have this race team, and they sell products. Each year they create this video where they've sort of orchestrated all these locations where they're going to go and race. *What that amounts to, is content that their end users would just think is cool.* That's pretty much it. We just spent over the last two days about $30,000 on Facebook ads just pushing that one video. It doesn't go to any sales pages or anything like that. But as a result, we built up this giant list of people that we can then use. Instead of just going to cold audiences, we've now got a multimillion-sized list of people that we can use for sort of in lieu of those cold audiences. That's something I've been doing more recently, is really just kind of pushing content that's not necessarily product focused, but it is going to appeal to the interests of your end users or your target audience.

RICK

If I go back and tie this into how you were describing the different levels of people by getting these people interested in that content through Facebook. These are people coming in the middle level of the funnel that they're interested in the product line and that's a great way of building a list. Let's talk about that for a second. Is that something that you're always trying to do is build a good list to market to. Talk about that a little bit because that's important for all e-commerce companies obviously.

KURT

Yeah, absolutely, we are always trying to build a list. And the way that I look at it is there's a few different objectives and different ways to build the list. One is just getting the pixel or the view because now they are segmented, and we can directly send messaging to them. In the case of that video that's what the objective was and I'm looking at really my cost per pixeling (adding pixels to track viewers) each of those people, that's the way that we're looking at that content. The other way is to send them to maybe a page where the video lives and then collecting their email address. But yeah, we're definitely always using content to try and either get them pixeled or get their email address so that we can then start giving them email and showing them messaging from other channels.

RICK

You work with a lot of e-commerce companies, and so a lot of what you're doing is, even though products might be different, similar type of marketing, right?

KURT

Definitely. Yeah, when we go in to work with a new client, we've got a framework that we're working from. We kind of build this trunk of the tree that is kind of the machinery we know is going to be applicable to essentially all of our clients and then we go and build out all the branches depending on their particular products and write those unique features.

RICK

Where do you see video going in the future, just kind of from your own perspective?

KURT

Well, I think that on these platforms, Facebook and Instagram, there's a lot of interesting things happening with 360 immersive experiences where you can look around the video and see what was happening in all directions. I've never run an ad that way because that's not possible yet, but that's a very interesting possibility. But in general, videos are just becoming more and more popular and powerful. One thing that I didn't mention is it is a little bit tactical, but it is a really powerful tactic. I use video at the top of my funnels a lot because I can then re-target people based on their engagement with that video, how much of the video they've looked at. It allows me to segment my audience very quickly. People that have watched 50% of the video, I know that they are interested in that topic to some degree, and I can segment them out from the initial list of 5 million people I was targeting, and now I've got a list of 1 million or a couple of hundred thousand people and focus my ad dollars on that.

As far as the future of video, I see Facebook just giving us more and more options to re-target and use video in our funnels. And I think that people are getting more and more used to that format. I don't know that I have any great predictions, *but video is definitely something that all of my clients are adopting and that I'm recommending they adopt because it's probably our most powerful ad format.*

RICK

That's awesome! One thing I didn't ask you about, have you done any or seen any feedback on length of videos that perform better or not? Or is it more content related than length related?

KURT

The answer I see, is that it is more content related than anything, but when I'm giving recommendations to my clients for top of funnel videos, a lot of times I'm asking them to do something that is in the 30-second range, no fade-ins, things like that because you need to capture attention right away. You've got a second and a half to two seconds before they scroll right past there. So that's what I'm recommending for clients for top of funnel. Then for middle of funnel videos, I'm saying longer formats work. Instagram is only letting you do videos that are a minute or less, so a lot of times that's the parameter that we're playing with on Instagram, which is where a lot of my marketing is happening right now. On Facebook, you can have really long videos. I'm not sure what the upper limit would be.

RICK

That's interesting because, in direct response marketing, there's a saying that long copy works better than short copy and so it's always a balancing act. I agree 100%, the content is more important than the length. I know you hear a lot of, "Oh, you can only make it a certain length. Otherwise, people will lose interest." If it's interesting and it's a topic that people want to know about, they'll stay engaged with the video. If it's not interesting, they won't. But that being said, I do agree with you that you need to capture their attention very quickly so that people know what you're talking about in the video they are about to see. I read a book a long time ago from Dale Carnegie called *How to win friends and Influence People*, and he said the secret to giving a speech is, *Tell them what you are going to say, say it and them tell them what you said,* so that people are not guessing about what you are talking about. I use that a lot in my videos, because people want to know right off the bat what it is you're talking about and if it's relevant to them and then if it is they'll stay more engaged.

KURT

I like that.

RICK

This has been really great. And I'm looking forward to working on a project with you real soon because I can see you're one of those guys that does a really good job of looking at an ROI based on your advertising and how to create the funnels and lead people thru them. It's obvious you are doing a great job and really know what you're talking about. I really enjoy getting the emails you send out. They're very informative, so for the people that are reading this, tell them how they can get in contact with you.

KURT

My email address is kurt@producedept.co, or you can visit our website, https://www.producedept.co, I appreciate you thinking of me and the chance to chat with you today.

RICK

Thanks Kurt.

LIST OF FACEBOOK & INSTAGRAM MEDIA BUYING AGENCIES:

- Produce Department; https://www.producedept.co/, Kurt Bullock, kurt@producedept.co
- Ad Baker; https://adbaker.de/, Patrick Dermak, patrick@adbaker.de
- Adrienne Richardson, https://www.adriennerichardson.com/contact/
- Nicholas Kusmich, https://www.nicholaskusmich.com/

INTERVIEW WITH SUSAN GILBERT OF ONLINE PR SUCCESS

Next is an interview with Susan Gilbert. Her company is called Online PR Success, http://www.onlinepromotionsuccess.com/

In this interview, we will look at an overview of using video on all Social Media channels, talk little more about Facebook and Instagram but then go into more detail about YouTube, including setting up your own channel, and also Facebook Live.

RICK

Hi, Susan. You run a company called Online PR Success. Before we talk about that, tell me a little bit about your background. How did you get to where you are today?

SUSAN

Well, I have always tended to go into businesses that are new and emerging. Way back in early 1980s, I had an opportunity to start selling personal computers. And I was selling IBM personal computers. I became the go-to person in the financial market for banks and securities in San Diego, and as a result, was recruited by AT&T because all the big companies were doing clones at that point. I headed up their data sales organization.

When it just became a box commodity, it wasn't so interesting to me anymore. I was running marathons to decompress from all the stress. I'd go into these early morning meetings where there were donuts served. I was like, I want a good bran muffin. I completely jumped ship from the technical world, and the sales world, and opened up Little Miss Muffins, which grew to be a five-location bakery café before coffee was the big deal it is today.

Long story short, that business became very successful, and it was an emerging market once again, but this time with coffee. Then I started writing. I published a gift book back when self-publishing was not considered what it is today, it was not the normal thing to do. I had wild success with the book, and it's an odd book because it's a gift book. As part of marketing that book, I became very astute in internet marketing. What I loved was search engine optimization. That was where my brain went because of the math and just all the juice in it. Interestingly enough, social media as we know it today was used early on for search engine optimization, because if we used Facebook, which goes back to 2004 if we brought the link into a Facebook profile, Google would index it. Then Twitter came right on the heels of that. We were using Facebook and Twitter, and of course, YouTube was great. Because it wasn't just YouTube, there were a lot of video channels at that point.

We would use it just to get websites ranked. For a long time, people didn't understand what social media was, and they certainly weren't using it or if they were, maybe not using it correctly.

RICK

That's a great background. What's the name of your current company, and what does that company help people do?

SUSAN

I really have my company broken down into two sections. I think what you are probably referring to is the digital marketing company, which is Online PR Success Incorporated. That agency does everything from website design, social media, platform building, helps authors with book promotions, and also search engine optimization because really search engine optimization used to be really about the Googles, and the Yahoos of the world. Now, search engine optimization is what's called social signals, which are being sent from the social media platform. We do SEO, but we do it very differently than we did years ago because it really encompasses the topic that we are talking about here, the social media.

RICK

Video and social media.

SUSAN

Exactly. I'm really excited for us to really dive in and talk about that because there are some amazing statistics on where video is today and where it's going.

RICK

OK, Let's dive in. As someone who's been in the social media marketing landscape for over fifteen years what's your view on using video on social media?

SUSAN

It's huge. It's estimated that by 2021, that 82% of all internet traffic will be for video, which is again so intriguing to me to see this evolution. If you think that that sounds unrealistic, it really accounts for about 73% of the traffic as of a year ago. That shows how fast it's growing. It's really now about needing to consider more formats than just text-based content. Any marketing plan, video marketing on social media, it comes down to what channels and the choices that we make is going to be based on a brand's demographics. *The bottom line is that video should be utilized in social media marketing in one way or another, hands down.*

RICK

Why do you think the video aspect is growing so much as opposed to print, stories, images, that type of thing? Why are people responding to the video part of it?

SUSAN

I think it's just in the society that we are in currently. It's all quick and dirty. People don't have the time to read. When someone wants to know more about a company, certainly they might delve more and read more. We want the information immediately. I think that's why video. We are so used to consuming content. Years ago on TV, there was just a few channels and now with all the Netflix and Hulus, and Amazon Prime people are used to watching information.

RICK

It's a format that they are used to.

SUSAN

Yes. My viewpoint is that when there is a creative, high-quality video posted on let's say Facebook or YouTube, that plays to what the viewer wants, and then motivates the target market that you are in to … It bridges that gap that we are just talking about, where people want that information fast because no matter what the video purpose is, let's say it's to explain a brand, product or what a service is, or to make a company announcement, or drive traffic to an e-commerce site. That the message is just as important as the actual content itself. We have to really clarify what that message is that we want the video in two, three, five minutes is going to say to the target market. That well-produced video, which is what you are all about when that quality information is created as an evergreen source of information. Then it gets indexed, and whether we use it on YouTube, which we'll talk a little bit more about that. Because YouTube viewers look at videos differently than people who are on Facebook, or Instagram.

On Facebook and Instagram the videos are done more like billboards, because think about it when you are driving down the highway, you don't drive down a road, a certain road, just to look at a billboard. It's that billboard has been put there, because that's where the traffic already is. Whether a video is placed on YouTube, or Facebook or Instagram, we want to think about how that video, we want to think about where your demographic of your brand is going to be consuming that video, because each of the platforms view it a little differently. Does that make sense?

RICK

Yes. It makes total sense. I love the analogy of the billboard and using traffic because that's just a really visual image that basically relates to what's happening online.

SUSAN

When we typically think of videos, we think of videos on, I think primarily YouTube, and we'll talk a little bit about Vimeo as an alternative. The really growing emerging market is on Facebook and Instagram. Here are some statistics that I jotted out. As of the third quarter of 2018, Facebook had 2.27 million monthly active users. Instagram now has one billion users worldwide, which has from 800,000,000 in September 2017. To go from 800,000,000 to one billion in a year. That shows the growth that's happening on social media for video. It's overall, Facebook and Instagram have more than video, but they are certainly utilizing it. Think about these platforms as online billboards, because Facebook and Instagram users are on there. They are using these platforms regularly. Because of the way which we'll talk a little bit more about, because of the ways Facebook and Instagram uses their video, which is very different than YouTube, I believe brands need to be on all of these, and video needs to be utilized on all of them, but just keeping in mind that the landscape changes on a regular basis.

We have to always stay on top of what the current lay of the land is because we are talking about what it is today. It's going to change because that's what I think keeps me intrigued with social media is because it's ever-changing.

RICK

That's awesome. You mentioned posting two-minute, three-minute, four minute-videos. In your experience, is there any desired length or any timing of videos in general?

SUSAN

It varies greatly depending on the different social media platforms. Let's talk about YouTube for just a second. On YouTube, think about, if you have a home project, this is non-brand information, but just in general. I do this all the time. If I have something that I want to get done, and I don't know how to do it. Let's say, even if it's something online. I go to YouTube, and I look for somebody who can step me through how to do something, which might be a five-minute video, and it might be a 30-minute video.

YouTube is giving me the answer to my question in whatever length it takes. I'm going to stay engaged because I want to know. Let's say I want to build a chicken coop. It's going to be a longer video. When we are talking about brand information, and we are just wanting to keep an audience engaged with the topics that our brand would be about, those can be very short and easily consumable bite-size pieces, because it's just a piece of information, and we move on.

When we get into Instagram and Facebook, then we get into where people are more on the go. When people are watching a YouTube video, they are usually on their computer, it could be on their mobile device. It could that they are on their iPad or their smaller device because they might be watching on Netflix. They are used to consuming information in large chunks. Think about it, when I was just in Los Angeles recently, and I'm waiting in line, because of the government shutdown.

There was a really big backup in security. Everybody had their phone out. I'm looking, primarily it was Instagram and Facebook. Those things are consumed, and they are scrolling. They are scrolling from one thing to another until they get something that catches their attention. When we consume, and there are criteria on Facebook and Instagram that says it can only be certain links. In general, we are going to look at small bite-size pieces of information on Facebook and Instagram versus YouTube having the ability to be all links.

It could be a short bite-size piece. It could be a five or ten-minute piece. It could be something that's 30 or 60 minutes if it's a topic that people are interested in watching. Does that make sense?

RICK

Absolutely. You are tailoring your video to your target audience. It is important for people to realize that the distinction between YouTube, and Facebook, and Instagram, because everyone ... There is a big generalization out there, your videos have to be short, and they have to capture the attention immediately, which is true. Like you said if they are looking to a specific subject, and an answer to a question, and if that answer takes twenty minutes the person will stay engaged. What you are saying is, you will find more of those types of videos on YouTube.

SUSAN

Yes. Think about this. Somebody has a cooking product, and maybe they are going through a recipe demonstration. That recipe demonstration could take a period of time to get from the beginning of measuring out the ingredients and the process of creating it, and then showing what the final dish looks like. Someone is going to stay with that.

RICK

Absolutely. Even though we probably talked a little bit about it, but which video platform should a brand use for their videos?

SUSAN

Yes. That question to me really comes back to the YouTube, because what we'll find, and you've experienced this as well, is that the two absolute video platforms, when I'm talking about videos that happen to be on Facebook or Instagram, or LinkedIn. The two actual video platforms that are best known is YouTube and Vimeo. Here is what the main differences are between the two.

In a nutshell, Vimeo has a mostly mature community. While it's got both free and paid options, pretty much people who are using Vimeo for brand, they are using the paid version. One of the nice things about Vimeo is that if you replace a video with a new updated version of that, you don't lose any of the stats, and you don't have any ads going on in Vimeo.

However, YouTube owns the masses when it comes to video. Again, we were talking about examples earlier. People are watching TV shows, they are watching comedy, they are watching movies on YouTube. People when they want to find how to do something, they go to YouTube. It's got a really large mix of users from all walks of life. And while you can enjoy an ad-free version for a small price, most people are using the free version, which again brings in the masses.

Unfortunately, you can't replace a video with a new version and maintain analytics. To me, the fact that YouTube has the masses, when people want to watch a video they go to YouTube, that YouTube is the better choice in my mind. They've been around the longest. YouTube was actually started by PayPal's former employees, and then Google bought the site in November of 2006. The fact that Google also, keep this in mind—when you have a video that's ranking in YouTube, it shows up in Google search results—you are getting two for one. And all of those reasons are why to me YouTube is the uncontested king, is that YouTube brand, the brand is so powerful, and well known that people often aren't even aware that there is alternatives that exist.

SUSAN

I mean, Vimeo has its places, and it can be seen as the more prestigious, but if your audience is used to watching YouTube videos, and they are going to use the search box in YouTube to find videos. Then the people are already there. They are already there, and to me, that's a defining factor for brands in terms of which ones do they use.

RICK

That's great. Let's go a little bit deeper into YouTube, what are the components of having a well set up YouTube channel?

SUSAN

Well, I think that is a huge thing, Rick, because a lot of people just create the channel, and they don't understand all the different ways that you are not only promoting your video, you are promoting your brand. I want to point people to your channel because we worked with you on your channel, and it's a really good example to see how it's been set up.

Here are the points that we've followed. *Number one, we used a header for you to create and reflect your brand.* Often people will just put up something that's entirely different as an image than what is on their website, or what's being used across their other social media. You should maintain your brand with the same image.

The second thing is that there is a place in the YouTube header, where you can connect the other social media channels in your website. Thinking again of people who are following a brand on YouTube. They know that. They say, "I use Twitter. Let me go see what that brand is on Twitter." If you haven't connected those things and somebody knows that they can often find it in a header, they are going to get a little frustrated with you. And they might not go off, and even though Twitter might be something that they use as a platform on a regular basis, you've just lost that potential person that's following you there.

The third thing that I see that doesn't happen very often is that each video should have a really good description that also includes your website link, along with any promotional information that's appropriate for your brand. It should also take one of the videos that is within your channel, and be placed as a featured video, which plays automatically when anyone who is not yet subscribed to that channel if they come to the channel it plays.

That should be a short video. When we talk about short and long, that little featured video should be two, three minutes, five minutes would probably be a little long. Then the final thing, and there is lots of factors that I wanted to cover, just what the main factors are. Is that your channel should have playlists. If somebody is watching a video on a particular topic, that there is more videos that will automatically start to play within the playlist, rather than the video when it finishes going off and going to a competitor's video, because that's the way YouTube works.

It'll go often begin to show other videos. Know that video that gets uploaded in YouTube, it's not the end of the game, because it gives you the opportunity to share that video across other channels. As in, you could put the link to your YouTube video on Facebook, even though Facebook has their own video option. You can use that same link in a blog post. You can utilize it in many different ways, and each time that video is played you are gaining the potential of views, more new followers that are going to follow your channel. Again, just kind of spreads the word across all of your internet marketing, and all your online marketing.

RICK

That's good. You used my channel as an example, rickcesari.tv. Do you have any other clients that if somebody was reading this and they wanted to check out the way a YouTube channel should be set up, they can find mine, but do you have any other examples of ones you'd like to share?

SUSAN

Yes. I could. And what I want to mention too, a little trick that we did for yours is that some, depending on how old a particular YouTube channel has been around. Branded links names aren't always available. A trick that we used with yours was to register a domain name, and then do a forward over to it. Yours is RickCesari.TV, because that's a good brand name. It's easy to remember. It's short rather than the YouTube that can be very, very long.

SUSAN

With the custom URL not available for all the channels, your actual channel link is:

https://www.youtube.com/channel/UCDp5-LwBgjvDaymxS5owbJA

This is the default channel URL. Changing the "Name of the Channel" (don't confuse with the URL) is very easy, but the actual URL is not always available. Since we could not change the URL on your channel, we suggested you register the name, rickcesari.tv, and we forwarded the long YouTube link to the long URL making it easier to promote.

Another win, branding is available through YouTube, and I'm actually looking up so I can give it to you specifically here. Could be found through the search box as well, is a client of mine who you've met who is an author, Robert DeLaurentis. His YouTube channel is Flying Thru Life, which is his brand. It's playing here in the background. One of the channels we were able to customize is http://www.youtube.com/user/flyingthrulife. The branding on YouTube can vary greatly based on what's available within how old the channel is.

RICK

All right. We covered YouTube. What about videos on Facebook?

SUSAN

I think the biggest thing with video on Facebook, and we'll talk a little bit about posting YouTube videos versus Facebook native. The biggest thing is you must look at what the finished, where it's going to be posted. If you aren't considering what that's going to look like, and how Facebook handles it when it gets posted. Just not having the fore-thought or keeping that in mind could be a barrier to the success, and it could undermine all the hard work you've put into and making it because it does make a difference. The biggest thing about videos on Facebook is that before you choose, make a choice of when you create a video, is this video going to go on Facebook, or is this video going to go on YouTube? Spend some time understanding what the differences are between these two dominant social media outlets. Knowing what approach you are going to take when you make that video. *Here is the question you want to ask is, what is the goal for your brand, and do you want to gain more views on YouTube or have more visibility for your brand on Facebook? The two really are not the same.*

Two different things. Facebook will grade, they are always going to favor a video that's been put on Facebook directly versus a YouTube link that's been shared.

RICK

That's good information. When you say that that's what you mean when you are talking about posting YouTube videos on Facebook, versus posting directly to Facebook native?

SUSAN

It is, and to just go a little bit further is that keep in mind we were talking about earlier is that there is also a difference in the way the audiences on Facebook and YouTube view the two different social media sites. Think about the people standing in line waiting to go through security. It's their time in line, you've lost them because they are not watching long involved YouTube videos. They are just scrolling through their newsfeed on Facebook.

When people visit YouTube, they are going with the specific intent to watch a video of whatever link is needed. They are already primed for video watching experience, and they are likely to have the time to watch it. When people are on Facebook, they are on the go. They are using their phone. Whether it's in line at security or Starbucks, they are in between meetings, they are jumping around. All of these scenarios are not ideal for watching videos that have been created with the need for undivided attention, just the small screen itself of the mobile device, and maybe even the audio limitations, maybe somebody is at work, and they've got their phone out, but it's muted, they are just watching something.

Keeping these things in mind when you create a video, where is it going to go? Then for product videos, keeping it short. Really on Facebook, because of these limitations we are looking at, a great format is 60 seconds. Even for some people on the go that's going to be too long. If somebody is just going to spend a few seconds on a video, and not engage the whole way through, what point can the brand get across? One thing, this could be the catchy title. Maybe it's the title that will compel a potential viewer to pause and watch the video. Does that make sense?

RICK

Yes. Absolutely.

SUSAN

Knowing that Facebook grades things based on, is it native, has it been put directly on Facebook? Versus ... Facebook, they won't tell you this Rick, but those of us that work with it know that Facebook will grade a video on how much attention is it getting...How many people are viewing that video in the first 15 seconds or less?

If the video is playing 30 seconds before anybody starts to notice it or starts to watch it. Well, Facebook isn't going to be so ready to put it in the newsfeed. We'll talk a little bit about Facebook Live next. They are all about grading that. I guess the message here is *when you are posting videos on Facebook, they should be short and sweet. And in my opinion, there is really no need to use Facebook to increase YouTube video views.*

You use Facebook to send traffic to either a shop that you have set up on Facebook or the main website. We also don't want to forget that even though we are talking about social media, that the main asset is always your website. That the social media should be directing traffic to that website instead of two other social media platforms. That's just my personal opinion.

RICK

That's great. It's interesting when you are talking about Facebook videos, and the engagement early. Actually, I spend a lot of time in chapter five of the book talking about how you can capture people's attention very quickly. It sounds like that that would be very useful information when you go to make a Facebook video.

SUSAN

You got it, Rick. That was really the point I was hoping to make when we first started to have the conversation is that when videos are being created, you want to think what's the end use? Who is the target market? Is that market on Facebook? If they are, then you want to make sure that the video is created with that market in mind, because the people who are viewing videos on Facebook, view them differently than videos that are being viewed on YouTube.

RICK

... You just said the same thing that several of our other experts have said, including myself, and that's *start with the end in mind*. Again, what viewer are you trying to target, and then tailor the video to that person, and you'll have much better results.

SUSAN

Yes.

RICK

Next question, what makes Facebook Live so engaging to Facebook users?

SUSAN

Well, it's the live thing that makes it special. I mean, think about how many reality TV shows there are. And people watch them, even though a lot of them are probably very much staged, but the idea is that it's done in real time, and without an editor with Facebook Live. It feels very intimate and connective. *Some recent reports also show that viewers of Facebook Live videos comment ten times more than they do on videos that aren't live because they are engaging with the person in a real- time conversation.*

I watch a lot of Facebook Live, and you see that all the time. People are liking, and you see the little thumbs up coming across the screen, or they are loving, and you see the little hearts coming up. The person who is doing the Facebook Live, they are watching the comments, and they are saying, "Hi students. So nice to see you here." It's just a very, very different kind of way of using video, and while you might not think it's good for brands, it's excellent for brands.

RICK

That's great. The word I think with live video is there is an authenticity to it, and I think people respond to that. That it isn't necessarily advertising that they ... Like you said, it's based on I think viewing habits of people watching reality television and responding to something that they are used to seeing, and also the believability of it, because it isn't staged. I agree one-hundred percent, and I'm not surprised to hear you say that Facebook Live works really well.

SUSAN

And one of the other things that I do want to make a point is that Facebook Live is very different than a pre-produced video because Facebook Live could be ten minutes, but it could also be 90 minutes long. People are doing actual course delivery information with Facebook Live. I think the average is closer to maybe fifteen to thirty minutes. You'll see Facebook Lives hugely vary in length, dependent upon the audience and the content that's being delivered.

RICK

Of course, Facebook, one of the beauties of it, it allows you to target your audience a lot more specifically maybe than other platforms.

SUSAN

Very much so. Even I'm sure you had your phone on the newsfeed portion of Facebook, and all of a sudden across the top of your screen it says Susan Gilbert is live. It's like a flashing neon light. You go, "I didn't know she was live. I'm going to go watch her right now."

RICK

That's awesome.

SUSAN

Facebook really wants people to do more of these lives, and they are rewarding them by making them center stage in the newsfeed.

RICK

So, is Facebook Live important for brands?

SUSAN

Very much so, because it's so easy to think, "It's just a person, it's a coach. It's an individual who is an author." All of those things is true, but one of the really big trends, and again we have to follow the new things that are happening all the time on social media, is that it's really ... You can build brand awareness now using brands. Here are some of the points. We are talking about how you can easily reach fans much faster, because of the targeting, because it's showing up as a neon light.

You can get a healthy dose of brand awareness. Any brand can get that by increasing the use of live video. You might be thinking, well, what would a brand share in a live video if it's not a personal coaching kind of situation? Here are some ideas. A business or a brand might want to share some company milestones. Talk about what's happening in the company, or they want to announce a new product that's coming. Either it's coming down the pike, stay tuned for it.

Apple is excellent for doing that kind of thing. They are always teasing people about what the new product is that's coming out. You could definitely do a teasing with the Facebook Live, and you could also do the announcement itself like it's here. What that does is it gives the brand instant feedback from the community that they serve, and it makes it easier to get the word out about a new product, or news about the company if people are tuned in, and aware that the brand is using Facebook Live.

Another thing, even though we talked about using YouTube as an instructional format, Facebook Live could also be teaching you how to do something. It could be an easy task, instructionally a particular task that you already know very well. We were talking about the recipe situation. It could be a product demonstration because there is no limitation on a Facebook Live.

If you have a company spokesperson, they can be the person that becomes very visible with Facebook Live. You can begin to host live Q&A sessions. That has been found to be a real winner. What it also becomes very interesting is when this authoritative figure begins answering questions within the video, because it's real time, and viewers know that it's real time.

If it's something that they are interested in, they are not going to say, "I'll go watch that video later on the brand's page." They might do that because they can watch it. If they see it's available, they'll go, "I want to go watch it live, because I have a question. I can ask that person that question, I might get an answer right away, right here on the spot." Which I think is incredible.

RICK

That is incredible. The instant interaction. I always like to tie into what's current today and see if we can learn anything with something that's been successful in the past. When you mentioned live product demonstrations, the best model for that is to look at QVC or Home Shopping Network and see how they do their live presentations, and how they create that video, *because they've spent years and years and years mastering the techniques of what are going to get people to respond to the product demos. You could take that information, and then use it on a different delivery platform, which would be Facebook Live.*

SUSAN

Absolutely and think about the power. QVC, and these models that you are bringing up which work take that model and make it live, so the person can actually communicate with the person delivering it. That's very, very powerful. Another part of this, because if you think about QVC, a lot of times it's two people presenting.

You can do that with Facebook Live also. You don't have to live stream by yourself. You might want to interview someone in your industry, which helps position your particular brand as the industry leader or expert, but it's cross-promoting, so that this person that you are interviewing, you are getting their audience as well as your own audience and vice versa. It's a win-win situation where you are helping both brands receive a larger viewing.

RICK

That's great information.

SUSAN

Here is the little caveat. In those situations where you are doing the interview right now, and it could change. Right now, Facebook Live you can't do it from within their platform. There is a special app called BeLive. When you use BeLive, you'll get a unique link that you send to your guests. Then the guests can click on that link, connect their camera, and immediately jump into the stream with you. You just need one extra step when you are bringing that second person in.

RICK

That's great information. Thanks for sharing that. Let's talk about Instagram a little bit. Instagram seems to have become a leader in social media. You mentioned it a little bit earlier about how fast it's growing. What can you tell us about best practices using video on Instagram?

SUSAN

Well, and this is something ... Instagram is gaining market share as I mentioned earlier. When I say market share, I mean usage. People that are using it, it has grown so much in the last couple of years. I mean, it's gone from a startup darling to of course we know that Facebook purchased them. It's really become quite a powerhouse.

When it first started, some people were on Instagram, and some people weren't. We would always the two platforms that you must be on is Facebook and Twitter, and if you are utilizing video, you need to be on YouTube. Well, now Instagram is becoming part of the bigger players, and we can definitely say that the big four should be in place.

The interesting thing with Instagram is that they are now, in addition to the visual, because that's always been the big thing, it's a visual platform. Now video is being added. There is a couple of different ways ... There is Instagram stories, and there is Instagram Live. Here are some basic differences, while Instagram stories gives you the option of publishing prerecorded videos, there aren't any retakes on Instagram Live.

You want to think about the prerecorded version, which would be the story, versus the Instagram Live, which is similar to Facebook Live. As an example, Facebook stories could be a way that a user would share pictures that maybe the user doesn't want to remain on the profile indefinitely. The stories are shared with followers at the top of the regular feed, but you want to keep in mind that these are deleted automatically after twenty-four hours. It's very similar to Snapchat.

The stories are, people know that they have to be engaged with it, because if they don't watch the story now, or soon it's going to go away. Facebook Live gets newsfeed priority. Like we talked about with Facebook, how it shows up. The same is true with Instagram, and so if you want to have a way to stay in top of mind with your fans, then you want to use Instagram Live.

With Instagram Live there is that increased engagement. Bringing it back to a brand, a company can respond immediately, either to client issues, to answer questions, to host valuable discussions with their followers, and forming the real-time connections, which you mentioned earlier with Facebook that are authentic. All of these are more important when you consider the power of the platform. Instagram demographics are changing, because the percentage right now is that 32% of teenagers consider Instagram to be the most crucial social media network. If your brand is aimed at that demographic, then, of course it's a match. You want to use this social media platform. However, that's changing. Just like Instagram wasn't very well used a few years ago, and now it's become the darling.

Watch for that demographic to change. I see a lot of weight loss exercising happening on Instagram. That's not only a teenager situation. Just keep in mind that the stories are going to disappear, but you have editing capability. Instagram Live is an excellent way for brands to demonstrate there, everything from individuality to inspirational content, all the things that's going to bring a company's personality to life.

I think that might be a keyword is *that Instagram has a lot of personality to it.* They want to bring that, where I think *Facebook is more community oriented. Instagram is more personality oriented.*

RICK

That's a good way of looking at it. What are some other social media sites that utilize video?

SUSAN

Well, we might not have thought about this one, because it is relatively new. I think it's only been about a year now. I think that LinkedIn should not be forgotten. I don't think it's one of the big four for video, but who knows a year from now, or six months from now where things are going? Because while most people might not think about LinkedIn videos for platform building. We definitely think about LinkedIn as kind of like a storytelling, talking about the story behind your business venture or giving a quick explanation about how you get started, how you got started in your business.

Some ideas for brands might be a LinkedIn video to promote a product. It could be a post on a how-to a demonstration, very similar to what we are talking about with the other platforms. They can maybe answer some frequently asked questions, or again to share some upcoming launch details, whatever might be in the pipeline for your product or service offering and allowing people to watch that video and get excited about it.

Again, just like Facebook, and Instagram, and YouTube all have their flavor of who's on that platform, you want to keep that in mind with LinkedIn, so that it's very professionally done, it's not going to be a fun party video. It's going to be something that's much more business venture oriented. I think whether it's the spokesperson for a company, and it's on the company profile, or whether it's the CEO, or the chief marketing officer of a company. I think videos on LinkedIn is something that's really going to be on the move, LinkedIn is going to reward people who are doing video, because they've seen the handwriting on the wall. They see what's happening across the other social media channels, and they want to keep up.

RICK

The statistics that you mentioned before about how much video is being consumed.

SUSAN

Exactly. They are not going to stay with that content marketing model. Even though that still exists for LinkedIn, and it has its place, I think we are going to start seeing a lot more of the videos.

RICK

You mentioned the big four. When it comes to video, right now in the present moment, what are the big four platforms?

SUSAN

Well, I think YouTube is number one because that's what people think of. We are going to find a video, we'll talk a little bit more when I get you the channel, but one of your clients Puriya, we worked on their channel. They want to rank for some of the same that people are searching for when they want to find a solution for psoriasis, a solution for eczema. People search, they use it kind of like an encyclopedia. They are searching for a solution on YouTube. To me, that's number one. Even if Vimeo exists, Vimeo is not used as an encyclopedia like YouTube is. The next one I think is Facebook. Just because it does have at this point a wider viewership and usage. I think a lot of people in their thirties, forties, fifties, sixties, use Facebook. Instagram still has that a little bit younger market share. I definitely would do Facebook. Twitter is not necessarily considered a video channel, and so I didn't talk about it here. Twitter, I think, has to be a platform that we use just for social media, not necessarily for video, even though you can post videos there. The fourth one, up and coming, keep your eye on it. If your demographics match, do it now, is Instagram.

RICK

Got it. This has been great so far Susan. If somebody wanted to contact you to hire your company, where can they find you or what's the best way for them to reach out to you?

SUSAN

Well, they could find me just about anywhere on social media by putting my name in, Susan Gilbert. A direct email would be susan@onlineprsuccess.com. Thank you for asking Rick.

RICK

One last question I always end up every interview, is there anything that I didn't ask you about that you want to share that you think is pertinent? This is a chapter in a book about creating video, video persuasion, we covered a lot of territory. Is there anything I left out that you wanted to just maybe add in that I didn't ask you about?

SUSAN

Well, one of the things we didn't talk about that I know you do extremely well is well-produced testimonial videos. One thing I would bring up is that while I've been to events, you probably have been to, where somebody is there with a videographer, and they'll say, "Can I get a video of you leaving the event right now and tell us why you like this event so much?" I think those have a place when they show up on websites because it's real time.

The polished videos—I know you have covered this in your book already—doesn't necessarily need four cameras and a big crew. Knowing the components of what a short video testimonial should include really has a very strong place in video content. I know you are covering that in other chapters. We didn't necessarily cover it here for social media. We do want to keep in mind that those testimonial style videos can be used on social media. We are using them right now on the Puriya website, https://www.puriya.com/ and YouTube Channel, https://www.youtube.com/watch?v=bBYb6e0ZfFg&t=19s.

There is a variety of different ways. Those short testimonial videos for a product can be utilized across social media and will do any brand very well to do so.

RICK

Well, that's awesome. This has been very informative. I know that the readers are going to really learn a lot from this information. I just wanted to thank you for taking the time today.

SUSAN

Thank you, Rick, for inviting me. As you can tell, I'm very passionate about the topic. I'm passionate about people understanding this is right for everybody. Everybody should be, every brand should have a good social media presence. Doing it correctly makes all the difference as to whether it's successful or not.

RICK

I agree. Thank you again.

CHAPTER NINE SUMMARY

- If you aren't already, start using video in your social media.
- Right now, video ads on Facebook and Instagram are getting the highest ROI.
- Content is more important than production value. You do not need to spend a lot of money producing slick videos for them to be engaging.
- Know your target audience, then create your video content to appeal to that audience.
- People will engage at a ten-times higher rate with Facebook Live videos, than a pre-produced segment.

CHAPTER TEN
Using Video Persuasion for Social Good

"Thaw with her gentle persuasion is more powerful than Thor with his hammer. The one melts, the other breaks into pieces."
—Henry David Thoreau

HARNESSING TECHNOLOGY

"How we manage and harness technology for the good of mankind is the key issue of our time."—Henry Timms, Executive Director, 92Y

"There's no doubt that technology empowers everyone – are we going to use it for positivity and change, or to close ourselves off?" —Pete Cashmore, Founder & CEO, Mashable

Up to now, this book has been about how you can harness the power of video to get your viewers to take the specific action you want. Hopefully, those actions will help you build your brand awareness, generate more sales, and increase business growth. But what happens if you harness this video knowledge and use it for social good? What is our greater responsibility—beyond the bottom line?

A CALL TO ACTION OF A DIFFERENT SORT

In 2011, I had my first open heart surgery, something I never would've imagined could happen to me, especially after being diligent about diet and exercise. I had incentive to be cautious after my father died young of a heart attack. He was only 46 years old. From what we know today, my dad's heart disease was preventable, caused primarily by poor lifestyle choices. He smoked two packs of Camel cigarettes a day, and he ate red meat regularly. From what my mom told us, he ignored common warning signs, like high cholesterol and high blood pressure.

My dad's early death, led to my passion for good health, including regular check-ups, as well as healthy lifestyle choices. One of the offshoots of my healthy eating habits led me to start drinking freshly extracted juices back in the late 80s. I turned that into Trillium Health Products and The Juiceman juice business, which launched the fresh juice revolution in this country in the early 90s. I continued to juice and stay active, which made an unexpected call from my doctor following a routine health check quite a shock. He said he'd found an enlargement on my Aorta artery and that he wanted me back for further tests. The tests revealed an aneurysm 6.5mm wide on my ascending aorta. They call this condition the "widow-maker" because there are seldom apparent symptoms. Had I not been vigilant about getting regular check-ups, it probably would have killed me.

I had surgery shortly after the discovery. The operation went well, and I walked away with 3" of tubing to replace my aorta where it met my heart and a new aortic heart valve. Everything was great until 2015. I was on a golf course in 90-degree heat, when I began shivering violently. This continued for the rest of the day and through the night. I knew something was wrong, but what? I went back to my doctor and she immediately started me on round-the-clock intravenous antibiotics. My replacement heart valve had become infected and had a colony of bacteria growing on it. I was admitted to the hospital, where my condition deteriorated. At one point my fever hit 105 degrees, with uncontrollable shaking from the associated chills.

The surgeons were at an impasse. While there was some urgency to get in there and clean up the mess, there was also concern about my persistent fever. Three days into the waiting game another complication emerged. I had a stroke! A tiny piece of the bacteria had broken off my replacement valve and traveled through my blood stream, lodging itself in a vessel in my brain. My family was notified, and a priest was called to my room for final rights. Things weren't looking so good to say the least! A 12-hour, Hail Mary surgery cleaned up the infection and a new mechanical valve replaced the porcine valve. I've never felt better. To say I was grateful to be alive and have a second chance at life would be a gross understatement.

A NEW KIND OF PERSUASION

Health crisis averted, I had some serious decisions to make. For thirty-seven years I'd been honing my craft, hustling to keep pace with evolving technology; anticipating trends in DM. It had been an exhilarating ride. It was also all-consuming. During my second recovery from open heart surgery, I began to seriously re-think my approach to life—one with greater balance, where work no longer singularly defined me. As I was recovering, I was also experiencing an overwhelming sense of gratitude towards my family and friends, of course, but also for the medical team that saved me. I wanted to do something to demonstrate my deep sense of respect for their care and remarkable achievements. This is where it occurred to me that I was in a unique position to give back using the skill set I'd developed over nearly four decades.

After I recovered, I started volunteering for the American Heart Association (AHA) in Seattle creating videos that draw more donors and helping to spread the word about the importance of regular check-ups and other key steps people can take to prevent heart disease. These videos are helping them reach their goals, which in turn is helping to save lives. The experience of making a difference in such a profound way inspired me to seek out other opportunities where video persuasion could be used for social good.

THINKING MORE GLOBALLY

My work for the AHA continues to be satisfying on a number of levels. It has been a rewarding way to engage with my community and a way to give back without tracking profits and losses. It also gave me an entrée into the world of philanthropy coming from a place in my heart (truly!) where I wanted to do more.

I recently got connected with a California-based organization that uses video to educate people in some of the world's poorest areas. The company, called OMPT (One Mobile Projector per Trainer), is led by Matt York, founder and editor of *Videomaker* magazine, who himself realized how his unique skillset as a video maker could be used for social good. Because Matt and I have similar training and experience with video, his work at OMPT really resonated for me. It has been a "way in" for me to do deeper and more meaningful work on a much broader scale, with video persuasion as the common link—from practical skill application to social good.

I interviewed Matt by phone for this chapter so readers could learn more about OMPT from his perspective; how Matt himself transitioned from using video for profit-centered work to now, through OMPT, using video to educate the world's "bottom billion" about making healthier choices.

INTERVIEW WITH MATT YORK, FOUNDER, OMPT.ORG

RICK

Hi Matt, can you tell me more about how you started using video for social good?

MATT

Absolutely, Rick. I'd be happy to. So the original inspiration actually was leveraging affordable video technology for social good, even though the first 20 years of my career was in a for-profit venture I started called Videomaker Magazine. The underpinning, though, was always this motivation to figure out how, as video gear became more affordable and easier to use, can mankind benefit? That's always been my mantra.

RICK

That's awesome. Let's start off just talking a little bit about your background with *Videomaker* Magazine, and how you got involved in video in the first place.

When I was in high school, 1973 maybe, I saw one of my fellow classmates had made a Super 8 film. I was just absolutely captivated by the fact that a lay person, a student, a kid could make moving images, either TV, or movies, or film, whatever you call it. It was a staggering idea to me, so I got really captivated and I started making films in high school. It was very expensive, like a dollar a minute, very tedious to edit, very difficult to show. You had to have an eight-millimeter projector, so you had to pull down the window shades. It was still a bit revolutionary, but it was still quite limited. You couldn't send the media to somebody, expect them to absorb the media, or the message, or watch the audio-visual presentation.

In college, at Rutgers in 1975, I learned that something called Betamax was percolating across the marketplace. I thought, wow, this is really gonna change everything. For someone to be able to watch that in their house, that really would be revolutionary, and I had no idea there would ever be something called YouTube that would live in my pocket. We live in a different era now.

All of that excitement that there was really a video revolution about to occur, I was just captivated. Okay, well what do I do about this? I didn't have a degree in business, my undergraduate degree was in film and video, so a newsletter seemed quite approachable, but in researching all the things that would require a successful newsletter, led me to believe that a magazine, would just be a little different. It's more expensive paper, four color ink, more expensive preparation, but it would be more attractive to advertisers.

We're here in a small town in Northern California. It was a big leap, to go from a small-town resident to seeing myself as a future magazine publisher, incredibly struggling first few years where we thought we were gonna go out of business multiple times, but we made it.

It was a very, very difficult classic start-up where you are under-capitalized, and overworked, but slowly we kind of eked our way into a break-even where we had incredibly tiny staff. I was probably making sub-welfare wages for a few years. By 1990, everything changed, we were experiencing explosive growth, along with the explosive growth of the camcorder sector in the consumer electronics industry. I was always driven by what would happen if there was this democratization of television. That was actually our mission statement for a long time, that we wanted to enrich and democratize television, back when there were four broadcast networks, and almost no cable TV. There's a long answer for your question.

RICK

I love the history. Not very many people have that entire perspective, which is great. I want to just go back to the name of the magazine you started, it's called Videomaker?

MATT

Yeah, it's still is an amazing work. Here we are in December of 2018, and we still are printing a paper magazine. Isn't that incredible? ... We're heading into our 32nd year.

RICK

I didn't know you were still publishing the magazine. That's amazing.

MATT

Yeah, more than half the revenue comes from social media, from email lists, from the website, but there's still sufficient demand for the paper magazine.

RICK

At what point did you, start to use video to do social good, when did you actually start acting on that idea or philosophy?

MATT

Great question. At the beginning, just the fact that we were enlightening people to make video, it was sufficient, my worldview was in America, I didn't travel that much, so I felt like I was doing my duty. I was achieving my calling, my vocation to enrich and democratize television by getting more Americans to participate in making video.

As the company grew, I realized that we were reaching into Europe, I hadn't been there, but was happy that we were inspiring westerners and people in the most developed world, the first world we used to call it, to make more video and to kind of dilute the power that was centralized in the entertainment industry in New York and in Hollywood, where just a few hundred people kind of dictated the opinions and the values that the rest of the world embraced. We launched our website in 1994.

RICK

Wow, you were early.

MATT

Very, very early, but there was no real interest from advertisers for many years. We had great metrics and great traffic, but it wasn't something that was important to ad agencies and Madison Avenue, or to Sony, or Canon, or Panasonic. Around 2000, there was this explosion of interest., My company went from stumbling along for years, then this rocket to stardom, where we kept growing dramatically, and had like 42 people at one point. I think we were like 5 million in revenues, but then we began to take a hit from the internet advertising category. That hit occurred on every metric, every month for 10 years, 120 months in a row. Newsstand sales, subscriptions, renewals, advertising sale, every single metric was heading south monthly. It was slow, it was kind of like water torture, where you drip, drip, drip on your head.

That really got me thinking about how do I resolve this? There wasn't a clear exit. I have an acute knowledge of video technology, and kind of where it's going, I knew a lot about hardware. I knew a lot of key personnel inside the imaging industry. I've been watching people learn how to make video for many years by that point, 15-20 years, so we began teaching people to make video, not just with the paper magazine, but with the website, and with VHS tapes. We had how-to videos about making video on VHS tapes, and ultimately you and I talked about the fact that we were kind of delivering that content by buying infomercial time on the Discovery Channel.

In any event, I had been watching people learn how to make video. I knew I wanted to help the entire world, so began doing some intentional travel to the least developed countries. We used to call it the third world. It was very difficult. It was not an easy path. Ultimately, what we did is we actually had conducted events at

Videomaker. We did four-day workshops in our headquarters in Chico, California, outside of the Bay area. I just took the four-day workshop from Videomaker, which we had done 100 times, I guess, by this time, and I just dramatically simplified it, and began offering it to staff members of charities around the world, like Save the Children, or Mercy Corps, or Catholic Relief Services. These organizations that their mission was to increase the quality of life, reduce suffering for the marginalized people in the world. It's just, let's empower those charity staff members to make videos that would teach people how to use latrines, or to read, or to spray soap on their tomato plants, that would kill the aphids.

Then we needed to give them the equipment to both create the video, and to share the video, and then there was this emerging market of cordless video projectors. Then we needed to recharge all of these devices, 'cause it was far off the grid. We came up with these three kits, the video making kit, the video sharing kit, which is primarily a cordless projector and speaker, and the recharging kit. I began to market it, even though we established a 501c3 non-profit. I began to market it using my business acumen, where we would gather email addresses from decision-makers at these NGO's (Non-Government Organizations) around the world and email them. Schedule a Skype call and articulate the value proposition.

Eventually, we began to have enough customers who would sign an agreement that we had a small enterprise, and we had three paid employees. My wife and myself were volunteers, but also donors. That's kind of how I transitioned from a classic for-profit publishing company, or training company, to a charity.

RICK

That's a great story. Tell me what OMPT.org ... the organization does?

MATT

So OMPT, what it basically does, is this four-day training, and provides the hardware to these charities and also ministries of government around the world. Sometimes we work directly with the government, the Ministry of Health in Afghanistan, the Ministry of Health at the country of Gambia. We train and equip them, that's really it in a nutshell.

RICK

Where did the name, OMPT come from?

MATT

When the company was founded, we incorporated as Polder, Inc. Polder is a Dutch word and we know from observing Holland, that they have a lot of low-lying sea water. They built a dyke around it. They put a windmill in the middle of it to pump the water out, and what's left is called reclaimed land in English, but in the Dutch language, it's Polder. We were reclaiming this one billion people, the bottom billion, people making less than a dollar a day back in 2008. There was a billion people, a sixth of the planet living on less than a dollar a day, so we were gonna reclaim them for humanity. But we had to have a practical initiative, so ... We needed a name for the initiative, and at the time in this category, the buzz was all about this professor at MIT, Nickolas Negroponte, and his One

Laptop Per Child, OLPC. He had this vision for $100 laptop that was going to revolutionize the international development sector...

RICK

Yes, they did a "60 Minutes" story about him.

MATT

Yeah, he was all the rage and he was the keynote speaker at the Consumer Electronic Show, and he came up with OLPC, four-letter acronym, One Laptop Per Child. We said, "Okay, one", and at the time it was Media Player Per Teacher, OMPT, One Media Player Per Teacher.

RICK

I get it now.

MATT

We prefer to call them cordless projectors, battery-powered projectors. Initially it was One Media Player Per Teacher, OMPT. About six years after the founding of the organization, we renamed our acronym. One Mobile Projector Per Trainer. We changed teacher to trainer, and media player to mobile projector, and we kept the same acronym. That's a long back story on the name of the organization.

RICK

Please give people an example of one of the things that OMPT does. I know on your website, there's a video about when you went to Africa to help educate about Ebola, as an example.

MATT

That's probably the most pungent example on multiple levels. Everybody can relate to the acute anxiety we had as a society at the time. My organization was still kind of embryonic, so I was making statements about, and proclamations to myself and my friends and family, and to the marketplace about what I intended to do, but when Ebola arrived, the rubber had to meet the road. I had to be willing to go there. The Center for Disease Control invited us to ground zero, almost. We went to Guinea. It was an enormous transaction. We had hundreds of kits, $100,000 worth of equipment. I got into my car with like 12 suitcases, went to the airport and ushered 12 suitcases through customs in Guinea. You can imagine when they were x-raying those suitcases, how that alerted them to the fact that this wasn't just a tourist.

We're usually met at the airport by our colleagues who usher us through customs, but I had to go to this place where people were dying, and people who were helping were dying faster than the residents. In the health sector, anyone in medicine, their contraction rate and death rate was off the charts, compared to a classic resident in West Africa. It was quite intimidating to go, but I went, and I taught 45 different local NGOs how to make video, and how to use battery-powered projectors to deliver the messages, the videos, to hard-to-reach places where no one was gonna go, because there was no electricity there, and it was very remote and distant, places that are off the grid.

There were some very specific behaviors in the Ebola crisis that needed to change, but the problem was that there were people with light colored skin, telling the locals, the dark colored skin people, that they needed to change their behavior, so it didn't go over that well. They lacked credibility. So, we put local experts in front of the camera to articulate what had happened when they first heard about the new behavior, decided not to adopt it, suffered a serious consequence, like a death of a child, and now after watching the video, they've adopted the behavior, and their babies are healthy.

That Ebola crisis really galvanized what we could do as a biggest project ever in terms of budget, in terms of risk, in terms of number of trainees, and it was a great example of we go to places that others don't want to go, so I'm kind of borrowing that moniker from Doctors Without Borders. We go to places no one wants to go, because where there's a deep need, there's usually high risk.

If we go to Bangladesh, or if we go to Darfur, Sudan, there are great risk, immense headaches, massive suffering on an enormous scale where the world has kind of forgotten about that part of the earth. We go there, and we help change behaviors. Ultimately, we're behavior change consultants.

RICK

How easy or difficult is it to train the local people to create these videos?

MATT

There's already an infrastructure in place, and has been actually for decades now, where experts go into the field, and they use their spoken voice to convince people to adopt a new behavior, Sometimes, they bring with them a flip chart, where they'll have a bigger flip and they'll illustrate the words that are coming out of their mouth. There's a number of institutions that do this. There are health advisors, so we just equip them with a battery powered projector. Instead of relying only on the spoken word, or a few still images that are on a chart, it's projected on a large screen. In ideal circumstances, there's a white wall with a 10-foot wide video image on it, coming from a battery-powered projector, a cordless projector, and every single nuance about the behavior and the consequences of the behavior is vividly illustrated.

Such as, wash your hands to avoid intestinal diseases. It's 'wash your hands with this much lather at least, for 45 seconds. This is what it looks like. When you do that, the bacteria living under your fingernails is more likely to be killed.' We show a close-up, a macro of the fingernail, and we can scrape the debris out from underneath it, and we never did this yet, but you could put it under a microscope and show that there's living things under your fingernails that are moving on to the people who you're serving food to. We vividly illustrate the consequences of bad behavior, and we model good behavior.

We show aphids eating a tomato plant, and we show when you spray soapy water, liquid water, the aphid dies within 20 minutes, 'cause it's suffocating. We make these incredibly specific videos for a very unique set of people, in a very unique place trying to achieve a very specific purpose. People, place, purpose. It was, at one point, all citizens in west Africa that were concerned about Ebola. It could be mothers in the Gambia, who want to be sure their children don't contract malaria. Purpose is keeping the kids healthy.

We had a vividly illustrated, what is the lifecycle of a mosquito and the malaria life form, and why this abstract behavior is really important to adopt. We would go into a hospital, and we'd show all of these mothers what their sick babies and close to death. It was really morbid and sad, but it's really a great way to motivate people to adopt a behavior.

RICK

You're using video, really for almost its highest and best use. It's just such a powerful communication tool….

MATT

A few things we learned, is that when these extension agents classically attempt to gather a crowd, they're kind of like carnival barkers. They just get to the location, and then they yell aloud. I'm hearing now the town crier trying to gather a crowd. When they began using video for this, a crowd gathered faster, a larger crowd gathered, and the mix of female to male changed to have a greater percentage of males. Something as simple as simply introducing the device changed the way in which a crowd is gathered, and then just the depth of understanding of what it is that's trying to be taught. Again, it's deeply illustrated, and accompanied with these testimonials of people who had a before and after story.

It's a fantastic application of video in the world, where we use it to inspire people to do things that save lives, or decrease suffering, so an incredibly wonderful altruistic pursuit. It's really heartwarming to be called to this kind of work.

RICK

That's really awesome. What type of goals do you have for OMPT moving forward?

MATT

We want to embrace smart projectors, so the upcoming generation of projectors will be android based. Smart enough to run an app, so that the app will keep track of where the projector has been, by

GPS, what videos were played, where they were paused for discussion, rewound and played it again, so lots of feedback to headquarters of Mercy Corps or Oxfam or Classic Partners. They can gather data about how to make the next video even more explicit, or understandable.

We have a program called Videomakers Without Borders. That's where a North American, or a European in a developed world raises some money, so they can buy plane tickets and pay for their own housing and meals. Maybe if they can raise even more, they can finance some kits. They will join us to help us train on the four-day workshop, and then after the workshop, they will continue to partner with the trainees, or the alumni from the Video Educational Workshop, the VEW and they will provide something called capacity development. They enroll in our Capacity Development Program where they become sufficiently skilled in making extremely simple videos.

In a classic workshop, where we're training maybe 30 people, the vast majority of them are under 30 years old. They're well educated, got a college degree. One of the few people in the country that have graduated, got a good job. Most of them have smart phones. All smart phones have cameras. Many of them have already shot video, but never really edited it, so in the workshop, you could see the people who either have done a bit of editing on their phone, or people who maybe never shot video before, that's really amazing, never had a smart phone. They're just blossoming and flourishing in this environment of learning how to make videos.

RICK

If somebody is reading this interview in the book, and they want to help. What's the best thing that they can do to either get involved, or help out? What are your needs from people that would respond to this message?

MATT

Go to the website, OMPT.org. Get a keener understanding of what we're about, and you could enroll in Videomakers Without Borders if you want some adventure travel. Again, we go to places that are like half-star hotels, the thread count is like 40. Sometimes we eat the same meal for breakfast, lunch, and dinner. In the Gambia, I had sardine salad served from a common bowl, and you eat with your hands. It's quite an adventure travel.

They can make a recurring donation on the website, so each month, they could have their checking account docked, or their credit card, for a recurring donation. Introducing us to people they may know in the international development community, to popularize our, what's called an intervention, they can volunteer, they can join the board of directors, or the advisory board. I'm glad to have you on our board Rick.

Making donations is very important, maybe like 80% of our income comes from contracts with Oxfam, or Catholic Relief Services, or Mercy Corps, or Care, but we always want to try to underwrite our own projects with very small in-country locally created enterprises that want to embrace this. Yeah, those are the ways in which somebody who is reading this could engage.

RICK

One last question, you talked a lot about countries in Africa. Where else do you go and do work?

MATT

When you register a non-profit, the IRS sort of requires you to say where you're gonna operate. We chose the 70 poorest countries in the world where the bottom billion are most likely to live, so there is an awful lot of them in Africa, but we've done work in Central America. We've done five or six projects in Central America, Southeast Asia. We did a project in Oceania, and Papua New Guinea, so we have no limit to Africa, just that it's a … We actually did a project in Macedonia, which is surprising, but as their economy's emerging, they needed some very specific videos delivered to obscure locations, so any of those 70 poorest countries in the world is where we operate.

RICK

Matt, I wanted to thank you for taking your time to share your history with us. I'm looking forward to working with you and wish you luck in everything you do in the future.

CONCLUSION

Matt's passion and conviction are an inspiration to me, not only because of the impact OMPT is having across the globe, but because of his fearlessness in pursuing something because it's the right thing to do.

For more than three decades, "work" for me was defined by the personal and financial goals of my clients. These kinds of transactional relationship benefitted my clients by helping them reach strategic business objectives. A client-centered focus also benefitted me directly, of course, through financial rewards and from the continuous thrill that comes from the challenge of anticipating the next product phenomenon.

While I have always been selective about the clients I take on, typically with some health and wellness or environmentally-sustainable attribute as a defining feature, I'd never pursued a job expressly for social good. In fact, it hadn't really occurred to me that my years of training and expertise in the field of DM and video marketing put me in an ideal position to positively impact social change.

In my case, it took a heart attack to persuade me to think differently about how I thought about work. It made me reprioritize my values in a way that is further enhancing my video-making skills, while also nurturing my soul. As you expand your own portfolios, I encourage you to think more globally about what you can achieve beyond the board room—about how your unique skill set can potentially improve the quality of life for others.

CHAPTER ELEVEN
Conclusion

"I think the power of persuasion would be the greatest superpower of all time."
—Jenny Mollen

WHY A BOOK ABOUT VIDEO PERSUASION?

I wrote this book to accomplish three things. The first was to let readers know that we are living in a video first society. Video is everywhere and is continuing to grow. It is already the primary means that we receive most of our information and if you are not currently using video, you need to start. Knowing that, I also wanted to help you understand just how powerful video can be as a marketing tool. With the information about video, that I shared in this book you can, increase your sales, grow your business, create more customers and/or clients, and build your product, company, or personal brand. I've shown you ways you can effectively use video for your content marketing, Facebook and Instagram advertising, how to use it on websites, video blogs, social media channels, e-commerce, TV advertising, Amazon, and more.

The second reason I wrote this book was to introduce you to the concept of Video Persuasion. I spent a little bit of time talking about ways you can create video and shared some good information and contacts to help in that area. But my primary focus is on the content of the video you are producing. *Good content will always surpass good production quality in getting your viewers to take the actions you want.* I've identified the elements that you can put into a video and techniques you can use to get people to take the action you desire. I've been using video to sell products and services for over thirty years, and I gathered the most important lessons I learned in that time and shared them with you in this book.

My third reason for writing this book was to give you a look from many different sources, what is working in the market place today when it comes to video marketing. I'm a big believer *in learning from other people's experience* and by interviewing experts in many different areas. I was able to share great information with you, and I also learned many new things myself. These expert interviews were my favorite part of doing this book.

PUTTING IT ALL TOGETHER

I would like to share with you a story about a company and a product that is using every aspect of video, for content, advertising, and live-streaming just about better than anyone else in the market-place today. As you read this next section look for all the different ways this company, Peloton, is leveraging the power of video. *I added italics for emphasis.*

About four months ago I bought my wife a Peloton® bike. She loves to work out and is very disciplined about it, rarely missing a day. Earlier in her life, she had been a spinning instructor, and so when she saw the *television ad,* she put it on her wish list. She had a birthday coming up, and so it was a no brainer for me on what to get her.

On the other hand, my exercise history could be labeled erratic at best, and so I didn't really plan on using the bike very much. We have various pieces of exercise equipment in our home, and I get bored easily with the repetitive nature of the workouts. I would do them for a little while then find that I just drifted away and stopped. That didn't happen with this particular stationary bike. I found myself looking forward to the workouts each day, and I am still going strong after six months.

I'm a curious marketer at heart, and so the more I got into exercising, the more I admired what the company has been able to accomplish through *video marketing*, especially since I had looked at this very same category many years ago.

BACKSTORY

In the early 2000s spinning was just starting to become popular in the United States. Spinning was created by a South African, a former special forces military man turned cyclist named Johnny G. He had just opened a new studio in Los Angeles. At the time I was still doing a lot of video production and video marketing projects for the company that bought my Juicer business, Salton Inc. They were always on the lookout for new products they could promote through a Direct Response TV/Retail model. Their CMO at the time, Barb Westfield, was a big road cyclist who had just started taking spinning classes and was raving about them. She reached out to Johnny G., who was *the spinning guru* at the time and set up a meeting at his studio. Thinking it was going to be a regular business meeting, I wore my normal business clothes at the time—slacks and a sports coat. The CEO of Salton, Leon, was also there in his best suit.

If you look at an indoor spinning bike, it's kind of big, heavy, and boring. It's a bicycle that doesn't move, hence the name stationary bike. I couldn't really see what all the fuss was about for spinning. Then Johnny G. suggested, actually insisted, that he take us through of one of his classes so we would get the full experience. Part of Johnny's success was his personality and passion for what he did. I've worked with some great pitchmen in my time like Billy Mays, George Foreman, and Jay Kordich. I would put Johnny G right up there with them for the energy and passion he brings. We had no idea what we were getting into. After a little struggle, he convinced us to take off our sports coats and get on the bikes. The music was turned up loud, and Johnny started urging us on...and it was awesome! Within ten minutes our clothes were drenched in sweat, and I said to myself, "Now I get it." We were sold on the concept.

Being a D2C marketer, I started to analyze what would be involved in the project if we moved forward. We had a very large, heavy product that would be difficult and expensive to ship. The margins were not great, and it did not pan out financially as a one-time sale. But, the biggest obstacle was the problem of how we could deliver the excitement we felt in the live class, with a live instructor and cool music playing. Technology at the time didn't allow it, and without that live experience, I did not think it could work. We passed on getting involved in the project.

FAST FORWARD

Several years ago, I started seeing extremely *nicely produced direct response ads on television for the Peloton® bike,* and I kept seeing them over and over. Usually, a good indicator that the ads were working from a positive ROI standpoint. Their ads are classic *"direct branding" spots using high-quality images with a call-to-action* to place an order or find out more at the end of each commercial. This was similar to what I helped GoPro do to propel their growth.

I realized that here was a company, which found a way to unlock the secret to success in selling indoor cycling. Let's look at video marketing techniques that helped make them successful.

RECURRING REVENUE MODEL

One of the main reasons many D2C campaigns fail is because the financial model will not support the advertising dollars being spent. As a consultant, one of the first things I always do is run a financial proforma to *make sure the numbers work before any video is shot.* One of the reasons I did not do the original spinning bike at the time was that there was only revenue from a one-time sale, the product was expensive to ship, and the margins were not good enough to support a D2C ad campaign. The financial model just didn't work.

With Peloton® it was different — when I bought my bike, not only was there the one-time cost to purchase but then *you could also purchase the ongoing video classes* at $39.00 a month for as long as you wanted to have access to them. This is a very nice back-end revenue stream. The spinning lessons, music, and instructors are so good that my wife and I are happy to pay this fee every month. It's way cheaper than a live class at a studio, but you still get all the benefits of a live class in the comfort of your home. With this ongoing revenue stream, the ROI model not only makes sense, but it is also an absolute home run.

INFLUENCERS / INSTRUCTORS

When I first moved to Seattle in 1986, I was walking through some shops in the Pioneer Square area just south of downtown. I went into a print shop to look at some of the pictures they had hanging on the wall. One of the framed posters had a headline that jumped out at me: "The Lures of Advertising." Since I like fishing and I was working in advertising I thought this poster was intriguing. I bought the poster, and many years later it still hangs on my office wall. The slogan at the bottom of the poster reads "The advertising club of greater Boston wishes you a good catch." It showed various fly-fishing lure images with names under them like; Hard Offer, Soft Offer, Celebrity Images, Appetite Appeal, The Beauty Promise, Jingles, The Lure of Sex, etc. Let's just say Peloton® has tapped into several of these lures to hook their customers and keep them on the line. *In the video classes they provide*, they use top male and female instructors who are very inspirational and easy to admire to lead the classes. They appeal to both male and female riders. You get to choose your favorite instructor every morning, afternoon, or evening workout. Being able to put *these instructors on streaming video set to great music is one of the secrets to their success. Using video, they can deliver that live-class feel right into your home.*

LIVE CLASS/COMPETITION

With the advent of spinning studios like Soul Cycle, which gets many people in the same room at the same time competing with each other, it helps make exercise fun. The live classes have a leader board up front to see how you are doing compared to the rest of the class, and this creates an atmosphere of both excitement and competition. *Using live-streaming video, you can join any class happening anywhere in the country. Peloton® is able to deliver the live studio experience right into your home.* Now you are not only competing against your class but with people nationwide.

VIDEO CONTENT MARKETING

It does not matter what level spinner you are, Peloton® provides workouts starting for beginners all the way up to advanced riders. You can pick the length of the workout you want, the type of music you like to work out to, and even your favorite place in the world that you have always dreamed of cycling. *There is constantly new video content being produced and made available to you as a subscriber to keep you happy and engaged.*

BEAUTIFUL BRAND RESPONSE ADVERTISING

By now it might seem like I am a paid spokesperson for Peloton®, but I'm not. When I see a great product, using an innovative and successful D2C marketing campaign, *that is using all aspects of video correctly, I like to talk about it.*

I mentioned earlier the company's use of brand response television ads. If you are thinking about doing a D2C product marketing campaign, go to YouTube and view the ones they have produced at Peloton's YouTube channel: https://www.youtube.com/user/ PelotonCycle. They have done a really good job of capturing the emotional appeal of being physically fit and also delivering the benefits to you of owning one of their bikes. Great work!

MY CALL TO ACTION; WHAT SHOULD YOU DO NEXT?

I would be remiss and not following my own advice if I did not ask you to take the next step. It's really simple, just get started! Using this book as a resource, start incorporating video in all your marketing and all your social media. Learn how to get started producing your own videos by reading Chapter 4. Use the existing resources that make it easy for you to produce video. If applicable, follow the advice in Chapter 7 and be your own spokesperson and you'll see results soar! Combine the information in Chapters 5 and 6 to build more engaging videos with stronger CTAs, and you will watch your engagement and response increase dramatically. Follow the advice in Chapter 8 and your Amazon sales increase. Finally, do not forget to give back, be grateful for any success you have and try and pass along something that will help someone else. You get it, the information is all here, now you just need to go out and start doing it.

Thank you and good luck!

ABOUT THE AUTHOR

Choose Rick Cesari as your guide as you consider how to build your corporate, product, or personal brand and how you can take it to the next level. He specializes in creating and implementing D2C marketing plans that are proven to generate robust growth no matter what your product or service.

Rick was the first person to use direct response television marketing to build a national brand (Juiceman® Juice Extractor). By applying similar direct response strategies and video marketing, he has been responsible for helping to create and market many well-known, iconic brands you use in your home every day. Products like Sonicare®, Clarisonic, the George Foreman Grill, OxiClean, Rug Doctor, and GoPro.

Having run one of the most successful full-service direct response marketing agencies for over twenty years, which provided creative, video production, media buying, interactive, and campaign management services, he is now offering his broad range of D2C experience, knowledge, and wisdom as a consultant to best assist your brand.

Specialties: Specializing in creating the very best, authentic and powerful customer testimonials for your business.

Additional services: Strategic Marketing Plans, Direct Response Television & Branding, Video Production, and Marketing.

Produced direct response marketing campaigns for Sonicare® toothbrush, the George Foreman Grill, OxiClean, Momentus Sports, Juiceman, Rug Doctor, Hunter Fan, Clarisonic, Jack Canfield's Dream Big, the GoPro camera, Silk'n beauty products, and Fortune 500 companies: Clorox and Microsoft.

To contact Rick about media appearances, consulting projects or speaking at your event, or to subscribe to his newsletter, visit: www.RickCesari.com

CONNECT WITH RICK ON HIS SOCIAL MEDIA PLATFORMS:

Facebook: https://www.facebook.com/rickcesaridrtv/

Twitter: https://twitter.com/rickcesaridrtv

YouTube: https://rickcesari.tv

LinkedIn: https://www.linkedin.com/in/rickcesaridrtv/

Amazon: https://amazon.com/author/rickcesari

BRING RICK TO YOUR NEXT EVENT!

As a keynote speaker, Rick will deliver an entertaining, engaging and inspiring presentation your audience will enjoy and learn from. Each speech is customized to meet your company or conference goals.

Topics include:

- Video Marketing Insider Secrets
- How to use Video to Build your Brand and grow your Business
- How to create great consumer Testimonials that will instantly increase sales
- How to produce video content consistently and inexpensively
- The 5 Keys to Building a great Brand
- 11 Timeless Marketing Tips that will make your Business Grow

Book Rick as your Keynote Speaker and you're guaranteed to make your event highly enjoyable and unforgettable!

PRAISE FOR RICK CESARI

Rick Cesari has nearly a decade of professional speaking experience and has wowed audiences across the country with his stories, case studies and marketing advice. He has spoken to both corporate clients as well as small business owners, masterminds and large conferences.

Rick was the Keynote speaker at both the Dan Kennedy Info-marketing Summit and the Prosper Show for Amazon sellers. He is invited as a guest speaker to many high-level mastermind groups and is a regular guest lecturer at the University of Washington business and marketing classes.

The following are just a small selection of the rave reviews that Rick has received from promoters, peers, and audience members.

"Rick, I am shamefully slow in sending you a note to thank you for a marvelous presentation. I got so much positive feedback about you and the content of your talk. We are very happy with our choice of Keynote speaker. Thanks for exceeding our expectations!"

—James Thompson, Ph.D., Founder, The Prosper Show

"Thank you so much for presenting at Prosper 2017. From George Foreman Grills to OxiClean and GoPro, your experience in marketing products blew me away."

—Jonathan Jesper, onefamilycorp.com

"When I listened to Rick Cesari's keynote speech at the Prosper Show for Amazon sellers, I couldn't believe how similar his proven process for marketing and developing great products for the direct-to-consumer market was to our process for developing great products for Amazon. Rick is a wealth of knowledge and a true marketing genius. I continue to learn from him, and I share with him my decade and a half of experience selling on the Amazon platform. It still amazes us how well so much of the processes that he developed translate directly into success on Amazon."

—**Jason Boyce, CEO Dazadi.com, Founder, Avenue 7 Media**

"For a number of years, Rick has been a guest presenter for my Marketing Management class at the University of Washington. Rick's presentations on direct response marketing and branding are especially illuminating as nearly every student in class has or has used one of the products Rick has successfully promoted over the years. This practical and approachable content helps the students get what marketing is really all about. Rick always gets rave reviews in student evaluations. Best of all, he has helped me turn students from finance and accounting to marketing!"

—**Richard Geasey, Lecturer, University of Washington Bothell School of Business**

DEAR READER

I hope you've enjoyed VIDEO PERSUASION: Everything You Need to Know | How to Create Effective High Level Product and Testimonial Videos That Will Grow Your Brand, Increase Sales and Build Your Business.

I've spent over 30 years, through trial and success, gathering the information in this book. I love being able to share it with you, so you can implement it in your life.

I want to say thank you for both buying and reading this book. I am so grateful to you. You have no idea how important your feedback and support are, so welcome, and thank you again for coming on board.

To keep giving you the best possible information that will keep you on the cutting edge of all your video needs, I'd love to hear from you. I want to know what you liked in VIDEO PERSUA-SION, what you loved, what you wish I'd written more of or what didn't resonate with you. Your feedback is important to me.

You can write to me at Rick@rickcesari.com.com, comment on my blog posts at my website www.rickcesari.com and connect with me on any of my social media platforms;

https://www.linkedin.com/in/rickcesaridrtv/
https://www.facebook.com/rickcesaridrtv/
https://twitter.com/rickcesaridrtv
http://rickcesari.tv

I'd like to ask a favor of you…

If you have ever tried to market an important, product, service out into the world in a big way, you know how important testimonials and reviews can be. Would you help me put my book, VIDEO PERSUASION, on the map and write a review on Amazon? Even just a sentence or two helps.

Thank you so much for reading and reviewing VIDEO PERSUASION. Let's create the next big success together.

With Health and Vitality,
Rick Cesari
Author | Speaker | Marketer

Made in the
USA
Middletown, DE